THE AM

# THE AMITYVILLE HORROR II

## John G. Jones

Based on the story of George and Kathleen Lutz

NEW ENGLISH LIBRARY

First published in the USA in 1982 by Warner Books, Inc.

First NEL Paperback Edition June 1982

NEL Books are published by
New English Library
Mill, Road Dunton Green, Sevenoaks
Kent, a division of Hodder and
Stoughton Ltd.
Printed and bound in Great Britain by
©ollins, Glasgow

British Library C.I.P.

**Jones, John G.**

Amityville Horror II.
I. Title
813'.54[F]  PS3560.0/

ISBN 0-450-05468-3

# THE AMITYVILLE HORROR II

# Foreword

Shortly after 3:15 on a cold November night in 1974, twenty-two-year-old Ronald DeFeo picked up his .35 caliber rifle and left the TV room of his home in Amityville, New York.

He was finally listening to the voices—the ones he thought were the voices of God. They had been hounding him incessantly for days—cajoling, whispering, shouting. They always told him the same thing:

*Kill them*, they said. *Kill them all*.

Ronald DeFeo's parents, two brothers, and two sisters all died that night, each one shot in the back of the head without any signs of struggle. Within days, Ronald DeFeo admitted to the ruthless execution-style killings, though he later claimed that the police had beaten a confession out of him.

· At the pretrial hearing on September 22, 1975, Ronald's counsel submitted a plea of mental disease or defect—a plea of insanity. Nonetheless, DeFeo was convicted of six counts of second-degree murder and sentenced to six consecutive terms of twenty-five years each. Today he is serving those terms at the maximum security prison at Danemorra.

Ronald DeFeo has never changed his story. He still claims that the voices were real—that he was possessed, a tool of some force that inhabited, and may still inhabit, his trim colonial-style home in Amityville. The murders were supernatural rather than psychotic in origin, he insists.

Despite the jury's unanimous conviction, there are some odd questions about the DeFeo case that have never been answered. For instance, a high-caliber rifle like the one used makes an earsplitting noise when discharged, particularly when fired in a large, echoing house like DeFeo's. Yet each of the victims died in bed without a struggle. Why didn't any of the family members awake at the first shot? And why were all six murder victims found in identical positions—lying on their stomachs, with their hands crossed under their heads? And more: the murders occurred at 3:15 A.M., on a cold quiet morning when sound carries well. But none of the neighbors, close as they were, heard anything unusual, even though the rifle was fired at least six times.

One theory that was quickly discarded by the jury and the media—at the time—had to do with the strange history of the plot of land on which the DeFeo house in Amityville stood. The Dutch Colonial house, built in 1928, was only the most recent structure on that site. Other buildings, with tragedies of their own, had existed there in the past. Could there, in fact, be some truth in Ronald DeFeo's bizarre stories of disembodied voices and malevolent spirits?

No one knows for certain, but it is reported that one John Ketchum, driven out of Salem, Massachusetts in the late 1600s for practicing witchcraft, lived on the land on which the DeFeo house stood. There, he purportedly practiced the rites that had forced him to flee from Salem . . . and he is said to be buried somewhere within the boundaries of the property.

Even before that, the land was said to be a "power-spot"—a burial ground for local Indian tribes. Though the Amityville Historical Society denied this at first, the facts have been independently confirmed.

Even Ronald DeFeo's father had talked about "strange feelings" at the house. He insisted on priests placing statues of Catholic saints around the yard.

Later—much later, after multiple deaths and another family's experiences in terror—accredited psychic investigators were invited to visit the three-story house in Amityville. Their experiences were incredible.

One "saw" an Indian burial ground and the spirit of an old chief whose grave had been disturbed.

Another saw an ancient well beneath the foundations of the house that had never been properly sealed—a fact that was also verified. He sensed an evil emanating from the black hole.

A team of renowned demonologists, with over thirty years of study and investigation in the paranormal, described their encounter with a preternatural being charged with a diabolical intelligence sealed in an inexorable and eternal rage against both God and Man.

Still another authority in the paranormal, who had spent the better part of her life in psychic research, saw something so evil and horrendous that she retired totally from the field. She said she never wanted to take the chance of evoking such horror again.

All the psychics "tuned in" to different aspects of the horrible entity at Amityville, but they all agreed on one point. The house contained one or more inhuman forces bent on destruction—forces that were vehemently opposed to any kind of religious ceremony or blessed object; demonic entities that manifested themselves in blood and death.

George and Kathy Lutz knew only a little of the strange history of the Dutch Colonial in Amityville when they decided to buy it—only that a poor crazy boy had killed his family there a year or so earlier. It didn't matter to them; they still wanted the house.

"The agent hadn't really thought of us as serious buyers," Kathy remembers. "I think she just got tired of having us turn down places because they didn't have what we felt we needed. So she decided to show us that what we *did* want was out of our reach. She was totally surprised when we said we'd take it."

The house was right on the water, complete with a boathouse, a garage, and a pool. It was even large enough for George to set up an office of his own, and it was available for a good low price, though it was more than they had hoped to spend. In short, it was everything they wanted—a perfect place to raise their children.

On December 18, 1975, only a little more than a year after Ronald DeFeo listened to the voices and murdered his family, Kathy and George Lutz, their three children, and their beloved mongrel dog Harry moved into the beautiful Dutch Colonial. It all seemed too good to be true.

It was. Twenty-eight days later, half mad and terrified almost beyond thought, they fled from their home. They have never returned.

George Lee Lutz was born and raised on Long Island, and if his birth is any indication, he was meant to be different from the start. Seconds after his delivery, doctors raced him into surgery and mended a large crack in his skull—one that should have killed him—and his mother often said that she thought his miraculous recovery was a sign that he was destined for something special.

At a very young age, George displayed a remarkable mechanical aptitude. At the age of twelve, he modified a hobby-kit hydroplane, adding his own custom-designed water-ski jets. It was the beginning of a lasting love for boats— canoes, rowboats, runabouts; sailboats, almost anything in the water. Later, the fascination grew to include cars, and today George can remember the color, interior design, make, and model of every car he has ever owned. And there have been many.

At nineteen, he volunteered for the Marines, and after he completed his hitch he took two degrees with honors and an F.A.A. course that led to a job in Boston as an air traffic controller. His father's death a short time later took him back to New York to run W. H. Parry, Inc., the family's land-surveying business.

He married for the first time in 1972; he was divorced in 1973. In 1974, after years of profitable business management and years of enthusiasm and training in the martial arts, he met Kathy. For the next eight months, he tried to convince her to go out with him.

Kathleen Lutz was also born on Long Island, and as a child she was an outgoing girl with spells of intense self-absorption, when she would walk alone for hours and stare into the clouds. For the most part, however, Kathy was a tomboy who couldn't resist a dare. Growing up with the boys in her neighborhood put her in constant competition with them, and she usually won the foot and bicycle races quite easily.

At twelve, she became interested in gymnastics, and later she developed her own fascination with cars. She remembers working odd jobs, trying to save enough to buy a 1956 Thunderbird, and later she fulfilled her dream of racing a dragster on an official quarter-mile track.

At eighteen, she married for the first time, and over the next six years she gave birth to three children: Greg, Matt, and Amy. When she was divorced after the birth of her youngest, she suddenly found herself faced with some harsh realities.

"I'd just been cruising through life," she says today, "not really thinking much. Now here I was, alone with three kids, and I began trying to understand myself. When I first met George, I was in the middle of some serious soul-searching, and I know it sounds kind of corny, but I needed to find myself—to find out who I was before I could face a relationship with any-one else. Finally I felt confident enough, and I agreed to go to breakfast with George."

They both approached the relationship very cautiously—they had been through it all before. George wanted Kathy's children to like him, and he didn't have to worry for long. They became good friends very quickly.

A year after their first date they were mar-ried, and soon they began searching for a house of their own. By the end of 1975, they thought they had found one—a three-story Dutch Colo-nial in the small Long Island community of Amityville, New York.

The day after they moved into their new home, a Catholic priest named Father Mancusso came to bless the house for them. But as he began the simple ceremony, he was slapped viciously across the face by an invisible assail-ant, and an unseen voice ordered him to leave the house. Later, psychics would say that the blessing provoked the evil in Amityville, and began a chain of events that would affect the Lutzes for years to come.

Still, Father Mancusso pressed on and finished his blessing, then fled the house. Later, at his rectory, he was physically attacked a second time. This assault, much more intense than the first, left him dangerously ill. He hovered at the edge of death for days, and though he was sick and frequently delirious, he tried to call Kathy and George to warn them about the thing he had felt. He wanted them to leave the house immediately.

He tried again and again to reach them by phone, but it simply couldn't be done. Every time the connection was completed, it would be cut off at a crucial moment or static interference would make it impossible to talk. And each time, a new bout of sickness would follow his attempt.

Meanwhile, at the house, strange things were happening to the Lutzes. They were slowly being twisted out of shape by demonic forces that worked in constant, subtle, invisible ways; and what had once been a warm and loving family gradually became a group of vicious, cruel, embattled strangers.

It was, in every sense, a nightmare. Even today, the Lutzes have trouble deciding what really happened physically, and what occurred only in their minds. Dreams, physical attacks, apparitions, and imagination combined, con- quered, and eventually shattered outside reali- ty. They rapidly came to realize that what they felt and saw, not what they could necessarily *prove*, was "real."

It began immediately after they moved into the house. As early as thirty-six hours after the Lutzes arrived, George began to consciously feel something "not right."

"Before Amityville," he says now, "I don't recall ever being really scared. I just wasn't the kind of person to jump at things that went bump in the night. But the attack on me started in such a strange way that it wasn't until after we left the house, when we looked back in retrospect, that I realized it was even an attack at all."

"I just couldn't keep warm," he recalls today. He began to spend more and more time in front of the large open fireplace in the living room, stirring only long enough to go into the yard and cut more wood, or to check the thermostats. He was sure the furnace had gone out, but it always read eighty degrees.

(Psychic researchers call this manifestation psychic-cold—the ability of a spirit to drain thermal energy from a victim or a room. They say this energy, which has been known to produce "cold spots" in haunted houses, is usually transformed into a negative power and turned back on the victim from whom it is taken.)

Kathy felt something, too. Even though she and George had been married only a short time, she was secure in the knowledge that she understood her husband well. Now, however, she saw them all changing for the worse.

"Even on the nights when he did finally pull himself away from the fire and come to bed," she recalls today, "he would wake around three in the morning, get dressed, and go off to wander around in the snow near the boathouse. And George was normally a neat and tidy person, too, but suddenly he started to forego even personal cleanliness in his mania for keeping warm. It became an obsession."

**15**

He was becoming a stranger, and he didn't even know it.

That was only the beginning... a deceptively quiet first round in what would become a battle for the Lutzes' souls. For the next twenty-eight days, they would all go through their own personal versions of hell.

"Trying to put into words what happened is impossible," George said later. "It seems too unreal to possibly have happened, even to me. And I was there; I went through it."

The psychic-cold intensified and affected them all. George would awake at 3:15 every morning—the exact time the DeFeo murders had occurred, though he didn't know it at the time—assaulted by dreams and visions of death. Hordes of flies swarmed in the sewing room, the room that had belonged to Ronald DeFeo. Toilet water in the upstairs bathrooms turned inky black and emitted a putrid smell. Furniture and objects were thrown about. Little Amy became friends with an invisible entity she called Jodie—a pig-thing that was more real than anyone could have imagined. Young Greg's hand was squashed flat by a window, and later showed no signs of injury. And all of them—even the poor half-breed dog— changed and decayed as the evil spirit of the house took them in.

The terror that the Lutz family endured is fully documented in the runaway best-seller, *The Amityville Horror*. More recently, the book was made into an equally successful movie. Both versions show what took place during that horrible month in the house.

One thing, however, is certain: on January 15, only twenty-eight days after a happy young family had taken possession of the house, the Lutzes grabbed what clothes were in easy reach and fled in terror. They left behind over $40.000 in antiques, cars, boats, furnishings, clothing, toys—even the deed to the house itself.

And that is where this book, *The Amityville Horror II*, begins.

*Amityville II* has been written in close constant cooperation with George Lutz and his family. Many hours of conversation, field trips as far away as England and Amsterdam, and intensive research and interviews here in America have gone into its making.

*Amityville II* is written in a narrative, novelistic style, in an attempt to communicate not only the facts, but the feelings behind the facts. Those feelings, after all, are the tools that the forces at Amityville used to torment the Lutzes and their friends; they are the weapons that caused an innocent family to abandon their home, and irrevocably changed their lives forever.

Toward that end, certain events and bits of information have been combined or reshaped to communicate the *effect* of the horrors that followed Amityville. In a few cases, the roles of two or three minor characters have been consolidated into a single fictional character, to avoid confusion and complications. Also, again in only a few cases, the names of certain participants and locations have been changed to preserve anonymity.

But it should be made clear: *Amityville II* is *not* a fictional account—not some flight of fancy cooked up by the writer, the Lutzes, or any other party. It is a horribly true recreation based on the facts and feelings surrounding the horror from Amityville. And it is, I think, ultimately a story of love, courage, and triumph.

The international notoriety of the Lutz family's ordeal has led to accusations of hoax, to suspicions about conspiracy or pointless publicity-mongering. More than a few skeptics have even questioned the very existence of certain principal characters in the account. These comments make little difference to Kathy and George Lutz.

"My husband and I know, without any doubt, that evil *does* exist in the world. And the fact that people argue over its possibility or its impossibility—well, that's totally academic to us. We have been *through* it. We have lived it, and we know it exists," Kathy Lutz said when she and George visited Amsterdam some time ago. Later she added, "Even though we try, it's quite impossible for us to put into words what *really* happened. Much of it is beyond words. You would have to go through it to even partly understand."

George added to her statement. "It's close to impossible for us to effectively put into words the horror that plagued us, first at the house and then as we continually moved in hopes of emancipation from it. The word *horror*, though explicit, is totally inadequate."

But it will have to suffice, as the story of The Amityville Horror continues. . . .

*John G. Jones*
*Santa Barbara, California*
*Spring, 1981*

# 1

It was an ordinary house in an ordinary American town. There was nothing particularly unusual about the time of night or the time of year... but that didn't matter. It happened anyway.

On January 13, 1976, all hell broke loose in this ordinary house in Amityville, New York. And George Lutz was caught in the middle of it.

He lay trapped in his bed while the world went crazy around him. The bedroom door slammed shut and flew open over and over, like a shutter driven by the wind. Dresser drawers spat out, then sucked themselves back into place, then spat out again. There were shouting voices, shattering glass, and the crash of metal against wood. There was even an invisible marching band that yawped off-key like a warped record-ing, screeching up and down the halls in a crazed and urgent rhythm.

*I'm not crazy*, George told himself. That would be too easy, and too much has happened to make it that simple. This is happening. *It's happening*.

But what about Harry? The Lutzes' mongrel dog was sleeping soundly as the bedroom door swooped and slammed behind him, close enough to ruffle the animal's fur, but he didn't move. He didn't flinch. Couldn't he feel it? George wondered. Couldn't he *hear?*

And what about Kathy? George's own wife, equally plagued by the evil forces hiding in the house, was sleeping peacefully at his side. Even his five-year-old daughter, who had somehow made friends with one strange and distorted aspect of the house's power, was snoring con-tentedly in the warm canyon between their bodies.

Not crazy, no. But what, then? What?

There was a new sound over George's head—a sharp scrape; a moan; an elongated complaint from the floorboards.

The beds, he thought. Something was moving the beds of his stepsons, dragging them across the floor of their third-story room.

"I've got to get up." George tried to rise, but a blast of icy wind slammed him back against the mattress. "I've got to get up," he repeated, and tried again. A smothering, invisible force, like a huge fingerless hand, pressed him against the bed. The box springs groaned at the sudden strain.

There was shouting upstairs. Something was

clattering in the halls. A door slammed. A drawer shot free. The band yattered and screeched on the staircase. And now he couldn't scream, he couldn't breathe. Something was stealing the air out of his lungs.

No! I've got to get up, I've got to get to the boys, I've go to—no! *No!*

The force closed over him. George blacked out.

"Daddy! *Daddy!*"

He forced his eyes open and stared blindly at the cracks in the ceiling. Was it a dream? A fever? Was this what it felt like to have a stroke? How long have I been asleep? he wondered. He could remember voices. He could remember the house flexing around him like a spastic muscle, but now—

The bedroom door flew open, and for an instant he thought it was going to start again. Not yet, he pleaded silently. Not yet!

"Daddy! *Daddy!*"

His stepsons, Matt and Greg, rushed into the room. Greg's blond hair was twisted into sleep-curls. He was pasty white and grim. Little Matt, barely old enough to understand what was happening, was shivering from the cold.

They tugged at George's bedclothes and screamed. "Daddy!" Greg shouted. "Daddy, wake up!"

He's only ten, George thought. He felt strangely distant and serene, as if the force that held him against the bed were a blanket or a shield. Poor Greg. He's too young to know what to do.

The boys jerked the covers off their father and pulled at his arms, but he wouldn't budge.

He couldn't. Matt threw himself on George's chest, and George could feel the boy's heart thumping against him. Matt's lips were next to his ear, his breath warm and harsh. "Please, Daddy," he whispered, "please wake up."

*Get up, dammit,* he ordered himself. *Get up!* He forced himself—he willed himself to move— but nothing happened.

A cold wind blew through the room a second time, and Harry started out of a twitching animal-dream. He jumped to his feet and barked at an empty space just beyond the open door of the bedroom, his ears flat against his head.

*GET UP!*

"Daddy, come on!"

Something dark was taking shape in the doorway—an inky cloud, thunderhead-ominous, that swirled and billowed to eclipse the light in the hall. George imagined he could see shapes in it; silhouettes that oozed up, froze for an instant, then disappeared.

A flapping crow. A mad grin. A hooded figure. And a huge claw—a grasping, bloody-fingered talon that filled the doorway and blocked out the last of the light.

It couldn't be real. Nothing he saw, or heard, or felt could be real by any sane standards. But the house had been built in a place beyond sanity, and George knew what the evil, real or imagined, could do to them. They were in danger. They could die. That much he was sure of.

Something snapped apart inside George Lutz. The tiny thread that had held him together during the last twenty-eight days suddenly gave way. He had seen what was happening all along.

He'd seen all his dignity and equilibrium and hope ebb away, but he couldn't stop it, he couldn't do anything to change. He had even tried to lead his family away from this house once before. But something inside him, something he couldn't fight, had held him there. It just wouldn't let them go.

But the chains were broken now. The shackles had snapped open, and quite suddenly he knew that he *could* go, he *could* break free. And he knew there was no choice. They had to leave now, or they would never leave at all.

In that instant, George Lutz could move.

He threw himself out of bed and the cloud-thing blinked out of existence. It didn't dissolve or disappear. It was simply, suddenly, *gone*— wiped away in an instant. George felt his new strength fading. His knees threatened to give way.

"Greg," he said as he groped for support, "take Amy. We're leaving now. We're leaving the house."

He forced his head to clear as he leaned forward and gathered his wife in his arms. Greg picked up the little girl.

Out of the bedroom, he thought. Through the hall, down the stairs, and out the door. It was that simple. Just a one-minute trip. Nothing to it.

He led the way through the door where the cloud-thing had hovered only seconds ago. The house was dead silent now, and icy cold.

He took the stairs carefully, trying not to shiver. He wished for eyes in the back of his head.

Kathy stirred in his arms as he reached the

bottom of the stairs. She passed a hand over her eyes and pushed her hair out of the way. "George," she said, still half asleep, "what's happening?"

"We're leaving. Right now." Just a few more steps, he told himself, fighting down panic. Through the hall. Out the door. That's all.

Kathy understood. "I'm awake, babe," she said gently. "You can put me down."

George eased her onto her feet, and as she leaned against him, he called to Greg and Matt: "Take your sister and Harry and get in the van. Lock the doors behind you and *don't open them* until we get there. Okay?"

They nodded and left the house. George held Kathy away from him and said, "You okay, babe?"

She nodded and stood on her own . . . and felt George suddenly turn cold and rigid under her hands. He kissed her mechanically on the forehead and turned away. He started back up the stairs.

"What are you doing?"

"Getting some clothes."

"We don't need clothes," she said, confused. Then she said it again, new realization in her voice. "George, we don't need clothes. *Let's just get out of here!*"

George barely heard her. It was crazy, he was telling himself. Crazy. They couldn't leave without coats and boots. It was freezing outside. And—and there were plans to make. Things to consider. Why were they leaving in the first place? There had to be something wrong with him, just up and leaving like this. *Quitting.* Was he a coward now, on top of everything else? Chicken-shit George? He—he—

*No*, he told himself, gripping the second-floor banister with both hands. That's not me. That's the house. The *house*. We have to get out of here. Get out *now*.

He kicked open the door to the boys' bedroom and threw the closet doors wide, muttering to himself as he ripped shirts and pants off hangers.

Downstairs, Kathy was standing uncertainly in the hallway and shivering. She was just beginning to understand. For a moment, whatever thing had been plaguing them had loosened its grip. Now they could leave, they could escape. But if they didn't go fast, they might never get away at all.

Somebody pushed her. She stumbled a step forward and turned, thinking one of the children had come back into the house . . . but there was no one there.

Something pushed her again, and she threw her hands out, afraid she was going to fall.

Another push, and she was in the front alcove. Another, and she was through the front door. Suddenly, painfully, the cold winter wind cut through her nightgown, and she found herself standing on the porch.

She spun and looked at the blue white facade of the house, at the flickering lights in the upstairs windows and the dark shape moving beyond the curtained glass.

She clutched at the doorjamb and screamed her husband's name. Something billowed in the hallway before her, and she screamed again.

George was alone in the house.

His arms were full now. He had jackets and

shirts for the boys, a jump suit for Amy, coats and shoes for Kathy and himself.

"*George!*"

He heard Kathy calling from downstairs. She sounded terrified.

He took the stairs two at a time, spinning so violently on the landing that he nearly lost his footing. Twenty more steps, he told himself, and I'll be out of here for good. Ten seconds more, that's all.

He skidded to a halt on the last flight of stairs and grabbed at the banister with his free hand.

The cloud-thing was hovering in the hallway below him, billowing and black as cinders. Beyond it, behind it, looking small and fragile in the night, Kathy was standing with her hands at her mouth.

"Look out, George!"

The black and bottomless cloud swirled forward. He blinked, then blinked again. His vision hazed, and for an instant he thought he saw shapes inside it again, a *feeling*, as tangible and deadly as noxious gas, swept into him.

I'm not going to make it, he thought, I'm not going to make it. He knew it, as deeply as he'd ever known anything. He started to lower his arms. It was no use. There was no point. He was trapped in this house forever. He knew that now.

Beyond him, behind the expanding black cloud, the front door began to close.

"George!" Kathy screamed. "Run! *Run!*"

He looked up, he shuddered, and for a moment, for a fraction of an instant, he cut through the shroud of brutal depression that the cloud-thing generated.

George exploded in a fury of motion. He lunged forward and dodged to the right, skirting past the thing and heading for the door. A numbing cold slashed into his shoulder as he passed it.

The door was closing faster. He rushed to catch the knob and stumbled.

*"Run!"* Kathy screamed again. *"Run!"*

He bellowed and lunged forward, jumping farther than he thought possible, and slipped through the narrowing crack an instant before it slammed shut. He ran headlong into his wife, and they fell heavily onto the porch in a single heap, clothes and boots flying in every direction.

They grabbed at the nearest items without a word. George was sweating as if it were summer. Kathy was sniffling and trying not to.

When their hands were full, they scrambled up and pushed each other toward the van. The children's faces were white and blank behind the glass. They unlocked the doors as their parents ran down the driveway.

Door relocked. Key in the ignition. The wind was rattling at the van, but George ignored it. The children were whimpering in the back but he blocked it out. They were leaving. Going. Nothing else mattered now.

"Where's Harry?"

George's hand froze on the ignition key, and Kathy said it again: "Where's Harry?"

"We tried to get him!" Matt said defensively. "He ran, though. He always runs when he gets scared."

"He's in the boathouse, Mommy," Greg said tearfully. "That's where he always goes. We saw him."

"We tried, though! We tried!"

"It's all right," George said. A rattling sigh escaped him, and his hand fell away from the keys. "It's all right, I'll get him."

He jumped out of the van and ran past the house, down the grassy slope to the river's edge. The wind scraped at his face. A broken branch twisted out and slapped him on the cheek.

Go now. Go, go! was all he could think. Leave! Get out!

He put his hand on the knob of the boathouse door, and a current of cold electricity cut through him. He turned abruptly and looked at the house.

Nothing had changed. The trees still danced around it in the wind. Lights still glared in the second-story windows. But he felt something new, something awful. He knew the house was watching him...waiting for a mistake. Crouched, hungry, dangerous as a wounded animal.

He forced himself to turn away and jerked open the partly closed door to the shack. Harry was crouched inside, growling and shivering, his eyes so wide they were rimmed in white.

George tried to pick him up, but the dog was covered with a slimy combination of sweat and mud. Or maybe it's my hands, he thought numbly. Maybe I'm the one.

He cursed under his breath and took a length of rope from a peg beside the door. He looped it through the dog's collar and murmured meaningless, comforting things as he made a knot.

"C'mon, Harry. We're going now. Leaving. C'mon, c'mon, let's go."

He dragged the dog out of the shack and started to run. Suddenly Harry seemed to get the idea, and he loped beside him, then in front of him. He made a beeline for the van.

The boys shrieked with delight and opened the sliding door. Harry piled in, and George slid into the driver's seat and said, "We're going. Leaving. Now!" He slammed the door and turned the ignition key.

Nothing happened.

Kathy stifled a cry, but he forced himself not to look at her. He gritted his teeth and tried again, digging the key into its slot.

Nothing.

"*Shit*," he said distinctly, and pulled the hood release. No one said a word as he opened the door and lunged at the front of the van.

A loose wire, he thought. That's all. No devils, no demons, just a goddamn loose wire. He looked for the manual starter button, trying to convince himself that that was the problem, and only that.

Please God, he prayed, please let the engine work. Make the manual starter work.

There it was. A little red button, no bigger than a fingernail. He took a deep breath and pushed the button . . . . and the engine caught on the first try.

George hurled himself into the van, and in one swift motion he closed the door, slammed the gearshift into reverse, and stomped on the accelerator.

A spurt of gravel went up in front of them as they bounced into the street. Metal scraped against concrete, tires screeched on the asphalt, and they roared into the night.

A few seconds after the van raced away, the clock passed twelve. It was January 14, 1976. The Lutzes had seen their house in Amityville for the last time.

# 2

Amityville was in the grip of a bitter cold snap on the evening of the Lutzes' escape. George could see his own breath cloud the air as he guided their '74 van out of town, winding north toward safety. The visibility was fair, but layers of nearly transparent ice on the highway made driving treacherous.

He lifted his hand from the steering wheel and ran it through his tightly curled hair. His eyes never left the road, even as he fumbled at the dashboard, searching for the heater's controls. He found the knob on the wrong side. It took him a moment to realize what it meant.

It was full on. Hot air was pouring into the car.

Then, why do I still feel cold? he wondered.

What's this rotten chill I can't shake off? It had invaded his arms and legs—his whole body.

Kathy felt the same eerie cold. She shivered in the seat next to him and tucked the blankets more tightly around Amy. Her daughter was no more than a small, dark bundle in her lap.

Kathy's grandmother had known what the chill felt like, she remembered. She would have said, "Someone just walked over my grave."

The thought was much too close to home for Kathy. She quickly pushed it away.

Greg and Matt were in the backseat, silent and watchful. Harry was asleep at their feet. There was an unnatural stiffness in the way the boys sat, and George realized that they hadn't made a sound since the van had left the house.

Don't let them be hurt, he pleaded. If something bad has to happen, let it happen to me. Just leave the children alone.

Less than fifteen minutes out of Amityville, the van hit a small section of icy road, and the car lurched slightly to the side as the tires lost traction. George tightened his grip on the wheel and kept control. Seconds later, the tires took hold again.

George relaxed a little and tried to ease the knot of tension in his stomach. It wouldn't go away, but he wasn't surprised. Who wouldn't be tense after what they'd been through in the last month?

It was hard to believe it had only been four weeks. All that fear, all that insanity in twenty-eight days? That's all? God, he thought, it felt like a lifetime.

But we made it. We got away, we're free. I won't have to feel cold anymore. I'll get my balance back. It'll be like it was before. We'll be like a family again.

But I do feel cold. I feel... strange.

It's probably just shock, he told himself. After all, that had been a close call at the door. It had hammered shut just a few inches behind him, and a sick feeling in his gut assured him that if he'd been inside the house when that door had slammed, he never would have gotten out alive.

He glanced at Kathy, and she looked back. I would never have made it without her, he thought. She was there all the way, right up to shouting that warning as the front door tried to trap me. Oh, she was scared stiff plenty of times, but she never was one of those hands-in-the-air screamer types. Even when she was really frightened, she kept it together. She saved my life.

Kathy smiled, and he smiled back. It wasn't hard to appreciate a woman like that.

George raised his eyes a fraction of an inch and caught a brief glimpse of the boys in the backseat. They looked small and gray in his rearview mirror.

They'd been terrific, too, he knew. As good as they could be, considering what had happened. There was a lot of inner strength there. He'd been hard on them in the house. Like when ...when...

Wait. He'd been thinking about something that had happened, about when the— But suddenly he couldn't quite remember. He knew it had been hard for them all. He—it had to be, it must have been, but...

Damn! So much of the time was a blur, a dream, a nightmare. Why couldn't he remember it?

The lights of an oncoming car raced at the van and flashed by. George dragged his tired thoughts back to the road and tried to concentrate, but weariness was like a solid thing inside him. Five minutes later he was drifting again.

They were good kids. He hoped to God that they hadn't been damaged somehow. At least it was over now. They'd gotten through it. And they could all put their lives back together again; they could decide what to do with the future.

Damn it, he thought with a mixture of anger and frustration, I'm already beginning to accept that insanity as if it were normal, as if I could ever really forget. What's wrong with me? Why can't I remember things clearly?

He sighed and rubbed his forehead with one hand. I'm just tired, he told himself. Really tired.

Kathy heard her husband sigh, and she touched him lightly on the arm. "Are you all right, babe?" she asked quietly.

She saw him straighten up in surprise. "What? Oh . . . yeah. Fine. I . . . fine, I guess." He smiled reassuringly but vacantly at Kathy and looked back at the icy road.

He's beat, Kathy thought. But at least we're out of the house. Now he can rest.

Thank God we got away. I couldn't have taken much more.

She wondered if George realized how close she'd come to completely cracking up back there. A couple of times, she had wanted to scream; just scream until her lungs hurt. But she knew if she had started screaming, she never would

34

have stopped. She didn't know what had kept her going.

George leaned forward, over the wheel, and sighed again. She looked at him and, in spite of it all, she smiled. Yes, she *did* know, actually. George had kept her going. Even in the middle of the craziness, even exhausted and terrified, she'd felt his strength holding her up.

And now it was over. Over and finished. She looked into the oncoming darkness and tried to forget the house and the horror of Amityville. The monotonous purr of the engine filled the van. The warmth of her daughter and her thick wool blanket penetrated the cold. Her eyelids shut lightly. She forced them open once, then again, and finally a third time. Still they drooped.

Suddenly Kathy's eyes flew wide open. She sat bolt upright, and Amy, still asleep, squirmed in her lap.

Something was in the darkness. She could sense it... feel it. Something awful was in the darkness ahead of them.

George had felt it a split second earlier. His foot was already on the brake pedal, but the van hadn't slowed a bit. He saw Kathy sit up and gasp, but he couldn't take the time to look at her—not now.

Is it paranoia? he wondered. It must be. There's nothing out there. We can't see anything at all. It must be a dream, a fragment of nightmare.

But real or imagined, he felt something—and so did Kathy. What did "real" mean now, anyway? The line between imagination and dream had disappeared during their month in Amityville, and if he had learned anything at all he had learned that whatever he *thought* was real, whatever he *felt* with this kind of power, was real enough to hurt them.

Another wave of terror washed over Kathy like an icy rain. A hopeless, sick feeling dragged at her stomach. This can't be happening, she thought. We're miles from Amityville. We left that craziness behind. It can't be reaching out for us. *It can't!*

George pushed on the brakes a second time, but nothing happened. They weren't slowing down, he knew that, but his mind wouldn't accept it. He stamped on the pedal again and again, until it went to the floor and stayed there, useless.

The van's headlights and dashlights blinked out. The car swayed wildly on the icy tarmac, and the engine roared. George lifted both feet from the floor, away from the accelerator, but the van rushed forward.

They were picking up speed.

No, he said to himself. No. He tugged at the automatic gearshift, tried to ram the car into PARK, but it wouldn't budge.

The speedometer was moving past eighty. The wheels were whining against the ice.

Finally, frantically, he took a tight hold on the wheel and fought to keep the van on the road. There was nothing he could do but try and keep them alive.

A heavy wind hit the front of the van, and the wheel twisted in his hands. Torrential rain poured out of a clear night sky and pounded on the metal body of the van, loud as thunder. George pulled at the windshield-wiper switch, but nothing happened.

In the rear, Harry was on his feet and barking madly. The two boys were crouched in their seats, their hands over their ears, too afraid to move.

As suddenly as the attack began, it ceased: the wind disappeared; the rain let up; Harry stopped barking and tried to hide under the backseat. The sound of the van's engine, revving higher and higher, was unnaturally loud.

George hesitated, holding his breath. He held the van firmly on the road as he waited for something more. Then a gust of wind whistled through the van, so cold it burned. It encircled each of them in turn, cutting to the bone, chafing the skin.

George looked around wildly, trying to find the source of the draft. All the windows were secured.

Seconds after it came, the wind disappeared. The Lutzes were drained and trembling.

Kathy tried desperately to keep control, but one word escaped her.

"George?" she said.

George didn't answer. He gripped the wheel even harder and tried to keep it steady. The van was still accelerating, bumping and sliding over patches of ice in the road, slipping sideways over the polished roadway. He had to ignore the rest of it. He had to keep them from running off the road.

In a strange way, he was almost glad. George Lutz was a fighter, he had always been a fighter; and now, finally, there was something tangible he could fight. He leaned into it, wrestling with the wheel, until his knuckles were white with the strain.

Kathy saw the struggle all too clearly. "What is it, George? What's happening?"

"Having trouble holding us steady," he said shortly. "It'll be all right in a minute." He tried to sound normal, but it didn't work.

Matt burst into tears. "Mom! Dad! What's happening?"

"It's all right," Kathy said tightly. "Everything's all right. There's a little problem, but George is taking care of it."

I'm no good at lying, she thought. There's no way they'll believe me. They aren't babies anymore. They've been through more than most grown men.

But the boys seemed to take comfort from the sound of her voice. They stopped crying and sat back, eyes wide with fear.

George's neck and shoulder muscles stood up like steel cables as he struggled to keep control of the van. He didn't know how much longer he could hold out.

Then, abruptly, the van began to slow. It was still moving too fast for an icy, nighttime road, but he knew he could keep it on the road now. He let out a sigh and loosened his death-grip on the steering wheel. It must have been wet ice, he lied to himself. Something like that.

Kathy saw him relax. "Is it all right?" she asked, almost whispering.

"I think we're through the worst of it."

"Are you sure?" It was Greg, the ten-year-old. His voice reflected the fear he was trying so hard to hide.

George put on a false, comforting smile. "Nothing to worry—"

Something slammed into the side of the van. Matt jumped away from the sound of the crash and screamed, and they swayed recklessly to the left. George grabbed at the wheel, and an instant later it hit them a second time. They lurched even farther off the road.

George leaned into the wheel to keep them steady.

"Daddy! Daddy!"

"Get down! Stay on the floor! *Get down, damn it!*"

It hit again, both sides at once. And again— and again. The steel walls of the van began to bend inward.

The children screamed and clutched at each other. The dog stood up and barked wildly. The roadway danced crazily in front of him, blue and black in the moonlight.

The blows were louder than thunder, louder than explosions. With each attack, the walls buckled further.

"George, what is it? *George!*"

He knew it was only a matter of moments before the van would collapse completely. His family would be crushed. We'll die, he thought numbly. We'll finally die.

Another blow. Another. Greg and Matt cried and Kathy clutched at George's arm, her nails digging into his skin. He could feel the panic rising up to choke him.

Please God, he thought desperately. Please God, don't let it happen. Please . . .

A thought occurred to him, slipping through the noise and fear. A single, inexplicable thought.

"Our Father who art in Heaven," he said, beginning quietly.

Kathy looked at him as if he were mad. But it was right; George could feel it. It was right and he said it again louder and stronger.

*"Our Father who art in Heaven . . ."*

The thing outside the van bellowed its defiance. The shrieking built to a scream and the pounding tripled its force.

Kathy remembered what Father Mancusso had told them both: prayer was their only defense. As she heard George's voice rising, thin and weak against the chaos, she joined in: ". . . *hallowed be Thy name.* . . ."

The boys heard their parents praying, and they picked up the chant: *"Thy kingdom come.* . . ."

The van shuddered; the wind groaned around them; outside the attack grew weaker.

*"Thy will be done on earth as it is in heaven!"* They shouted it now like a victory yell, like a cheer. George led them through it as he slashed at the steering wheel, cutting and sliding over the icy road.

". . . *The kingdom! And the power! And the glory for ever and ever! Amen!"* He said it again, shouting in triumph. *"AMEN!"*

The crashing stopped. The screaming died away. The night turned dead and quiet, and only Harry's frenzied barking remained.

"Shut up, Harry!" Harry paused, gave two more sharp barks, then was silent. The final words of the prayer echoed in the night, and very quietly George said it a third and final time: "Amen."

The hum of the engine faded. The headlights and dashlights flickered on. The wipers jumped and began sweeping the dry windshield, and George switched them off. The sky was clear again.

Amy, who had slept through it all, suddenly squirmed in her mother's lap and began to cry.

"It's all right, honey," Kathy crooned. "Everything's all right." Amy whimpered again, then lapsed back into sleep.

George tested the brakes. They worked normally now. He pressed them gently until the van was moving very slowly.

"Keep going," Kathy said harshly. She was bent over her baby, wide-eyed and trembling. "Get as far away from that house as you can."

"Don't worry," he told her, "that's exactly what I intend to do."

He punched the accelerator to the floor and kept it there until the speedometer's needle passed fifty.

There were no stops that night. No breaks at gas stations or all-night coffee shops. George drove steadily, as fast as he dared, until they reached their destination: a small suburban house in East Babylon, New York.

# 3

Joan Conners had lived in the same house for over twenty-six years. When she had first moved in, it had been part of a suburban tract development made up of small two-bedroom houses, but over the years, as the East Babylon area of New York State became more prosperous, the house had grown. Joan added a bedroom, a den, and a dinette to her ranch-style house. Others in the neighborhood expanded considerably more. It was a good house, a fine community—a happy life.

But tonight, after a strange and disturbing telephone call from her daughter Kathy, Joan was not a happy woman. Kathy had sounded frantic. She would only say that she and George and the children had left their house in Amityville—that they were coming to stay with her.

But that had been well over an hour ago; they should have arrived by now, she thought. Unless something had gone wrong.

She hated that house. The memory of her last visit to Amityville still sent a cold shiver up her spine. From the moment she'd walked in the door, she had felt as if someone—or some*thing* —were watching her. At first, she'd tried to push it aside, but the feeling stayed with her. And it hadn't been her imagination. It couldn't have been. She recognized the sensation.

As a small girl, Joan Conners had been alone in the dark of the woods only once. There had been a primeval fear hiding there that had terrified her so badly she had never gone out alone again. That *thing* she'd felt in Amityville was very much the same . . . and it was more than she could stand.

She had been invited to have dinner with the family her first evening in Amityville, but after five minutes in that awful house, she'd made some lame excuse and fled. She had actually *run* to her car to escape that horrible feeling.

She remembered how George had looked that night: the vacant expression, the unkempt appearance, the obsession with the cold. It wasn't like George—not like the George she knew, at any rate. It was true she hadn't been too sure about him at first—after all, Kathy had three children, and he *did* seem a touch irresponsible—but she'd been quick to see the error in her first impression. Why, these days no one would guess they weren't his natural-born children; he loved them that much. But that evening in Amityville, he had been different, somehow.

It must have been the house, she thought. Whatever could have prompted them to buy it in the first place, knowing its tragic history as they did?

A car horn sounded in the driveway just outside, and Joan hurried out of the kitchen. In the few seconds it took her to reach the front door, her worries disappeared. At last, she thought. At last.

Her son-in-law's van was rolling to a stop just a few feet from her door. It looked normal enough: she could see George and Kathy in front, and the boys in back, strangely immobile. They were all there, all safe. But still... something was very wrong.

The instant she thought it, something hit her. A rush of horror, a wave of fear as real and awful as it had been at Amityville struck her with an almost physical force.

The feeling was coming from the van.

Joan began to fall. She grabbed at the doorframe for support, and for an instant she thought her heart had stopped. She couldn't breathe, couldn't move, couldn't—

Then it was gone. Passed by. She could stand by herself again. She forced herself to walk through the doorway and down the porch. She blinked her eyes and took stock of the occupants of the van, trying to forget it, to put it aside. They all looked unhurt but frightened, and she could see from the tight, walleyed expressions that this wasn't the time to ask what had happened.

It was obvious that her grandsons needed her most. She steeled herself, put on her best "grandma" smile, and opened the rear door.

"You poor dears," she said, trying to sound warm and calm, "you must be exhausted. Come on inside now. Come on. How would you like some cookies and milk?" The boys piled out of the van without a word.

At least they're here, Joan thought, wondering at her own overwhelming sense of relief. At least they're safe.

But what had she felt at the doorway?

An hour later they were all together in the living room, where pillows and blankets had been hastily bundled together to serve as makeshift beds. Amy, Greg, and Matt had already been warmly tucked in. They were sleeping fitfully, tossing back and forth under the covers.

Kathy finished assembling the last bed, the one for her and George. "There," she said, "all done."

"Are you sure you'll be comfortable enough?" Joan asked. She didn't like them sleeping on the floor. It didn't seem right, somehow. "The kids could bunk together in the spare room. I'm sure that would be better."

"This is fine, Mom," Kathy said wearily. "We'd prefer to stay together, at least for tonight." She touched her mother on the arm. "And I'm sorry we busted in on you like this."

"Nonsense. You know you're always welcome here, Kathy." Joan gave her daughter a kiss on the cheek and a quick hug. "Always." When she straightened up and smiled, there were tears in her eyes. "You know where everything is," she said, trying to make it sound light. "I just hope it's comfortable enough."

"It's the most comfortable we've felt in a long

time, Joan," George said, just a little annoyed. Joan realized she was being a fuss-pot.

She took one last loving look at her sleeping grandchildren and said good-night. It must have been awful, she thought. Worse than I can imagine. I can see it in their faces.

She stepped outside her room and turned off the hall light. They need to be together, she thought. But is it really necessary to have Harry sleeping in the den?

Harry, however, was far from asleep. Over the last month he had gotten more than his share, and now he was wide awake, nervously padding back and forth at the end of a leash that was tied to the leg of the piano. Every few moments, he whimpered softly, sensing something no one else could.

George and Kathy were exhausted, but they decided to meditate for a while before going to sleep. Kathy crossed her legs and put her back against the wall; George sat on their makeshift bed. Within seconds, their breathing slowed and grew more regular; their thoughts blurred and began to turn inward. . . .

Two hours later, George's eyes snapped open. He sensed something—something he couldn't comprehend quite yet.

He was slumped forward, legs still crossed, but as he awoke his body grew tense. For an instant he couldn't remember where he was; then shreds of memory began to surface.

Kathy's mother's. He was at Joan Conners' house. The realization came quickly, piercing his sleep, but somehow it seemed to take forever. He leaned forward and rubbed his eyes, sighing heavily. We were meditating, he thought. I must have fallen asleep. More tired than I realized.

Harry's loud barking from the den made him jump in surprise. He looked up, his eyes taking in the darkened room, and he lurched shakily to his feet at what he saw.

Kathy—her back to the wall, her legs still crossed—was floating five feet off the floor. Her hands were clasped tightly over her head. Her body was stiff—almost brittle, somehow—and absolutely still. She was fast asleep or unconscious . . . and she was rising toward the ceiling.

George's legs were unsteady and numb from his sleeping position as he put his hands around his wife's waist. He tried to pull her down, but she was anchored in the air—fixed, immobile. He hung on her, dragged down with all his weight, tried to force her to the floor—

And collapsed under her sudden release. He tried to recover, to catch her or break her fall, but they both landed heavily, thumping on the makeshift mattress.

He turned her on her back and tried to wake her. "Kath? Can you hear me? Come on, babe, open your eyes!" He shook her roughly. "Kathy!" There was no response. She was in some kind of trance.

George felt a new and painful fear seep into him from somewhere outside himself. What is this? he wondered. Why—

It was the sound, he realized. He couldn't hear any sound. His ears strained at the silence, but there was nothing there.

He could see the second hand of the wall clock out of the corner of his eye, moving through its full circle. But he couldn't hear it ticking as he had earlier. Kathy's chest rose and fell with her slow and steady breathing, but he couldn't hear that, either—even when he laid an ear to her chest. The room was empty of sound, a vacuum of sound.

Something happened. George felt it. His vision flickered, the air itself flinched, but he couldn't tell, he couldn't see—

His eyes darted to Kathy, and he gaped in horror as a deep green welt appeared on her leg, inches below her short pajamas.

He looked wildly around the room, searching for some invisible hand, some source of pain. But all he could see were patches of shadow, the blue white illumination of the moon and nothing else.

No sound broke the silence, but the air twisted around him again, and two more welts appeared on Kathy—one on her leg, another on her arm.

He was frozen, unable to move. Two more ugly scars marked her.

George threw his body over Kathy and tried to shield her. "Stop it!" he shouted. "In the name of all that's holy, *stop it!*"

Every muscle tensed as he lay waiting. Could he shield her? he wondered. Would the unseen attacker move through him somehow, and hurt her again? Or would it turn its assault on him, instead?

Nothing happened. Nothing. With a maddening slowness, the normal sounds of the room gradually returned, sifting back to him as if a volume control were being turned.

It's strange, George thought, how much warmth simple sounds can give. He listened to the ticking of the clock, to the steady breathing of Kathy and the children. It sounded good. *Right*, somehow. Then Harry's urgent barking dragged him from his reverie.

"It's all right, Harry," George yelled toward the den, reassuring himself as much as the dog. "It's all over. For now," he added grimly to himself.

Harry whimpered once, then dropped to the floor and lay quiet. In the stillness, George thought his voice was loud and harsh, but Greg and Matt and Amy slept on peacefully.

He checked them carefully. They looked okay, he decided. Just in a very deep sleep.

Kathy stirred next to him and began to wake. Her eyes blinked as she tried to focus, and she peered at him warily, as if she knew something was wrong. "What is it, babe?" she said indistinctly, struggling against sleep.

"I had to pull you down from the ceiling," he told her. "Your arms and legs are covered with—"

He looked down at her legs and saw that all signs of the attack had disappeared. Her skin was clear and unblemished again.

"I don't remember anything," Kathy said. "I—" Suddenly George's words seemed to sink in, and she was wide awake. "Oh, no," she said. "It's following us, isn't it? *It's following us!*" She buried her head in his chest. "What are we going to do, George?"

They held each other tightly for a long time. Then, finally, George eased her gently to the mattress. "Let's get some sleep," he whispered. "We'll talk about it in the morning."

Kathy put her head on the pillow. She was asleep in an instant.

George lay next to her, but now that the immediate danger had passed, a new frustration was tearing at him. This—this *thing*, this terror from Amityville, seemed to strike when it chose to and where it liked. He knew he was incapable of defending his family, and that realization hurt him more than any physical attack.

He couldn't remember ever feeling so helpless, so weak. He broke out in a cold sweat and shook uncontrollably, and even when he calmed his body and forced the muscles in his jaw to relax, a black depression still engulfed him.

Kathy turned in her sleep and touched him gently. He moved closer to her and let the warmth of her body loosen his twisted nerves. Still, he couldn't sleep—not for a long time. He stared into the darkness for hours, hearing every small sound the house made and waiting for something more.

As the first light of dawn filtered into the room, he drifted off to sleep. There were dreams there that he couldn't remember—dreams that left him clammy and sick in the morning.

But they survived. The Lutzes' first night away from the house in Amityville was over.

# 4

The first golden beams of light were filtering through the living room windows when Amy Lutz stirred. She wasn't in her own bed—she saw that right away. The room was cold and unfamiliar.

Amy didn't like that. She cried for her mommy, and then she waited. Mommy would answer soon, she knew. Everything would be all right then.

There was no response at first, so she cried again.

Kathy heard her daughter in the depths of sleep. She tried to answer her, but she couldn't seem to move. She tried to waken, but she was too tired, too exhausted. Too much had happened. She drifted back to sleep even as she struggled against it.

Amy was a very independent five-year-old, and what she couldn't get her parents to do for her, she did herself. Now she climbed from her makeshift bed and went to them. She shook her mother and called her name, but there was no response from Kathy at all. She tried George too, but the best she could get from him was a sleepy mumble.

Her five-year-old patience was at an end. Amy tried once more with no luck, and with a huge sigh she turned away and walked off, in search of something slightly more interesting than sleeping parents.

Halfway to the kitchen, she stopped. Her eyes lit up and she smiled widely. "Jodie!" she said happily. "You came with us!"

In the kitchen, she stood on a chair and got a box of cookies out of the cupboard. Then she found the milk on a low shelf in the refrigerator and sat at the table, preparing a small feast for two.

Joan Conners looked at her reflection in the bathroom mirror as she brushed her teeth. Age had been kind to her, she thought. Even now, in her late fifties, she had few wrinkles and no gray hair at all. She looked at her watch and smiled. It was only 6:30 A.M., but she felt refreshed and ready for a new day.

She looked in on her sleeping daughter and her son-in-law and her grandchildren. Amy's bed was empty, but she could guess where the little girl had gone. She turned and moved quietly to the kitchen.

She'll be needing some breakfast, Joan thought

busily. I hope she likes the bran cereal I've been using lately. I guess it won't seem very exciting to a five-year-old.

She hesitated when she heard the sound of voices coming from the kitchen. A visitor? she thought. So early? Then she realized it was only one voice, and a very young one at that. Amy was having a conversation with herself.

She smiled, remembering her own daughter's imaginary friend. When Kathy was four, Joan had had to set a place at the table for him and tuck him into bed with Kathy every night. She even had to give him a good-night kiss before Kathy would go to sleep. The friend had stayed more than a year.

She knew how important invisible playmates could be. Sometimes they were very real to children. So she was careful to enter the kitchen very quietly, and she smiled as she framed an appropriate greeting for the "two" of them.

Amy was sitting at the table with a glass of milk in her hand, talking to a space in the air above one of the empty chairs. Joan opened her mouth to say hello, to greet the friend, and something violent and invisible struck her across the face with a fierce, almost physical, force.

She fell back a step, her head swimming. Just like yesterday, she thought numbly.

Amy hadn't noticed her before, but now she turned and looked at Joan for the first time. In the same instant, the empty chair at her side slid back from the table with a loud scrape. A moment later it overturned and clattered to the floor.

A new wave of terror engulfed Joan Conners.

A blast of intense cold cut through her. She tried to scream, but her body refused to respond.

My God, her thoughts stuttered, what's happening? Am I dreaming? Am I asleep?

She staggered back another step and the kitchen wall hit her solidly in the back. She tried once more to shout a warning, to shout anything, and then the wave was past her, rushing through the door, disappearing into the house behind her. It left her unsteady on her feet, short of breath and trembling. She felt as if she had been released from the grip of a tremendous fist.

She slumped against the door, realizing in some dim corner of her mind that only a fraction of a second had passed since Amy had turned to look at her.

"Good morning, Grandma," the little girl said, smiling sweetly.

Joan took a huge breath and forced herself through the door. "Amy, were . . . were you talking to someone just now?" she whispered.

"No, Grandma."

"But I—" Joan hesitated. "I was sure I heard you speaking to someone as I came in."

"No, Grandma." Amy casually brushed the question aside. "Would you like a cookie?"

Joan looked at her granddaughter blankly, confused by the offhand attitude. It must be all that's happened lately, she thought. It was affecting them all.

She moved slowly across the kitchen and righted the overturned chair as Amy chattered happily about the weather, and her toys, and her plans for the day.

"I'm fine," Joan told herself as she put the water on to boil. "I'm just fine."

Five minutes later, she had convinced herself that nothing had really happened at all.

Kathy was the last to wake that morning. She showered slowly, almost luxuriously, and went into the kitchen for some breakfast. A note on the table explained that her mother was out shopping, and she could hear George in the driveway working on the van while the children played quietly in the front yard and Harry dozed in the den.

She was more than happy to spend a few minutes alone. She made herself a cup of coffee and went into the backyard, wandering aimlessly around the lawn, taking in the morning and warming in the winter's sunshine. Eventually, she found herself at the old swing set she had loved as a child, and without thinking, she sat on the seat and swung herself gently back and forth.

This yard held many memories. She remembered how Mr. Mandel from next door had helped assemble the swing, and how a few months later she'd fallen off for the first time and broken her arm. It didn't stop her, of course. She'd spent hours learning how to swing higher and higher, always pushing to reach that incredible weightless feeling that came for an instant when the swing reached as high as it could.

I was a real tomboy, Kathy thought. She looked up at the almost mystical weightless space and wondered how she had ever had the courage to do that. She could have fallen and hurt herself badly.

Childhood had been a daring and adventurous time, but watching Greg, Matt, and Amy reach out and touch life was her joy now. Parents may not have the reckless abandon they had when they were young, she thought, but helping their children through their growing pains was the next best thing.

George came into the backyard, wiping his hands on a rag. "Mornin', babe," he said. "How are you feeling?"

She smiled. "Fine, now that I've finally had a full night's sleep."

George fought to keep a look of shock from his face, but Kathy saw his consternation.

"Are you all right, George?"

"Just a little headache. Nothing serious." This wasn't the first time Kathy hadn't remembered an attack on her, and in a way he was glad. Why worry her unnecessarily? His earlier conversation with Joan had convinced him that *she* hadn't heard anything during the night, either. Maybe it was best if the incident was just forgotten.

He looked at Kathy dangling her feet, and impulsively he moved behind her and said, "Let me give you a push."

"No, George. I'm too heavy for the swing now."

"It'll hold you, don't worry." He pushed her forward.

"George, don't!" Kathy squealed, trying to pretend she didn't like it. But it was a good feeling. Silly, she knew, but nice, somehow. Comforting.

She moved up and down, back and forth, enjoying the sunshine and the feeling of George's hands on her back. She didn't push the swing to its limit—that was for children—but it was fun just the same.

She laughed loudly, and realized how good it felt to laugh again. It had been a long time.

George felt like hell the next morning. He sat alone at the kitchen table and watched the steam rise from his coffee cup, scowling at it as it rolled into the air and disappeared.

If only this headache would drift away like that, he thought. It's as bad as the ones I had at the house. The slightest movement brought nausea and a sick pounding between his temples, and even the reflection of the morning sunlight in his cup sent flashes of pain through his forehead.

George had never had a problem with headaches before Amityville. Now they were regular occurrences—a legacy from the house.

Kathy hurried into the kitchen. Her face was pale, her eyes alive with an old familiar fear. She stopped when she saw George's face. He looked terribly drawn, and something about his expression made her think of Amityville. "Are you all right, babe?" she asked quietly.

George didn't answer immediately. He was fighting to calm the pounding in his head.

"Is it the same as at the house?"

"I'll be all right. What is it?"

She had to force it out. "Flies," she whispered.

He pulled himself up, and Kathy led him to the bathroom that was next to the back door. In it there was a beige washer and dryer, and on top of the washer there was a neat pile of clean, folded clothing.

The outside screen of the bathroom window

was covered with thousands of large black flies. George's skin crawled at the eerie buzzing moan they made as they swarmed over each other, two and three deep.

Kathy tensed violently at his side. She squeezed his hand so strongly that he had to pull it loose.

*Calm*, he ordered himself. *Stay calm.*

"There's too many of them for a swatter," he said as steadily as he could. "I'll roll up some newspaper. If—if Joan has some fly spray, that might help, too."

It came out better than he expected, but inside his thoughts were spinning. These couldn't have come from the house in Amityville, he thought. They *couldn't* have. But here they are.

"I'd better get rid of them before Joan gets home," he said stiffly. "No need to worry her about it." The words seemed to fall from his mouth, cool and nonchalant, but he was cold inside, cold clear to the bone.

What are we going to do? he thought as he turned away from the window and tried to block out the incessant roar of the insects. *What in God's name are we going to do?*

Kathy said nothing. She couldn't. She only stared wide-eyed at the living black curtain, horror holding her frozen in its grip.

At the Amityville house, she had managed to keep going somehow. But not now. Not today. It was supposed to be over. She had actually begun to relax. Not . . . now. . . .

George tried to break her out of it. "Kathy!" he said sharply. "Kathy, it's all right! I'll get rid of them." She watched his lips moving, but her mind was drifting in a silent, separate world.

Please, he thought, fighting down panic. Please,

**60**

God, let her be all right. He took his wife and led her gently from the bathroom, glad that his children were playing next door and that Joan was visiting friends. He'd have to get rid of the flies before they got back, but Kathy came first. Always.

He sat her in a chair in the living room, horrified at the stiff, lifeless look in her eyes. Her hands were icy cold, and he rubbed them rapidly, talking to her, saying anything that came into his mind. After a few moments, warmth began to seep slowly into her fingers. She looked up at him with a tiny spark of new awareness.

"Feeling better, Kath?"

"I'm fine, George." Her words were distant and expressionless. "I'm fine."

How much more of this could she take? he wondered. How much more could any of them take?

Kathy seemed to improve as the day wore on, and by late in the afternoon, as she sat with her mother at the kitchen table having coffee and buttered rolls, she was almost her old self.

Greg and Matt were down the block, playing with newly made friends. Before the boys had moved on to yet another playground, they had used huge cardboard boxes and plastic ray-guns to transform the backyard into a space station. The small blue pedal-car that Amy loved hadn't fit into that scene. It had been pushed into the driveway and forgotten.

Now Amy was alone in the yard, and quite content. She pedaled the car across the driveway, to the porch and back again, over and over, humming happily to herself as she drove.

It's nice to have children around the house again, Joan thought. She sipped her coffee and realized for the first time that she hadn't seen her son-in-law for over an hour.

"Did George go into the office?" she asked her daughter.

Kathy took a bite from her buttered roll. "Yes. He said something about more problems with the tax audit."

"He didn't look well this morning, Kathy. Is he up to all that?"

Kathy frowned. "Well, things haven't been too good with the business lately. I think he feels as if he *has* to go in."

She cleared the table and put the dishes in the sink, and as she turned on the hot water to fill the basin, something outside the window caught her eye.

Kathy stopped and stared into the yard, frozen in place. Scalding water burned her hand, and she pulled away without thinking.

"Kathy?" her mother said, standing in alarm. "What is it?"

She didn't answer. Without another word, Kathy turned away from the sink and ran through the back door, leaving the water to gush through an unstoppered sink.

"Kathy!" Joan said again, and followed her outdoors. She found her daughter standing on the porch, swaying and silent, staring at her little girl.

Amy was in the middle of the yard, and the blue pedal-car was making a tight circle around her. Its pedals twirled furiously, its steering wheel twisted, its hard rubber tires crunched and hissed in the grass. As they watched, it completed a circle around Amy and began another circuit.

But there was no one in the seat. The toy car was moving by itself.

Amy laughed happily, her blond hair blowing lightly in the afternoon breeze. She was talking to the driverless car.

"Faster, Jodie!" she said, excited. "Go faster!"

Kathy's hand came to her mouth to stifle a cry. She tried to move forward, but she seemed rooted to the spot. Something was forcing her to stand still.

The car suddenly slowed, weaved out of control, and came to a stop.

"Jodie! Where are you going?" Amy asked the empty air.

Kathy strained against the force that held her. "Let me go to her," she pleaded. *"Please!"*

She broke free and rushed to Amy's side, taking her roughly by the arm.

"Who are you talking to, Amy?" she snapped. *"Who are you talking to?"*

"No one, Mommy," she said innocently. "I'm just playing." She tried to change the subject. "Will *you* play with me?"

Kathy shook her roughly. "Don't lie to me, Amy! I heard you talking to someone. Was it Jodie?"

Amy didn't want to answer. She stuck out her lower lip and softly said: "Yes."

"I thought we left Jodie in Amityville."

"No, Mommy. Jodie's my special friend."

Kathy bent closer to her daughter. "Amy, we have to leave all that behind us. You have to tell Jodie to leave."

"But Jodie's my friend," Amy repeated. She

couldn't understand why everyone seemed upset. Jodie was *nice*.

"Kathy!" Joan's voice had an edge that approached panic. Kathy turned quickly and looked toward the kitchen. Her mother was standing in the doorway, her face ashen.

"It's all right, Mom," she said, not believing it herself.

As she turned away, Amy looked at a space just above her mother's head. She listened for a second, then whispered, "I don't want to leave *you*, either, Jodie."

Kathy turned back to her daughter. "Amy, tell Jodie to leave. *Now*." The tone of her voice left no doubt—this was an order, not a request. Then she hurried to the kitchen door to help Joan. She could not remember ever seeing her mother more frightened. "What is it, Mom?"

"This morning. In the kitchen. I heard Amy talking to someone. I thought—I thought I saw a chair move by itself, and I felt terrible..." She stumbled on the words. "A cold feeling. I thought I'd imagined it. I guess I wanted to *believe* I'd imagined it. But..."

Joan didn't finish her sentence. Instead, her eyes looked blankly at the innocent blue pedalcar. It was rocking back and forth on its hard rubber wheels. Back and forth.

She didn't need to say anything else. Kathy knew what she meant. Her mother had finally become part of the nightmare.

*It's following us*. Her thoughts slowed and teetered as they had that morning. *It's following us*. Her mind began to slip again, drifting, turning cool and slow, in circles, like the pedalcar. *It's following us*.

What could she tell Joan that might help her understand? Nothing. Nothing would help. She didn't understand it herself. Kathy put her arms around her mother and drew her close. Joan returned the embrace, but neither of them spoke. There was nothing to say.

Amy stood by the car and listened. She smiled and nodded at a voice only she could hear.

"All right, Jodie," she said. "It will be our secret."

# 5

Kathy knelt beside the makeshift beds and listened to the slow and steady breathing of her two sons. They were fast asleep. Amy too was snoring softly, her knees drawn up to her chin as she dreamed. Kathy tucked in the blankets and brushed her lips across the little girl's forehead.

So pretty. So peaceful. Would they ever really know what damage the last weeks had done?

Kathy sighed and moved a stack of library books off the cushions where she and George had made their own bed. Her husband scarcely noticed her as she slipped under the blankets and nestled close to him.

A few days before, George had visited the local library and returned with a load of books on psychic manifestations and demonology. He had been lost in them ever since, devouring page after page with barely a word to his wife or children.

She put a hand on his chest and moved closer, but George was completely absorbed in his reading. As she watched him, wondering what he hoped to gain from the books, he seemed to find something particularly important. He nodded to himself, and his brow creased in concentration. He scratched at his thick beard and grumbled.

"Anything interesting?" Kathy asked softly.

He nodded absentmindedly. She doubted that he had heard her at all.

Then, abruptly, George marked his place with a slip of paper, sighed deeply, and laid the book aside.

He looks tired, she thought. As tired as I feel.

"It seems that our experiences aren't unique," he said, running a finger over the stack of heavy books at his side. "There are hundreds of documented cases of houses with . . . *problems*." He scowled at the word.

"Problems like ours?"

"Similar."

Why did that sound hopeful to her? she wondered.

"What did they do about it?"

George rubbed his face with both hands, washing away fatigue. "Different things, but it all boils down to finding someone who understands this kind of situation—somebody who'll go into the house and 'cleanse' it."

"Do you think that can help us?" she whispered. "Even now?" Kathy felt cold and a little lost, and she moved even closer to her husband.

George slipped an arm around her and kissed the top of her head. "Of course it can help. We're going back to our own house, and soon. It's our home, Kathy. We aren't going to give it up without a fight."

Kathy smiled and laid her head against his chest. He's a fighter, she thought. A strong man. It was one of the qualities that had attracted her to him when they first met. And that seemed so long ago now; so long ago.

"Where are we going to find someone to cleanse it?" she said.

"Well, Linda Murillo suggested a team of . . . I guess you'd call them psychic investigators. John Davies and Laura Harding. She told me they've been dealing with problems like this for better than thirty years, with a lot of success. Maybe they'd be interested."

He was trying to sound positive—he wanted to be positive, despite his doubts.

Kathy too was intent on finding some thread of optimism. "Can she contact them for us?"

"I think so. I'll call her in the morning and ask her to give it a try."

George laid back against the pillow, and for a few minutes neither of them spoke. Kathy was drifting off to sleep when he broke the silence.

"I think I'll go to church tomorrow," he said softly, "and see Father Mancusso."

Kathy didn't answer. Father Mancusso was the priest who had blessed their house in Amityville only minutes after they had moved in. Later that same day, he had tried to call them. "Get out," he had said. "You're in danger!" But before he could explain, a strange static had distorted his voice, and no matter how often they had tried, they hadn't been able to talk with him again for weeks.

He had been right. In the month that followed his warning, awful things had happened to the Lutzes—things she never wanted to think about again. And now the sickness that had infected the house seemed to be following them, tracing their path.

No. She wasn't going to think about it. She wasn't going to start trembling and crying again. She thought about Father Mancusso—a good man, a kind man—and felt an unaccountable warmth flood through her. Maybe he can help, she thought. He's a man of God.

George was thinking, too. All the bits of information, all the cases and quotes and theories he had absorbed over the last few days clicked and trickled through him. Then something unexpectedly fit into place, and his arm tightened around Kathy.

"Kathy?" he said softly. "Babe?"

"Mm-hum?"

"I've been thinking. Maybe we should get a tape recorder and put down all the experiences we've had over the last month or so."

She looked up at him, a little confused. "You mean talk onto a tape? Record it?"

"Right. I've been reading how that can help sometimes. Release fears and anxieties that are rooted deep down in the subconscious. Like written affirmations can strengthen positive thoughts." Kathy looked doubtful, but he pressed on. "Besides, when Laura Harding and John Davies —or whoever we can get to help—want to know

70

what's happened, we won't have to go over it again and again. We can just play them the tapes."

"All right," she said firmly. "If you think it will help, let's do it." But thinking about those days in the house was the last thing she wanted to do.

Maybe it will help us get away, she prayed. Get it behind us, destroy it, erase it.

She was drifting into sleep now, and for an instant she saw the shadow of a shadow: the outline of what she imagined Amy's pig-thing to be.

Maybe now that Jodie was gone, the influence of the house would disappear as well. Maybe they really were safe now, for the first time in a long time.

She held that thought tightly as sleep enclosed her. It felt good.

# 6

Harry was the first to sense it: the trace of an odor, the first stray particles of ash and expanding gas.

His black eyes flicked open. His ears snapped up and swiveled. He jumped to his feet and lurched forward, claws digging into the dirt, chain rattling like a winch.

He barked shrilly and leapt for the outer cellar door, but the chain at his collar yanked him back. He struggled to stand again, straining against the leash and yelping. He pulled so tightly at his collar that his barking squeezed into a strangled, desperate yap.

Inside the house, George Lutz snapped awake. That damn dog barks all the time, he thought. Ever since—

He sat upright and remembered where he

was. Joan's house. East Babylon. But what was bothering Harry?

He sniffed at the air, and something faintly unpleasant tickled his nose. He threw his covers off and inhaled sharply again . . . then again.

It's very faint, he thought. Maybe it's my imagination.

No, he had a good sense of smell. It was smoke.

He took Kathy by the shoulders and shook her, but she only winced in her sleep and tried to hide under the covers. He shook her again, so sharply her head snapped forward on her neck.

She was suddenly wide awake. She tensed under his hands and looked up. "George! What is it?"

"I smell something burning. I think it's inside the house."

"My God." She struggled to her feet, feeling numb all over. I might be dreaming again, she thought. It had happened so often in Amityville, and had seemed so real.

She wrapped herself in a robe as George padded barefoot down the hall and through the kitchen. The smell kept getting away from him. He was too groggy with sleep to track it down; and the barking was driving him crazy.

He stumbled out the back door, and Kathy followed him a moment later. She saw Harry straining toward the house, his chain pulled tight as a wire. There were flecks of lather on his jaws that glinted in the moonlight. His bark was little more than a gasp for air.

"Harry! Take it easy," George said, forcing the dog back, to take the pressure off its neck. "I'm awake now. It's all right." George knelt beside Harry and patted his head. "You can smell it, too, huh?" George looked around slowly. "Where's it coming from, Harry?"

The dog sat trembling under his master's hand for a moment, his sides heaving. Then he barked again—a wild, yowling sound—and leapt for the cellar door. The chain snapped tight, ringing like a bell, and forced him to the ground.

Kathy started to turn on the overhead kitchen light, then thought better of it. She switched on the small light over the sink instead. No need to disturb the children, she thought. Not unless something is really wrong.

George rushed back into the kitchen, hugging himself for warmth. He was in his underwear and a T-shirt, and it was cold enough outside for his breath to show up in the moonlight.

"Can you smell it?" he asked. Kathy nodded. He sniffed at the air, then sniffed again, and turned to the door that led to the cellar stairs.

He put his hand on the knob. It seemed cool. He laid his ear against the wood. Nothing.

What the hell, he thought, and in one swift movement he threw the door wide open.

A fist of dense black smoke gushed through the doorway and engulfed him. Without thinking, George rushed forward, through the cellar door and beyond. Suddenly his bare feet were on the stairs. He was stumbling down into the blackness.

*No*, he ordered himself. *Wait*. He threw out his hands, found the banister, and pulled himself to a stop. *Wait*, he commanded again, and tried to turn around. Behind him, he heard Kathy calling.

It was hard—much harder than it should have been—but he turned and began to climb the stairs, one at a time. His mouth was clamped shut. His nose was blocked. He had to get back to fresh air.

Abruptly his head and shoulders emerged from the smoke. It seemed to stop just beyond the cellar door, rolling like a cloud but not moving forward. Kathy, pale and remote in her dressing gown, was only a few feet away, untouched by the smoke.

"Wake your mother," he grated. "And get the kids outside."

He thought he saw her nod before he plunged back into the smoke. His feet found the stairs again, and he felt wetness on his cheeks. My eyes must be watering, he thought.

He hit the bottom of the stairs with a *clunk*, and a sudden updraft pushed the smoke away. He saw the fire itself for the first time.

Five parallel horizontal lines of fire climbed the cement wall on the far side of the basement. That's wrong, he thought dully. How could it burn like that? Then the image teetered, shimmered, and resolved itself into something recognizable.

It was the shelves where they kept the tools and old magazines, the boxes of unidentified papers and clothes. The shelves themselves were on fire, and *they* were causing the parallel lines. But the cartons and lumber and scraps of cloth on top of the shelves were just beginning to flare. Why would the wood burn before the paper? he wondered.

He didn't have time to think about it. The fire was already spreading. Even the cold cement slab under his feet was heating up. George glanced around and saw a filthy tarpaulin crumpled in a nearby corner. He seized it and beat at the flames, but the canvas was too heavy and pockmarked with holes, and the fire was already over his head and lapping at the beams. It chattered along the molding, chewed on the drywall. It was slowly swallowing up the discarded pictures frames, newspaper, and broken furniture.

He fell back, gasping for breath, and let the canvas fall. No good. No point. He coughed shallowly, trying to clear the smoke from his mouth, and concentrated.

Smoke rises, he thought, and fell to his knees. He was on all fours now—like Harry, just outside the cellar door but miles and miles away. He gulped at the relatively clear air only inches from the concrete slab, but even that tasted brackish and dirty.

There was a sound above and behind him, at the top of the stairs, as if a door had opened or closed. He wondered if there was a lock on it, or a knob on the inside.

A bad way to die, he thought. Trapped in a burning cellar.

Something cold and wet touched him on the arm. George almost screamed in spite of himself and turned to bat it away.

It was Kathy, holding the brass nozzle of the large garden hose. The swollen green length of the water line snaked up the stairs behind her.

"The water's... already... on," she said in small, gulping breaths. She was red-eyed and smeared with soot, and an abrasion on her knee was leaking blood. She saw George looking at it.

"I tripped," she said shortly, and thrust the nozzle into his hands.

The fire roared at his back, and George turned on it, twisting the nozzle as he spun. The water gushed out in a thick stream—thank God the water pressure's strong! he thought—and tore holes in the wall of flames.

The flames nearest to him turned red and shrank. Good, George thought. Here was something he could fight, something he could beat. He took a step forward, blasted a bit of burning wood away, then took another step.

Behind the dying flames, half obscured by the billowing smoke, the shimmering core of the fire was untouched. That's what I have to get at, he thought, feeling the heat under his bare feet grow more intense; sensing Kathy close at his side. If I can smother that area with water, the worst will be over.

He took another step forward and directed the water higher, aiming for the bright center of the blaze—and incredibly, inexplicably, something *changed*.

The water pressure decreased, or the heat violently intensified—maybe both, George thought later, maybe neither—but between one breath and the next, he was losing the battle. The fire was reaching forward again, and the water was steaming away like droplets thrown on a griddle.

George blinked, tried to clear the sweat and soot from his eyes, then blinked again in disbelief.

The orange white center of the fire seemed to be taking on a human shape, as if a skeleton had wrapped itself in flame. As George watched, it seemed to grow and solidify into limbs, hair, musculature. First shoulders over a torso, then a head over the shoulders, and finally a set of vacant, bottomless eyes—holes in the heat— that stared at him through the smoke.

First there were two fire-creatures. A moment more, and there were three of them. And four. And five. Not like imagined faces in a fireplace, he knew, or ghostly images or blazing inkblots. Real things. Demons of fire, with arms and fingers and gaping, toothless mouths. Were they real? *Could* they be? Or had the last shred of George's sanity finally torn away?

He crashed into Kathy as he threw himself back to the stairs.

It wasn't just a fire anymore. It was something else—something that was part of the monstrous thing that had followed them from Amityville. Fire he could fight. Burning wood, strangling smoke, even death—he could challenge even that. But not the power from Amityville.

"Get out of here!" he shouted at Kathy, and he felt her hair brush the back of his neck as she shook her head no. He opened the nozzle on the hose as wide as it would go, but the water trickled comically from the opening.

The flame-things moved forward and surrounded them. In desperation, George grabbed the smoldering tarpaulin and flung it at the nearest creature. The canvas wound around it like the wings of a bat, hissing and smoking, and pulled the creature to the floor.

It thrashed like a dying animal for one long moment, then lay still, flickering and steaming in the heat. It was dead. The tarpaulin had smothered it.

They're *not* invincible, George realized. It's just fire after all! The instant the thought flashed through his mind, the hose bucked in his hands and the water pressure increased again. He shot a hole in the nearest creature and breathed a huge sigh as it withered. Then he sliced it in two with a thinner, more powerful stream, and it flickered out.

Did it make a sound? he asked himself later. Maybe. Or maybe it was the crackling rip of wood tearing free, or paper crinkling in the heat. There was no time to think about it.

Another creature took its place, and George cut that one down, too. He was moving steadily forward now, the water breaking up the creatures into random patterns of flame. "Finally!" he shouted to himself.

The fire-creatures were gone now. Only one area of fire was left. It licked feverishly at the roof, but George hit it at its source with a full blast of water and it too twisted and sizzled, and finally faded away.

The fire and the fire-creatures—if they'd ever really existed—were defeated. Now there was only the crackle of the wood as it cooled, the stink of burnt plastic and rubber, the film of smoke that thinned and rose to disappear.

"Kathy? George? Come out of there! I'll call the fire department!"

It was Kathy's mother, standing at the top of the stairs with the children, peering anxiously into the smoke.

George threw the hose away and put an arm around his wife. She leaned against him, gasping for breath. "It's all right," he said as they climbed the stairs very slowly. "It's over."

Joan helped them into the kitchen and sat them down at the kitchen table, then ordered the children to sit with them. Everything looked abnormally clear to George, as if he had lived in smoke all his life and now, for the first time, it had lifted.

"Are you sure you don't want me to call the Fire Department?" Joan asked, running water in the sink and soaking a washrag.

"I checked it," George said, coughing up dust. "It's completely dead."

Dead? he thought. That seems appropriate. But those . . . *things* he saw, or thought he saw— had Kathy seen them too? Should he ask her about them, or just let it go?

He looked at his wife, huddled in a blanket and shivering at the sudden change in temperature. No, he decided. Why make matters worse? Just let it pass, try and forget, and—and keep running. Keep running until the hideous power from Amityville grew tired of toying with them, until they reached a place far enough away. A place beyond its reach . . . if such a place existed.

Was that the future he had to look forward to? Was that what his children would inherit from him?

"Amy?" Kathy said. She sounded strange.

The little girl, all eyes and uncombed hair, looked up expectantly, then looked away when she saw the expression on her mother's face.

"What is it, babe?" George asked. He was almost too tired to care.

"Yesterday, Amy asked me how we would get out of the house if there was a fire," she said, staring at the little girl.

George was dumbfounded. "But she was asleep

with us, Kathy," he said as gently as he could.

"I know," Kathy said reasonably. "It's just that she asked about a fire, and she's never asked anything like that before. I was busy at the time, and I put her off, but it was yesterday she asked—"

At that exact moment Amy looked quickly at the boys, a mischievous twinkle in her eyes. As if on a silent command the three of them leapt to their feet and raced off toward the lounge room to play, laughing happily all the while.

George's mind was spinning. Of course Amy didn't set the fire, he thought. That was impossible. But how could she have known about it? It's ridiculous, he told himself. He wouldn't even be considering it now, except for the look he'd seen on her face. It had reminded him of something.

*Relief*, he realized, is an emotion for grown-ups. All too often, it can be tied up with lying and fear—with getting away with something. Innocence has nothing to do with it.

Is that what was bothering him so much? To see his five-year-old daughter run away from him at the first opportunity, looking relieved?

Kathy touched the soles of his bare feet very lightly, and he jumped at the unexpected pain. "Come into the bathroom, babe," she said. "I'll put something on those burns."

"They're okay," he said, vaguely surprised that he had been burnt at all. "They don't hurt."

"Let me put a little cream on them anyway. In case they hurt later."

George nodded and stood up awkwardly, walking on the sides of his feet to the bathroom down the hall. "At least it's all over," Kathy said hopefully. "And there's no great harm done."

George smiled grimly at that. He knew Kathy understood what was over, and what wasn't. And they both knew how much harm had been done.

"The body of Christ."

First: an old woman with bright, penetrating eyes. She comes twice a day, he thought as he laid the host on her tongue. I wonder why so often?

"The body of Christ."

A fresh-faced novitiate from the convent. What awful thing must she have done, to come so far for the sacrament? He noticed his hand was trembling.

"The body of Christ."

A young man with curly brown hair and a full beard. His familiar face was etched with lines of worry and fear that made him look ten years too old. The priest recognized him: George Lutz.

He smiled as George's mouth closed over the wafer of unleavened bread, and George smiled in return.

"The body of Christ."

A boy just out of catechism. And a grandmother from Italy who barely spoke English, though she had lived in New York State for fifteen years. And a construction worker praying for his wife, who was dying of cancer.

He offered each the body and blood of Christ. He blessed them all and finished the sacrament, while his thoughts wandered away into stranger territory.

He was tired—very tired. More tired than he had a right to be. And though he was happy to see George—thank God the Lutzes had finally left that hideous house!—he despised the memories that George brought with him.

Something was wrong with Father Mancusso. It had begun the day he visited that unpretentious Dutch Colonial in Amityville—the moment he stepped across the threshold and tried to bless the new home, and a voice that came from no human throat had ordered him to leave.

There had been physical illnesses and fevers. There had been the stench of defecation that had filled only his rooms at the rectory, and no others. There had been physical attacks that had left him cut and bruised, visitations by night creatures that some called hallucinations and others called the assaults of demons. And more—more than he could bear to think about.

Even his brother clerics, who could have given him strength and helped in the fight, had refused to help. So all the talk of the church's place in protecting the immortal soul was just that—*talk*, and very little else. The church still taught the secret rites of exorcism to certain advanced men, supposedly for those rare instances when the need for it might arise, but even highly placed members of the church's hierarchy didn't believe that such things really happened. They couldn't face a real confrontation.

He had tried to ignore the manifestations, tried to explain them away. He had even tried to exorcise them himself, with the help of one loyal, if frightened, friend. And when George Lutz had called him and told him that they had left Amityville forever, he had thought that the horror had finally passed him by.

But the directionless, pervasive exhaustion that had weighed him down since his first visit to Amityville was still with him. It was turning him old and bitter before his time, and somehow he simply couldn't believe that the rest of the horror had vanished. It was still with them all. Hiding. Waiting.

I'm too young to feel this old, he thought as he finished the sacrament.

"In the name of the Father, the Son, and the Holy Ghost. Amen."

Father Mancusso met George at the foot of the altar as the congregation filed out of the sanctuary. "Let's go to my rooms," he said, and George nodded.

They sat opposite each other in a simply furnished, slightly overtidy study on the second floor of the rectory and drank their tea very slowly. George was taking a long time to answer any questions, even the most innocuous ones.

"I can't tell you how happy I was to see you at Communion, George," he said warmly. "I know you weren't raised Catholic, but it will give you great comfort nonetheless." He looked at George very closely. "I assume that is why you're here? For my help?"

George stared into his cup and thought hard. "I had to come see you," he said slowly. "I'm sorry, but I didn't know where else to go."

"You haven't gone back to the house?" Father Mancusso said sharply. Good Lord, if they had done something as foolish as that, there was nothing more—

"No, of course not. We left it better than a

week ago, and we haven't been back. We may never go back. But Father—" George looked up, and Father Mancusso felt as if he were looking through him, at some horrifying thing hiding beyond the walls of his room. "Father, the attacks haven't stopped."

Ah. As simple—and as awful—as that. The power, the *thing* that had found them, would not release its hold. And I am as threatened by it as they.

The thought nauseated Father Mancusso. The horror from Amityville was still at his heels, still ready to spring. If the Lutzes' flight from the house hadn't sent it away, or at least placated it, then what would? Could they expect more attacks? Would this innocent discussion itself be followed by another withering sickness?

He resisted a shudder and forced himself to look at it from a more positive angle. Perhaps George had instinctively done something that would put this all right—if, in fact, it could ever be put right at all.

"The sacrament of Communion is a very powerful thing, George. It opens your soul to God. And if it does not make you a better, stronger person—well, at least it inclines you toward the light rather than the darkness. Do you understand?"

George nodded. "But I'm not Catholic."

"Nonetheless, take comfort where you can. Faith, after all, is faith. That's what you must have."

"I hope you're right, Father."

"I am," he said, putting a hand on George's shoulder. "Have faith in that, too."

● ● ●

He stood on a vast, featureless plain of blue dust. He turned to the south and saw nothing. There was nothing to the north or the east or the west. Only blue dust, stretching to a skyline as flat and sharp as an incision, splayed open under a swirling gray green sky that was clogged with edgeless, fetid clouds.

He was alone. He could see it, feel it—*taste* it. He was completely alone.

A whip-crack of emotion flinched through him, and he twitched at its impact. It came again, in a slow, more painful wave.

It was fear—fear like an electric current coursing through him.

He cried out and began to run in no direction at all. It was stupid, he knew, running from nothing to nowhere, running because something he couldn't see might be chasing him. Still, he ran.

There was something up ahead now—something bright against the dull blue dust and gray green sky. A light...a thread of warmth. If I can reach that, he thought, if I can—

Then the fear was back, plunging deeper than before. He hunched his back against it; he lowered his head and ran even harder.

He was starting to black out. He was starting to lose control when something hit him and nearly brought him down. The air gushed out of him and he rolled back, peering at the thing that had hit him as he gasped for breath.

It was a human figure in a cloak as gray as ash. No eyes. No face. Only a bottomless black hole beneath the cowl.

It took a step toward him.

He screamed and ran away from the hooded thing. The warm light had disappeared now, swallowed up by the dust, but still he ran. This can't go on much longer, he told himself. It can't.

He threw a glance over his shoulder, and the thing was right behind him. He looked forward again and shouted, throwing his hands out, trying to stop, trying to avoid the collision—but he ran into the harsh wooden wall and bounced away like a rubber ball. He stared at the structure in front of him, and the fear gushed up again.

It was the house. The house from Amityville.

What's it doing here? It shouldn't *be* here! He shook his head like a punch-drunk fighter and turned. The hooded thing was still sliding toward him.

Gotta get away, he thought. This way. He ran along the edge of the house, away from the wall and the hooded thing. Without warning, there was a billowing of inky black smoke, and as he passed the corner of the house, something reached out for him—the cloudlike thing that had tried to trap him in Amityville.

"No!" he shouted, and ran again. The house was behind him now. The hooded thing and black cloud were both giving chase. But it was clear in this direction. Clear, except for—

The house. It was in front of him again.

He skidded to a stop and looked over his shoulder. Still there. Closer now. He ran parallel to the wall, past the stairs leading to the front door.

But, as he moved, the front door flew open

and a black, gnarled figure lunged at him. It had eyes as red and alive as embers; a broad, twisted body so black that its features were swallowed in its own shadows; a snout like a boar, squashed flat and dripping.

A pig-thing, he thought numbly as he spun out of its way. My God, is this what little Amy sees? Is this Jodie?

He was running out of directions, but he ran once more. The terror lashed at him like a physical thing; the smell—a thick, sickening stench—dragged at his feet like a weight.

*Run*, he told himself. Your legs are giving out, your feet are cut and bleeding, it hurts to breathe, but *run*. It's clear, it's clear, there's nothing but—

The house.

He cursed at it and pounded on the wooden walls, then pushed himself away and ran. Only one direction now: no house, no hideous things, no fear in *this* direction only. He ran and ran, ignoring the smell, ignoring the terror, ignoring the pain that sliced into his legs . . . and saw a light up ahead. The warm light, the good light he had glimpsed before. He shouted and scrambled forward, stumbling in the dust, and the pig-thing touched his shoulder. He screamed at the cold pain and lurched away. Just a few more steps! he thought. Only a few more steps!

The light was a circle now, throwing out a radiance that made the dead blue plain glow as if it were on fire. The monstrosities at his back screeched and growled at the illumination. They don't like it, he knew. It hurts them somehow.

Now the circle was a door, like the door to a vault. As he ran toward it, the door swung open and the light inside blinded him with its brilliance. The things behind him fell back, howling in frustration. The smell washed away. The terror receded.

There was a figure in front of the light, dressed in robes that flowed like water. Father Mancusso? he thought. No. Another priest? Or is it human at all?

Now he was only steps away, and in the white figure's hand he saw a Communion wafer. He smiled at that. It was familiar to him—real, somehow.

He threw himself forward, across the gleaming threshold of the vault door, and the things at his back yowled like wounded animals. The light blazed around him with a heatless, penetrating brilliance. The hooded figure screamed, the cloud shivered, and the pig-thing bellowed and screeched.

And they shrank. He watched them twist as they withered and blackened. He watched them fall into heaps of smoldering ash and bone, and as they disappeared completely, the vault door slammed with a loud, almost comforting *thud*.

He was safe. Safe for the first time.

Warmth flooded into him. He turned to the figure of light and smiled; a hand reached out to touch him.

"Thank you," he said, and the figure smiled.

Kathy Lutz awoke when her husband screamed. She clutched at him in the darkness, groped for a light, and when the lamp came on she saw what nightmares could do.

George had thrown all his covers off. He was bathed in sweat and bleeding from tiny cuts where his nails had dug into the palms of his hands. The tendons of his neck and the muscles of his arms and calves were all as tight as stretched wire. And his legs twitched and scuttled against the mattress as if he were trying to run.

He screamed again—a sound that degenerated into a mumbling whisper—and his legs moved even faster. Kathy had the awful feeling this was more than just a bad dream, that he was in physical danger. She knew people could die of fear, and her husband's features were twisted by it.

She put her hands on his shoulders and called his name. I have to wake him up, she thought. Now. She shook him roughly. "George, wake up! *Wake up!*"

Suddenly, without warning, he stopped moving. His shoulders relaxed under her hands. The tension drained out of his body in a rapid, almost instantaneous wave. For one horrible moment, Kathy thought she was too late. Then he moved comfortably in his sleep . . . and smiled.

It was an expression his wife had not seen in a very long time. Not a weary smile, or a forced one. There was no element of irony or grim determination in it. It was an innocent, beatific smile. As if George had found something very special . . . and very comforting.

Tears filled Kathy's eyes. She held them back long enough to pull the covers around her husband, then she slipped beneath the blankets herself and curled into the crook of his arm. She cried herself to sleep, weeping with a strange, unsettling mixture of relief and dread.

It had to get better, she thought as she drifted away. Please God, let it get better.

## 7

There must be ten thousand pizza places in the United States, Linda Murillo thought, and they are all exactly the same. The size and decor changes, but they all *feel* alike. In St. Louis, in L.A., in Fort Worth, in Brooklyn—all the same. She knew that for a fact. During her career as a television news reporter and producer, she'd been in all those places—and in restaurants in all those places.

So with all that sameness running clear across the United States, she thought, with all that bizarre unity in aroma and menu, why does this place feel different?

She stood in the doorway of the pizza joint in Amityville, New York, and shook off the cold. It was a weekday afternoon, and the restaurant was nearly empty. A teenage boy with a set of very free hands was talking to his girl friend at one table near the back. They didn't even look up when she came in. The sixteen-year-old behind the counter was working on a huge wad of chewing gum and reading *People* magazine, and the cooks were mumbling about the Jets. And sitting at a table in the exact center of the room was a normal-looking middle-aged couple who smiled and waved as she entered.

Those are ghost-hunters? Linda thought, amused in spite of herself. She'd seen their pictures before; they were John Davies and Laura Harding. But God, they looked so—so regular.

John was heavyset and robust, with silver hair that was neatly trimmed and carefully combed. He looked like a friendly uncle who probably had a nice, steady job with the government. Laura was slim, svelte, and very attractive in her late forties—a sharply dressed woman who had blossomed in maturity.

Linda waved back and worked her way through the empty chairs to the couple, thinking about these two demonologists. She'd read the clip file on Davies and Harding that the station's research people had put together, but how true could it be? Experts in the occult, it said. Thirty years of experience in everything from ghosts to demonic possessions to overactive poltergeists and the occasional haunted house. And both Davies and Harding themselves had confirmed it all during a telephone conversation with Linda just a few days earlier. It had been a disarmingly casual acknowledgment.

"Of course," John Davies had said, "we're concentrating on the study of demonic forces in all its manifestations these days, but we'd be more than happy to talk with you."

Weird, Linda thought. A little too weird for me. But she greeted them with a smile and introduced herself without a hint of discomfort. Keep an open mind, she thought. You never know, you just never know.

"We're so glad you called us, Ms. Murillo," Laura said in a low, confidential voice.

What remarkable eyes, Linda thought. They were deep, calm—a little awesome.

"We've heard your reports on the tube. Is that all right, calling it 'the tube'?"

Linda laughed in spite of herself. "I call it worse than that," she said.

John nodded, his cheeks flushed. "Well, we saw your reports. And we've read a little in the papers, too—but not too much." He glanced at Laura, and Linda felt as if some personal communication passed between them. "We don't *want* to know too much," he said.

Oh.

The door of the restaurant opened, and she turned to see a bearded man better than six feet tall hustle into the waiting area. He was dressed in blue jeans and a denim jacket, with a thick leather coat around his shoulders and worn, reliable leather boots climbing halfway up his legs.

Linda raised a hand, then stood up as he came toward them.

"Sorry I'm late," he said as he came to the table, looking speculatively at the three of them. "There were some problems at the office."

"That's all right," Linda said, and turned to the seated couple. "John Davies and Laura

Harding," she said, "this is George Lutz. George . . . meet John Davies and Laura Harding."

George too had felt something unusual when he'd come into the pizza place. He didn't like coming back to Amityville at all—the drive was alternately boring and tense. He couldn't quite shake the memory of that awful run out of town such a short time ago, and it was cold everywhere for him—in his office, in his car, even in public places where everyone else seemed to be very cozy.

But here, in this quiet, normal little fast-food place, where he had eaten a few times before, here it was warm. It felt good, very good. But strange.

He took John's hand in his own and felt something more. There was a tangible sensation of something *good*, something clean coming out of this man. He smiled broadly, and George smiled in return. He took Laura's hand with something approaching eagerness. And it was there too. Strength. Maybe even hope.

Linda pulled a chair around and they sat together. George realized that he felt comfortable here. That was something he hadn't felt in a long time: comfortable. Linda was part of that, too. After all the reporters, all the nuts, all the questions and crazy stories, she seemed to be the only one who had any real interest in *them*, in the Lutzes. He even trusted her, he knew, and these days he trusted almost no one.

He took a breath and looked back to John and Laura. "Linda has told me a lot about you both," he said, and they nodded. "What with all your previous experience in—in this kind of thing, and with the reading I've been doing . . .

well, I think we need someone like you. I really don't see any other way." He looked at them closely, and they didn't turn away. He liked that. He *needed* that. "Do you think you can help us?" he asked, surprised at the urgency in his own voice.

"Well, Mr. Lutz—"

"George."

"George. It's hard for us to make any promises until we've been in the house."

Laura must have seen his disappointment. "But we *have* been able to help a lot of people with some unusual problems," she said encouragingly. "Maybe we can help you too."

"You know, George," Linda said, "it may be cold comfort, but John and Laura told me that a lot of people are having troubles like this. In fact, it seems to be on the increase."

Laura nodded. "Just from the numbers of times we've been asked to help—and from the severity of the problems we've encountered— we're beginning to think there's some sort of trend developing. There's been a tremendous upsurge in demonic psychic manifestations in all forms over the last ten years."

The phrase stopped George cold. Demonic phychic manifestations? He'd resisted labeling the problem until that moment, as if giving it a name would give it an even stronger hold on him. But now the terms sounded so inadequate. *Demonic. Psychic.* What did those words mean, anyway?

Linda put a hand on his arm and he looked up abruptly. He had been drifting.

"We only want to be told the barest details of your experience," John said gently. "Much more than that, and things tend to get confused. So please: describe, just a little, what happened to you in Amityville."

"*No!*" George shouted. It was loud enough for the teenagers in the corner to look up with flat, slightly annoyed expressions. When they looked away again, George repeated himself, more softly but no less intense. "No!" he said again.

John was surprised at the harshness of the response, but he pressed ahead very gently. "If we're going to help you, George, we have to have some idea of what took place."

George's face went hard. "If you want to know what happened, go spend a night in the house." He was articulating very carefully, biting out each word. "Then *you* tell *us* what the problem is—and if you can get rid of it."

There was uneasy silence. George looked at the scarred table top. Linda looked at John. And Laura stared intently at the bearded man's shadowed face.

"Your problems didn't stop when you left the house, did they?" she asked.

He nodded. Feelings he'd kept tightly in hand were threatening to break free, and he couldn't let that happen. He couldn't.

"TV reporters. Newspaper people. Thrill-seekers, crazies—you name it. It's getting worse every day." He rubbed his eyes with one hand and coughed. "After they found us at Kathy's mom's, we tried to head them off, and after a while we stopped talking to them completely. But that didn't phase them. They just make up any story that suits them."

He sighed and looked up again—looked at

Laura. There was warmth and understanding there. "Most of the reporters decided it was just a hoax, though nobody has explained what we're supposed to gain from a hoax like this. Others are even worse. They're the condescending ones. They pat us on the head and say, 'I'm *sure* you are *honest* people, and I'm *sure* you really *believe* what you say, but really now.'" He imitated the complacency and scorn with a precise accuracy, and John had to smile and shake his head.

"I know the feeling," he said. "Believe me, we both know the feeling."

"Even our leaving the house has been distorted. I read a paper yesterday that said we hadn't run away at all—that we just went on a skiing holiday." He laughed shortly. "A skiing holiday!" He gestured at Linda, and she involuntarily backed away from him. "Linda's the only one who's noticed that this is our life they're tearing apart—not some freak show or publicity stunt."

The teenage boy grumbled under his breath and slammed down a tip. He dragged his girl friend out of the restaurant and threw a dirty look at George's table.

George barely noticed them. "That's our house up there, you know. Everything we own is in it. All our furniture, most of our clothes—even the deed to the house itself is still up there. We didn't leave because we wanted to. We left because we *had* to, because there was no other choice. And the only reason I'm sitting here right now is to try and get help, to make it right. Because *we can't go back*. Not the way it is. Not now."

George realized his fists were clenched, that

his jaw was aching with tension. Calm down, he told himself. Take it easy. These people want to help.

John Davies nodded. "We'll do what we can," he said, "but you will come with us to the house, won't you?"

"No!" George snapped.

"You could be a great help to the investigation," Laura said softly.

"I can't go back there," he said, shaking his head. He hated the unsteadiness in his voice. "I can't go back there."

Linda put a hand on his arm and squeezed gently. She'd seen him like this before, when he had first told her about the house—and whenever he'd tried to talk about it since.

George's head was thumping with pain. He felt sick to his stomach. I can't go back, he told himself. I can't. If they want to go, let them, I don't care. If they can get rid of the things in the house, let them do it. Just *do it* and leave me alone!

The restaurant seemed to be closing in on him. The walls were drawing inward, the ceiling with the fake beams and the phony carving was crushing down on him. He had to get out of there. He had to get the hell out of there *now*.

Linda said, "Are you all right, George?" But he barely heard her.

"I'm sorry," he said to no one in particular.

"George," she repeated, "are you all right? You look ill."

Too close, he knew. Too close to the house. Gotta get away. He stood up suddenly and his chair overturned. The cooks looked up warily and the waitress closed her magazine.

"It'll be dark soon," he said with difficulty, ignoring the astonished looks from Linda, John and Laura. "I'd better be going. Kathy's expecting me." He turned and took two steps toward the door, then forced himself to stop. He dug his hand into his coat pocket and found something so cold and hard it almost burned his fingers. Then he spun around and dropped the key to the Amityville house in the center of the table. The next moment he was knocking chairs out of the way as he ran to the door.

Linda watched George slam through the door and fumble frantically with his car keys. As he roared out of the parking lot with a scream of the tires on the icy pavement, she turned back to John and Laura and tried to apologize. "I don't know what—"

Laura waved the words away. "Don't explain," she said. "We see a lot of fear in our work. It does different things to different people. Though I have to admit, this is far worse than I expected."

John toyed with his coffee cup. "You know, until this moment, we weren't sure if there was a real case here." He looked up, slightly embarrassed. "A great many of the cases we see can be explained in rational, very *un*supernatural terms." Now he looked out the empty window, too. "But seeing a man like George Lutz, affected as deeply as he is...there's no question in my mind. Whatever it is, it's no hoax."

They're right, Linda realized. George was terrified, pure and simple. As frightened as a man could be and still be anywhere close to sane.

Their stay in the house must have been an ordeal. He'd tried to explain some of it—the fear, the horror. But how *could* he explain it? And even if he could, how could she really understand what actually happened in that ordinary house in Amityville if she hadn't been there?

George was exhausted. Within minutes of arriving at his mother-in-law's house, he had collapsed into an armchair in the lounge, and he had barely moved since then.

Now it was after midnight in East Babylon, and he was sleeping deeply. The children were asleep, too, and Joan was reading in bed while Kathy watched television in the den.

A tiny sound—maybe the rustle of fabric or the whisper of a slipper on the carpet—triggered George's senses. His eyes were suddenly wide open. He could see the silvery light of the television spilling in from the den, and he could hear the hiss of the static from a station that had signed off the air.

Kathy was standing in the archway between the den and the living room, silhouetted against the light. He could see the dim outline of her body beneath the modest nightgown.

Seeing her standing there relaxed the reflexes that had abruptly awakened him. She's part of my strength, George thought lazily, as his wife took a step toward him. My anchor. My hope.

The woman standing there wasn't Kathy. It *couldn't* be Kathy.

The skin of her face was stretched drum-tight over rigid, stony muscles. The eyes were blind and bulging. The lips were black stains. The skull showed through in icy, chiseled perfection.

It was a death mask; a human face twisted

beyond recognition. Something had stolen his wife's body . . . and it was coming for him.

He started to jump from the chair, but sleep had slowed his reflexes. Before he could rise, the thing that looked like his wife was on him, her outstretched hands reaching for his throat.

George had spent many years in the study of the martial arts. After endless hours of training, his mind and body had acquired skills—a fluidity of action and movement—that he could never consciously understand. Normally, these abilities lay dormant, peaceful, but now his subconscious mind sensed a violent attack, and he reacted without thought.

The intruder was kicked away, and George snaked behind her almost before he knew what he was doing. One arm came out and wrapped around her throat. The other caught a flailing wrist and pulled and twisted. There was a tight, painful sound from the woman, like the sound of ripping paper, but George held her firmly.

"Kathy!" he whispered in her ear. "Kathy, what are you doing?"

She jerked forward faster and more strongly than he thought possible. It threw him off balance for an instant, and an instant was all she needed. She broke his grip and spun around. Her hands clawed at his throat and squeezed.

George was ready this time. With one violent swipe, he broke the stranglehold and slapped this hideous caricature of his wife sharply across the face. The woman staggered back, but the rigid death mask didn't falter. She hissed and raised her hands to his throat once again. George hit her twice more, as hard as he dared.

It threw her back into the chair where he had

been sleeping. Her hair billowed forward and covered her face as she crumpled, and George stood over her for a moment, not sure what to do.

She wasn't moving. He wasn't even sure she was breathing. Then slowly, a hand reached up—a soft, uncertain hand—and scooped the hair away from her face. In that single, familiar gesture, he saw Kathy.

The fight was over.

She looked up at him in confusion and fear. "George?" she said in a very small voice. "What am I doing here?"

She stood up very quickly and came toward him, and involuntarily he caught her by the wrists and held her away from him. His mind believed she was all right now, but his body, still pumping adrenaline, was not quite so trusting.

Her eyes grew wide. "Wh—what is it, George? How—how did I get in here? I was watching television . . . I must have fallen asleep."

George felt his own body relax, and he folded his trembling wife in his arms. "It's all right, babe. Everything's okay." He stroked her hair and she seemed to wither in his arms. "You were sleepwalking, that's all. I . . . was afraid you were going to hurt yourself, so I was holding you until you—until you woke up."

She buried her head in the rough cloth of his shirt. "I've never done that before, George. Never. Why should I do it now?"

I wish I knew, George said to himself. I wish I knew something—*anything*—that would help.

"We've been through a lot lately," he said as convincingly as he could. "I'm sure it won't happen again." He turned and led her through the archway, back into the silvery television light in the den. He switched off the set and headed back into the lounge. "Come on, babe. Let's go to bed."

She went along quietly, still puzzled and afraid. Moments after George laid her in bed and pulled the covers to her chin, she was asleep.

A few minutes later, George gave up as well. He was too tired to think about it, too tired to worry. But not, he realized in the last shadows of wakefulness, too tired to be afraid.

## 8

"It's just a house," Al Kittery told Larry Berne. "Hell, our family had one just like it for years, and nothing weird ever happened to us."

Larry was pulling the portable video camera out of the back of the company station wagon while Al was grumbling about the assignment. He was a solidly built, broad-shouldered man with a wife, a child, and a job he liked. Exciting things happened just often enough during his work as a TV cameraman, and he was content. There wasn't very much more he wanted—or expected—from life.

Today, however, he wasn't quite as content as usual. He'd gotten a last-minute assignment to work with Linda Murillo on a follow-up story, and he didn't like it. Even the inclusion of his old buddy Al didn't cheer him up.

He hefted the camera onto his shoulder and looked through the eyepiece at the Lutz home in Amityville.

Your typical Long Island house, he thought. A three-story Dutch Colonial with a big porch, a new paint job, and a long backyard that ended in a small river. Similar to the house next to it, and the house next to that, and the one next to that.

"So what's the big deal?" Al mumbled, fiddling with the sound equipment.

Larry couldn't blame him for being nervous. Neither of them was too thrilled with this particular job. Not that there was anything to this haunted house stuff, but— Damn, they had better things to do, that's all.

And besides, it was cold. The wind was whipping angrily around the station wagon, tugging at his coat and blowing Linda's dark, tightly curled hair into clumps and bald spots. At least the weather could've been decent, he thought. That would've helped.

Larry looked at the reporter/producer through the eyepiece of the camera. Not a bad-looking lady, he decided. Not quite your beauty-queen weather-girl type, thank God, and smart enough to know a good story when it hit her between the eyes. He watched the tallish, well-built woman struggle against the wind as she got out of the car and pulled her lambs-wool coat tighter around her shoulders.

A smaller car pulled up behind the station wagon, and the middle-aged couple Larry had met before climbed out, bundling up against the freezing wind.

John Davies and Laura Harding were your typical, average, everyday ghost hunters. Larry shook his head in disbelief. Damn, this was one crazy assignment.

He adjusted his heavy belt with the extra equipment and kicked the car door shut.

"It looks pretty normal, huh?" he said to John Davies, trying to sound jovial about the whole silly thing.

"They usually do," John said grimly, "from the outside."

*Terrific*, Larry thought sourly. This is obviously going to be a lot of fun.

John flipped up the fur collar of his coat and thrust his hands deep into the pockets. The group assembled on the front lawn, all looking terribly uncomfortable.

"Are you both ready?" Linda shouted over the wind. She sounded unexpectedly thin and shrill.

Larry and Al nodded, then Laura Harding led the way into the house. Larry noticed that Al was lagging behind.

"Damn witch hunt," Al grumbled. "That's what it is."

The key rattled in the lock, the door swung open without so much as an eerie squeak, and the team found itself hurrying into the house to get out of the cold. John and Laura looked grim and slightly detached—like surgeons getting ready for an important operation, Larry thought. The older man was carrying a small leather pouch drawn closed with a string, and the cameraman had a crazy image of snake oil, lizard's teeth, and assorted exotic herbal ingredients hidden inside it. He laughed to himself at the absurdity of the thought—of the entire job, for that matter.

But it *was* his job, after all, and he got to it. He snapped off a few feet of tape—the living room, the pictures on the wall, some shots of John Davies and Laura Harding—as he moved deeper into the house.

Everything was in its place. All the pictures were straight, all the tasteful, expensive antique furnishings were arranged and coordinated. Nothing was broken. Nothing was scorched. There was no evidence of dangerous spirits, dead or alive—or anything else out of the ordinary, for that matter.

"I thought you said the family had moved out?" Al asked Linda skeptically.

"They have."

"Well, what about all their stuff?"

"They left it behind."

"*Everything*? There's some nice stuff here. Expensive, too, I'd say."

"I don't think they were worried about their 'stuff' at the time," Linda snapped back.

Larry thought it was weird. Not just that they would leave such expensive items behind, but that so much of it must have been personally important to them—heirlooms, mementos and such. Another thing bothered him, too: here it was February, and there were still Christmas decorations all over the place.

Brightly colored ornaments hung in the doorways. A yuletide wreath, now slightly brown around the edges, was standing over the hearth. Christmas cards were taped to the inside of the kitchen door, and rolls of wrapping paper were sitting on the sideboard.

He didn't know exactly why, but it all made him feel—well, *weird* somehow. And he couldn't place it, but he knew something important, something normal, was missing from the house.

*The clocks*, he realized. None of the clocks was working. He looked at the grandfather clock in the hallway through the lens of his camera, and zoomed in on the face. It was stopped. He joined Laura as she checked in the kitchen, and saw that the little clock on the wall of the breakfast nook was dead, too.

Well, of course, he told himself. They're all wind-ups, and if nobody's been in to tend to them, they'd have to have run down.

But the sound, or rather the absence of sound, was strangely disturbing. Any house that's lived in, he realized, has its own mechanical heartbeat. Clock-ticks, the rumble of a water heater, the thrum of a furnace—*something*. But it was quiet in here. Like a tomb.

"Look at this," Laura said to John. She was standing in front of the open refrigerator.

Larry snapped off a few more pictures. "Full," Laura said. "Kathy must have gone shopping just before it—just before they left." John nodded but didn't answer her.

The faint trace of a chill rippled down Larry's spine. For some reason, even the full refrigerator unnerved him. Why would anyone stock up like that and then leave, if it was some sort of hoax? There had to be a hundred dollars' worth of groceries in there—plenty of food and liquor. There were even some fresh vegetables and fruits, though they were beginning to wrinkle. A few more weeks and they'd start growing hair, he thought.

Laura shut the refrigerator door and he snapped out of his reverie. They joined the rest of the company back in the living room.

"There's a very negative aura here," Laura said. "A very strange feeling." She pulled John off to the side and they spoke together in low whispers. Then she came back and spoke to Linda.

Very cool, Larry thought. Very professional.

"John's going down to the basement," she said. "From what you've told us, this 'red room' the Lutzes found might be important."

Without another word, she headed for the staircase that led to the upper sections of the house. Larry and Al followed her; John headed for the basement alone.

Larry had been resting the camera on his hip, but now he pulled it back to his shoulder and recorded the start of their climb. Behind them, Al was still muttering to himself, and that worried the cameraman as much as the eerie silence in the house itself. It wasn't like Al at all.

"That must be quite a little handicap," he whispered.

"What?" Al grunted.

"Being a sound man who talks to himself. Don't you end up recording your own voice a lot?"

Al was usually a pretty happy-go-lucky guy, and he and Larry usually teased each other unmercifully when they worked together. It helped relieve the boredom. But Al didn't seem to think it was very funny this time.

They climbed the stairs guardedly, warily, as if they expected something to jump out of the shadows at any moment. Everything in the master bedroom seemed normal. Combs and brushes lay on the antique dresser, undisturbed. Clothes were strewn haphazardly but innocently over a nearby chair. The unmade bed was rumpled and uneven, as if the couple who had been sleeping in it had been there only moments before.

Laura walked around the room, quick-eyed and attentive. She laid her hand lightly on the dresser, on the bedpost, on the closet door.

"Feel anything?" Linda asked, with a small shiver in her voice. Larry dutifully recorded the question.

Laura shrugged. She walked across the room to the large chest near the bed and opened it. After sorting through papers inside, she took out a manila folder and handed it to Linda. "Those are the papers George asked us to get." Without any further discussion, she left the room.

They followed.

The sewing room was just down the hall. As they approached it, Al started grumbling again. Larry glared at him and his voice trailed off.

Laura stopped short, her hand only inches from the knob of the sewing room door.

"What's the matter?" Linda asked.

"I— I can't go in there."

Al had just switched off the tape recorder. Now he quickly turned it back on and extended the microphone toward Laura. Larry hastily rolled the videotape.

Linda glanced at them and nodded. "You say you can't go in there? Into the sewing room? Why not?"

"Something dark. Something dark and . . . and . . . bottomless is in there."

She wasn't talking to them. She wasn't talking to anyone, Larry realized. Before Linda could ask another question, the older woman turned and pushed past them, hurrying to the stairs.

She knocked into Al as she passed, and he nearly dropped his rifle microphone. "Damn it," he said, "what the—"

"Laura! What do you mean?" Linda hurried down the hall after her, and the technicians followed closely. Laura stopped at the staircase and looked up and down, unsure which direction to go.

"This . . . way," she said hesitantly, and began to climb the stairs to the third floor.

Larry moved quickly. He slipped past Linda, graceful in spite of the twenty-pound camera on his shoulder, and joined Laura Harding as she moved up the stairs. This time he wanted his camera to see exactly what she saw, each step of the way. He was going to be right there, right on—

"Ouch!"

Something hit the front of his camera and nearly drove the lens opening into his eye. "What the hell was *that*?" he said, and pulled his head away.

Laura was standing next to him, puzzled.

She moved forward, trying to walk up the stairs, but something— Jesus, Larry thought, something stopped her. It looked as if she'd hit an invisible wall, as if she were some grotesque mime defining a make-believe barrier. She leaned flat against it, tried to push forward, but she couldn't gain a single step.

"What the hell?" Larry said, and put out his free hand to probe the space in front of him.

Laura shouted "No!" but it was a second too late. His fingers found something in the empty air, and suddenly, completely, all the blood drained from his face.

He stumbled back from the barrier, as if he had been punched in the chest, and fell against the banister. A film can flew from his belt and dropped past the handrail, falling beyond the light and past the second floor landing. It crashed loudly on the first floor.

Larry was teetering on the edge of the stairwell, pinwheeling his arms as he tried to keep his balance. He was losing the battle; he was going over the railing.

Al Kittery cursed, dropped the mike, and grabbed for his friend, clutching at the cameraman's shirt and yanking. He heard it rip under his hands, but he pulled harder, and Larry jerked forward, away from the stairwell. He fell heavily onto the stairs and skidded down as a muffled, numb thought pounded in his head.

I nearly fell, he thought. I nearly fell down the stairwell.

Then he felt strange, panic-stricken. He pulled away from Al's hands and ran down the stairs, stumbling on the landing, almost losing his balance. He pulled himself up by the handrail and kept running.

"What's happening here?" Al demanded shrilly. "Why can't we get up those goddamn stairs? And what the hell's wrong with Larry?" He looked after his old friend as he ran into the shadows of the first floor, and when he turned back to the women there was confusion and fear in his eyes.

"Look, we've worked together for years, me and him. We've covered all kinds of messes, and nothin' could make him act like that. Nothin'." The women just looked at him, wide-eyed. "Godammit," he said, almost shrieking. *"What's happening here?"*

Laura Harding shook herself, as if waking from a dream. "We'll look after him," she said. "You find John. Tell him what's happened."

They left Al spluttering on the stairs, glaring at the thing he couldn't see, though it was only a few feet above him. He heard a door open and slam. He heard his friend beginning to moan. Then he heard him throwing up.

As John Davies left the others, he wondered about the Lutzes' story all over again. He had to admit that, except for a vague feeling of something being not quite *right*—whatever that meant—he hadn't seen or felt anything out of the ordinary. Not a thing.

Of course, the house was spooky, but he'd seen others like it, when people had fled because of gas leaks or other equally mundane reasons. There wasn't anything supernatural about that. It was just an indication of a very troubled family with some very real problems.

He switched on the lights at the top of the basement stairs and climbed down into the cellar.

Nothing.

He moved to the far wall and opened a large freezer he found there. It was packed with undisturbed, unaromatic food. Nothing unusual here, he thought.

He closed the freezer and turned to look at the far wall. Now here, he knew, there *was* something odd. A secret compartment—the "red room" that George had discovered.

He stepped into the room and waited, half-expecting something strange and fearful . . . and found nothing. Nothing at all.

He ran his hands along the crimson walls. Still nothing. True, he thought, not every house in Amityville—or anywhere else, for that matter—had its own hidden room with walls, floor, and ceiling all painted bloodred. But that in itself wasn't proof of anything. It was eccentric, yes. Even bizarre. But evil? Supernatural?

Still, his years of experience had taught him not to make hasty judgments about these things. They hadn't been in the house for very long.

He took the leather pouch from his large coat pocket and loosened the drawstring as he moved to the center of the room. Carefully, almost reverently, he removed the contents and lined them up on the bare concrete floor.

A crucifix. A vial of holy water. A cameo of Padre Pio, a revered holy man with extraordinary powers. A sanctified Bible.

In his years of study, John had come to recognize how few guarantees there were. But one thing was more likely than most: demonically activated spirits—and if the stories were true, that was what they were facing—could not stand the presence of blessed objects. It was the nearest thing he could devise to an acid test.

He lined up the last of the relics and waited.

After a moment's thought, he began to recite the Lord's Prayer. A little extra push, he thought. One final provocation . . . and possibly some protection as well.

"Our Father who art in Heaven . . ."

The light in the red room began to dim. John turned and looked into the basement beyond, and he saw it there, too: an inky blackness filling the space, as if it were oozing up through the floor.

He forgot the prayer and watched in fascination.

A few seconds later, he shivered at the sudden cold. Something was happening.

Suddenly it was hard to breathe. John put a hand to his chest and gasped, trying to fill his lungs, but no. It was as if air were being drained from the room. As if the darkness were clogging his throat. He tried to start the prayer again. Prayers had often saved him, and this prayer had helped the Lutzes in their van. But this time, he couldn't . . . he couldn't quite remember the words.

The pounding of his heart filled his ears. The gasping engulfed him. His hands clutched at his throat.

John fell on his side and gasped for air. There was only a little light now, a sliver of light. He forced himself to his knees and began to crawl, but the pounding in his head forced him to the ground again.

"Lau-ra!"

It was less than a whisper. He rolled onto his back, gasping as the sweat poured out of him, and he saw the thick blackness ooze across the room to cover his legs, his thighs, his chest.

Death, he thought as the blackness seeped into him. This must be death.

"*Laura!*"

"*John? John, where are you?*"

The light flared in front of him, and in one electric crackle, the darkness disappeared. Air gushed into his lungs. The pounding in his chest subsided.

It hurt too much to answer. John lay there, soaked in his own sweat, and worked his chest with his hands. He listened gratefully to the sound of his heart as its labored pounding slowed.

Not yet, he knew now. It wasn't his time yet.

Al Kittery stood in the opening to the red room. When he saw John on the floor, he hurried to his side.

"John? Are you all right?"

John coughed and forced himself to sit up. "Will be. In a minute." He slowly gathered the relics and put them in his leather bag.

"Jesus, you look awful," Al said. "For a second there, I thought you were hurt or something."

"So did I." He took a deep breath and let it out very slowly. "Is everything all right upstairs?"

"No. No, it's not." The frightened sound-technician told him what had happened: the sewing room, the staircase, the invisible barrier, Larry's sickness.

Then Al repeated the question he had asked upstairs. "Look, this don't make sense. Not even a little. Just tell me, please, what in God's name is going on around here?"

John shook his head wearily. "I don't know. But now, at least, we *do* know that the Lutzes

**119**

weren't chased away by something explicable. And this is no hoax. There is some negative force at work here, and it's strong. Incredibly strong." He stared at the red walls of the windowless room. "And something else, too. It doesn't like strangers. Not at all."

Al helped him to his feet, and John stowed his pouch in the pocket of his coat. "Come on, let's join the others. We know what we need to know for now. There's no need to stay any longer on this trip."

"Good," Al said shakily.

John went on as if he hadn't heard him. "We can get a group together and come back later for more serious study."

"Okay, okay, whatever you say." He helped John to the stairs, his mind whirling. Al Kittery wanted to break and run, to scream his lungs out and leave the house that instant, but he forced himself to walk slowly, to keep his voice calm and steady.

Just a few minutes more. He could handle that. And John Davies could come back to the house for "serious study" if he wanted to. Al only knew one thing for sure: he wouldn't be with him.

He was never coming back to this house. Never.

Larry rinsed his mouth out with cold water and tried to wash away the taste of vomit. Then he rubbed his face with a wet hand, took one last unsteady breath, and left the bathroom. Laura was waiting for him, smiling sympathetically.

"The others are waiting for us at the front door," she said quietly.

120

"What was that?" he asked, not really knowing what he meant—the barrier, the sickness, the house itself, or all that and more. "What was it?"

"I don't know," Laura Harding said. "I really don't know."

## 9

*Your future, like your past, will be filled with joy and peace.*

That should be funny, George thought. Hilariously funny. But it's not.

He dropped the broken pieces of the fortune cookie onto his plate and rolled the slip of paper between his fingers. The Chinese restaurant was buzzing around him: waiters chattered in the kitchen, customers arrived while others paid their bills, a brass dragon sat on a pillow and glared at him from across the room. His plate of vegetables and sauce was steaming invitingly, but he barely noticed it. His thoughts were on a different, darker place.

He pushed his plate away and reached for a cup of coffee, and his dinner companion asked him a question: "George," he said, "are you sure?"

He looked up in surprise, as if seeing his friend for the first time. "Excuse me, Father? What?"

"You've both been through a lot these last few months, I know. But are you sure?"

He grimaced. Even the coffee tasted bad. Everything tasted bad these days. Bitter and stone cold. "Father Mancusso," he said wearily, "you didn't see the look on her face last night. It was twisted, grotesque. It looked as if she were possessed, demonically possessed. That's the only word I know for it."

George saw the frightened, wary expression on Father Mancusso's face and mistook it for doubt.

"Look, you know how small-framed Kathy is. Usually I can hold both her wrists with one hand if I want to. But last night it took everything I had—I mean *everything*—just to keep her from hurting me. I finally had to slap her more than once—and hard, really hard—to get her out of her trance, or seizure, or whatever you want to call it. And less than a minute after she woke up, she couldn't remember any of what had happened."

Mancusso felt the horribly familiar nausea rising up in him again. He turned pale and cold. His head ached, his breath came in short, painful bursts, his hands began to twitch and tremble.

*No*, he pleaded. Not here. Not now. No no no . . .

George thought he was having a heart attack.

"Father, what is it?" he said, beginning to stand. "Are you all right?"

A weak hand came up and motioned him away, and the priest took a deep breath. He straightened and tried to smile.

"I'm fine," he said. "Just fine. It's a little bug I've picked up over the last few months. Can't seem to shake it."

"You're sure you're okay?"

"Fine, really. Fine." He took another deep breath and tried to stop shaking.

It's part of my own legacy from Amityville, Father Mancusso thought. But why put more worries on poor George's shoulders? He's barely surviving as it is. Still, this new attack of the sickness was a horrid confirmation. What George was telling him must be true—at least in some part. And it must have its roots in the house in Amityville.

Maybe if we stop talking about it, he thought, the sickness will go away. Sometimes that helped—but not always.

"George," he said, "I know how painful this must be for you. I promise, I will try to do something to help Kathy."

"Thank you, Father."

"I'll try, George. I can't promise anything."

George insisted on picking up the check, and as they left their table and waited in line at the cash register, Father Mancusso brooded over the problems that he and the Lutzes faced.

"George, I think you should seriously consider getting away. Permanently. Moving as far from Amityville as you can."

George looked shocked. "We can't do that.

Even if we could afford it—which we can't—all our friends are here. And the family business, and the schools for the kids. No, it's not possible."

The cashier said, "Nineteen sixty-five," and George handed her a credit card.

"Look, Father, we really had to stretch our finances to get that house in the first place. It was everything we wanted, and we're not going to give it up without a hell of a fight. I just can't afford to—in more ways than one."

Father Mancusso shrugged and put on his overcoat, and they walked out of the restaurant together. It was a strange night in New York. The intense cold had swept all the clouds and fog from the sky, and the stars, defying the city's brilliance, were shining bright and steady from horizon to horizon. Father Mancusso and George Lutz moved quickly along the icy streets, silent and troubled.

Hope was something Mancusso prized very highly. It had sustained him in the worst of times; it was a key concept, a central requirement not only for the priesthood, but for all Catholics. But he had to admit it, if only to himself: he had no hope to give to George Lutz. He did not believe for a moment that he, or anyone, could conquer the thing in that house.

An impossibly evil entity was using that plot of desecrated ground as a point of entry—as a gateway from some dark and hideous world to Earth itself. Mancusso had felt the smallest touch, the tiniest fraction of the power that black thing wielded, and he knew he was helpless against it. The only alternatives, he knew, were flight . . . and death.

No, my friend, you'll never get your house back. We may be able to break the thing's hold on you—temporarily. And perhaps over a long period of time, it will grow bored with its game and release you once and for all. But we can't face up to the full force of that thing. We can't possibly win.

Still, there may be something I can do to help, if only a little.

The priest stopped in front of an old-fashioned spice shop. "Let's go in here," he said, and ducked into the doorway. George, a little puzzled, followed him in.

It smells good in here, he thought as the door jangled behind them. Good and warm.

Father Mancusso disappeared into the back of the store, and George wandered down the aisles, looking at the colored tins and paper bags and glass jars that held teas, coffees, spices, and more. He didn't even recognize most of the names—or even the places they came from—but the warmth of the rich smells was strangely comforting to him. It's a weird way to feel better, he thought, but I swear, I like it here.

The priest found him standing in the center aisle and smiling at nothing in particular.

"George," he said, "go buy a pound of coffee."

George looked at him strangely, and the priest patted him on the arm. "I'll explain later," he said. "Just buy your favorite brand."

When George returned to the house in East Babylon, he found the windows dark and the rooms warm and quiet. He let himself in the back door and made the preparations in the kitchen without waking anyone. Then he tiptoed into the living room, balancing two pottery mugs and a coffeepot on an antique tray. He put the arrangement on the floor next to the makeshift bed where Kathy was sleeping.

For a moment, he almost thought better of it. She looked so peaceful—no tossing or turning, no nightmares. But he could see what the dreams were doing to her even now: the deep creases in her forehead, the black smudges under her eyes. And in a room that was barely warm enough, beads of perspiration were forming on her brow and staining the pillow.

No, he decided, something has to be done.

He shook her gently by the shoulder and said, "Kathy. Kathy, honey, wake up."

She awoke with a start and grabbed for him. "What is it? What's wrong?"

It's come to that, he realized. She can't even wake up without being afraid. "Nothing," he said soothingly, "everything's fine. I just brought you something warm to drink."

She relaxed in his arms and leaned against him. "Milk?" she said, trying to stifle a huge yawn.

"Coffee."

"Coffee? George!" She pushed her hair away from her eyes and looked at the alarm clock on a nearby table. "George, it's almost one-thirty. I just got to sleep a few minutes ago. Coffee? What's the matter with you?"

"Here you go," he said, pouring a full cup from the pot.

Kathy was whining. "You know I haven't been sleeping well, George. These dreams and these headaches, and the kids all the time. You know how tired I've been, and now, just when I get to sleep, you wake me up for *coffee?*" He tried to put the mug in her hands and she pushed it away. "No, George. I don't want any. What's the matter with you?"

"Look, babe, I know this sounds crazy, but Father Mancusso blessed it. He said that it would help you relax. Help you sleep."

She rubbed her forehead with one hand. "Father Mancusso? Oh, George, I don't know."

"Kathy, he's worried about you. We're both—"

"You didn't tell him about my sleepwalking, did you?"

"I had to."

"You promised! You promised you would keep that between us!"

"I said I wouldn't tell the kids or your mother," he reminded her. "But he helped me when I couldn't sleep, remember? And he thinks he can help you, too. Really."

She still looked doubtful.

"Really, babe. Really."

He felt her relax against him, and he smiled when she took one of the mugs and warmed her hands with it. "At least you could have told me why you were going to New York," she grumbled. "I would've liked to have seen Father Mancusso, too." Then she smiled back and took a sip of the coffee.

George picked up his own mug and held it out. The two cups clinked in the silence of the living room, and the Lutzes laughed softly.

"Sweet dreams," he said, and they finished their mugs without another word.

● ● ●

George rinsed out the coffeepot and put the cups in the dish drainer, trying not to hope, trying not to expect anything at all. Then he turned out the kitchen light and padded into the living room.

He slid between the covers and eased an arm around his wife. She moved closer to him, molding her body to his, and mumbled something comforting in her sleep.

Thank God, George thought. Thank God. Then he slipped into a peaceful, dreamless sleep of his own.

# 10

The yellow cab screeched around the corner and bumped to a stop in front of a man with a small pile of suitcases at his feet. A round, pasty-faced cabbie with a fringe of hair under his nose appeared in the passenger window and said, "Youda wondat cold?"

Father Mancusso looked at the cabbie in confusion. Then the syllables rearranged themselves into "Are you the one that called?" He smiled and nodded. "Yes, it was I." *I'll never get used to New York accents,* he thought, *no matter how long I live here.*

The driver climbed out of his cab and unlocked the trunk with one simple, economic motion that spoke of long experience and monumental boredom. A moment later he scooped up three of the priest's four suitcases and dumped them unceremoniously into the well.

The priest looked nervously at both street corners, and checked his watch for the tenth time.

"So where to?" the cabbie said as he opened the passenger door.

"Kennedy International Airport . . . eventually," Father Mancusso said.

"Eventually?"

"Do you suppose we could wait here for a few minutes? Some old friends of mine were going to see me off."

The cabbie scowled. "For Chrissake, fella, I ain't got all day. You wanna get to Kennedy, let's get the hell to Kennedy and quit this screwin' around."

Father Mancusso was taken aback. He wasn't accustomed to hearing language like that, even from New York cabbies.

Then he realized for the first time that he was in street clothes. His clerical collars were packed away with the rest of his belongings in the leather suitcase at his heel. It's strange, he thought, smiling to himself as he looked down at his jeans and sportshirt, I always thought I looked like a priest, even without the collar. I certainly feel like a priest.

"What's so funny?" the cabbie wanted to know.

"Nothing. Excuse me. Please, you can start the meter running right now, if you like, and if my friends aren't here in five minutes—"

"Hey, whatever you say, buddy. I start the meter running, I'll stay here till doomsday."

"I don't think it will be quite that long."

The cabbie stumped around the car, threw himself into the driver's seat, and shoved at the meter's lever with a little more force than necessary. Then he glared through the dirty windshield at the empty street in front of him, obviously uninterested in conversation.

Father Mancusso often wondered why the street in front of his church was always so quiet. Was it because the good people of New York didn't want to disturb a place of worship unless it was absolutely necessary, or because they felt uncomfortable with a holy place in the middle of the noise and filth of the city? Something to think about, that.

He thrust his hands inside his corduroy jacket and stood back on his heels. What could be keeping George and Kathy? he wondered. His plane would be leaving in a little over two hours, and what with the traffic and the check-in, he was going to be late if he didn't leave soon.

But he had to see them before he left. They had been in his thoughts more than ever the last few days—they were even beginning to interfere with his other duties at the church— and he had to talk to them, at least *see* them, before he left.

Maybe it was just an overblown sense of responsibility. He sometimes felt vaguely responsible for all the awful things that had happened to them in Amityville. After all, if he hadn't gone to the house, none of it might have happened. Then again, it might have been all that much worse without his help. He simply didn't know.

Mancusso sighed and shrugged inside his coat,

trying to keep the warmth next to his skin. The cabbie threw him a dirty look and went back to staring at the street.

It would be nice to get away, he decided. Nice to visit friends and relatives in California. It would feel good to lay aside his obligations and relax for a while—or at least try to relax.

But the Lutzes would travel with him in his thoughts and prayers. Especially in his prayers.

A frumpy old woman with a microscopic dog waddled in front of the van, and George laid on his horn with both hands. "*Damn* it," he said, glancing at his watch as he stamped on the accelerator. "We're never going to make it!"

Kathy resisted the temptation to ask him the time. When she had asked him five minutes earlier, George had nearly bitten her head off. It's the traffic, she decided. They both wanted to see Father Mancusso before he left, and they thought that they'd had plenty of time, but now . . .

George tapped the horn one last time and swooped around the corner without signaling. Half a block away, they saw a yellow cab idling at the curb and a middle-aged man in jeans and a brown jacket standing patiently in the middle of the sidewalk.

It took Kathy a moment to recognize Father Mancusso. This is the first time I've ever seen him dressed like *us*, she realized.

The van pulled up opposite the taxi, and Kathy was out of the car almost before it stopped. She rushed across the street without checking for traffic, her face flushed with cold and excitement.

"Sorry, we're late," she said, smiling at the priest. "The traffic was ridiculous."

"I was beginning to think I wouldn't see you before I left," Father Mancusso said, hugging the woman warmly. "I'm very glad you made it."

George huffed up behind her, still slightly annoyed by the drive. "You should have let us take you to the airport," he grumbled.

"No, George. Taking a cab is much simpler, believe me." The cabbie snorted at that, but didn't take his eyes from the windshield. "You would have to drive all the way back through town, and then to Babylon, and that would take hours and hours. Besides, I don't mind taking a taxi. Not *much*, anyway." He glanced good-naturedly at the driver, and the hackie hunched even lower in his seat.

"Well, all right," Kathy said, still a little worried, "but at least we can pick you up at the airport when you come home, can't we?"

Mancusso couldn't resist the look of childlike anticipation on the young woman's face. He'd come to know her family a few years ago, and since then he had developed an almost paternal affection for her. Since the problems at the house on Long Island, his worry, love and concern had increased steadily. "All right," he said gently. "I would like that very much."

"Great!" the cabbie said, jumping out of the car, "now that *that's* settled, you think we could make a couple'a tracks?"

Mancusso glanced at his watch and frowned. "I'm afraid he's right, George. I really have to be going."

George nodded, and took hold of the priest's

last suitcase before Mancusso himself could get it. The cabbie opened the back door and George eased it into the gap between the front and rear seats.

"He your father or what?" the driver asked as George ducked out of the cab.

George looked at him very strangely.

Father Mancusso didn't hear them. He was saying good-bye to Kathy. "You look good, Kathleen," he said, looking deeply into her eyes. "Better than I've seen you in a long, long time. Leaving that house was the best thing you could possibly have done."

Kathy knew it was much more than that. She knew the peace George had found in the sacrament of Holy Communion that Father Mancusso had administered. She also knew the special coffee he had blessed had freed her in a unique way.

It wasn't just leaving the house that had helped them. It was this good, modest man right in front of her.

She kissed him on the cheek. "Oh, Father," she said, "George told me where he got that coffee. And it's been over a week now, and I haven't had any headaches, or—or dreams, either." The memories of the nightmares still made her shudder. "They were bad dreams, Father." She shrugged the feeling away. "In fact, there haven't been any dreams at all, except one. A very beautiful one, right after I drank the coffee you gave to George." She looked at him very closely and smiled a secret smile. "I'd like to talk to you about that dream sometime," she said. "Sometime soon."

He nodded and smiled in return, and the cabbie said, "Hey, buddy! All *right*, already!"

Kathy gave him one last, fierce hug and let him go. "Thank you," she said, "for everything."

The priest blushed and looked at the toes of his shoes. "Don't thank *me*," he said shyly. "Thank God." Then he looked at her with unexpected frankness and power. "Thank God."

He turned away and climbed into the cab without another word, trying to hide his embarrassment. When he was settled, he rolled down the window and looked up at his friends.

"Have a nice trip, Father," George said. There was more he wanted to say—much more—but it simply wasn't the time.

"We probably won't recognize you when you get back," Kathy said, grinning. "All that California sunshine. You'll look like a movie star."

Father Mancusso smiled and shook his head. These were good people. He loved them more than they knew. "God be with you," he said.

"And with you," Kathy replied. George nodded and thumped on the side of the car.

"At last," the cabbie said, and screeched into the street.

They stood on the curb and watched the taxi roar without hesitation through a stop sign, screech around a corner with a squeal of brakes, and disappear. George put his arm around Kathy and squeezed gently.

"You okay?"

"Fine," she said, feeling sad and a little empty. "Just fine."

Put it away, she ordered herself. Father

Mancusso will be back almost before you know it, with stories to tell and presents for the kids. Just don't let it get you down.

(Two blocks away, a yellow Mack truck ground its gears and rumbled around the corner. The driver was tired. He had been on the road for almost nineteen hours without so much as a break, and now he was roaring through the back streets of New York, so he could get to his station before closing time. I don't wanna pay no goddamn penalty, he thought. No way.)

Kathy shrugged away her depression and smiled brightly at George. "Can we stop at the market on the way home? We need a few things."

George nodded, then glanced up and down the empty street and started to cross to the car.

(The truck cruised through an empty intersection, and the driver blinked again. It was going to take better than an hour just to unload. Hell, at this rate, he wasn't going to see any food or sacktime until way after dark. Well, he thought, peering at the street ahead of him, at least there ain't no goddamn traffic out here. And no pedestrians.)

"I'd like to go to California some day," Kathy said. "You know, I've never been that far from New York."

(The truck was a hundred feet away.)

"Neither have I," George said. "Not since I was in the service, anyway."

(The truck was fifty feet away, accelerating.)

"Do you think we could—"

Something *pushed* at George. It was a twinge at his right, a needle of awareness on his blind side. It came from years of experience in martial arts training, and in a single instant all the caution and skill and reflex narrowed to a simple, brutal command:

*"Look out!"* he shouted, and shoved his wife forward, out of the street, out of the way, into the narrow canyon formed by two parked cars.

(The truck driver never saw them. There was a strange little sound, a kind of warbling shout just outside his window, but he ignored it. There was even a quick little kick of cold air that cut through his heater for a second, but he shrugged that off, too. Then he was at the corner, thinking, No goddamn way I'm gonna make it. No goddamn way.)

"George? George, are you all right?"

Kathy was sprawled on her side between the cars. Her winter coat was stained with oil and grease from the gutter, and a lump was already forming on her chin where she had knocked into a hood or bumper as she fell.

George was on top of her, breathing rapidly, almost panting like a dog. He didn't answer her.

"George? My God, are you all right?"

He jumped up and shot out of their hiding place with both fists raised. *"Idiot!"* he shouted at the yellow truck. "Damn fool idiot, you could have killed us!"

The truck was already more than two blocks away. "He didn't even honk his horn!"

Kathy stood up unsteadily, and then George was at her side, supporting her. "I'm sorry, babe, I didn't see it coming," he said bitterly. "I didn't even hear it!"

"You couldn't have," she said, dazed by the blow to her head, but thinking very clearly,

**139**

feeling very certain. "You couldn't hear it, George. It didn't make any sound."

She stared at him, and suddenly her eyes narrowed—the certainty gone. She looked at her husband, her tone almost pleading. "It didn't make any sound, George. Did it?"

George didn't answer immediately. He wasn't sure. He couldn't remember hearing anything until the truck rolled by, but they were talking, and . . .

"I . . . I'm sure we were just preoccupied," he said with little conviction.

My God, Kathy thought. Is this what it's come down to—total paranoia? Will we blame everything bad or out of the ordinary on that house? We're finally succumbing to something even worse than Amityville itself: fear. We're beginning to think it's everywhere—waiting, watching, stalking us.

No. They could not go through life this way. They couldn't let that happen. And now was as good a time as any to prove it. She might be frightened, even terrified, at the prospect of being dogged by some powerful, unseen force, but she wasn't going to give in to fear. Not this time. Not ever.

She forced herself to straighten up, and put her lips against the hollow of George's neck, but only for an instant. Then she pushed herself back onto her own feet. "Well, I guess we'd better be more careful about crossing streets from now on," she said firmly. "Look both ways and all that?"

George smiled weakly. She could see that he was trying, too. Trying and winning.

"Right," he said. "Safety first."

She took his hand and squeezed it. He squeezed back, and without another word they walked to their van and started the trip back to East Babylon.

# 11

"Bud, you've got to take care of this. It's driving me crazy."

"You know how these things are, George. I've tried everything to get it straightened out. It's just not that simple when you're dealing with the IRS—even when they're wrong."

"I don't give a damn how simple it is, just *do* it!" George Lutz slammed his fist on the desk top, and the seven stacks of paper he had arranged so carefully on the blotter jumped and shivered. All the stacks but one had pink slips clipped to them, and there was a single word stamped on each slip: CANCELED.

Okay, calm down, he told himself. This man is trying to help, so give him a chance.

He forced himself to lean back and look out the window of his Syosset office at the busy street beyond. A late-model sports car slipped by. A man in an overcoat with the *Wall Street Journal* wedged under his arm moved in the opposite direction. The wind plucked at the slit skirt of a young professional woman on the far side of the street, and a new foreign compact drove into the small parking lot that adjoined George's office. It all looked very normal. Very peaceful.

Why does *normal* seem so alien to me? George wondered. He sat at his third-generation antique desk, much too aware that both of his equally beautiful antique filing cabinets were rapidly filling with canceled orders and overdue bills, and just as aware that his surveying company, handed down from grandfather to father to son, was failing for no damn good reason at all.

His accountant's voice buzzed out of the telephone.

"George, are you still there? I told you, I'm doing the best I can."

George sighed. "I know that, Bud. And I'm sorry I blew up. But you're my accountant. You've got to convince these IRS guys that they've made a mistake. I do not owe four thousand dollars. I didn't even take any questionable deductions on last year's statement, remember? You were the one who prepared it."

"I know, George. I've been trying to tell the IRS agent that for the last week and a half, but—"

"Well, what the hell do we have to do, anyway? Give them blood?" He could feel himself starting to babble, but he couldn't stop. "I can't go on like this, Bud, I mean I just can't keep working and working and not see anything come out of it, it's driving me out of my mind, I mean *out* of my *mind*—"

"George!"

It was the first time George had ever heard Bud Masters' voice raised to anything even close to a shout. It drew him up short. Now the accountant continued, more slowly and calmly. "George, I know you've been under a lot of strain these last few months. I've seen some of those stories in the paper and on the TV and all. Now, I don't claim to know what that's all about, but really, George—*really*—we're going to get this all figured out."

George took in a long, rattling breath. He felt as if he were breaking up inside, but he wasn't going to let that happen. Not now. Not over something as stupid and pointless as this. "It's just that I don't have the money, Bud. It's that simple: I don't have the money."

"Business picking up at all?"

"Not at all. Two of our regular clients canceled; one went out of business; one's under investigation and the project is frozen; and I can't even get the one other prospect on the phone. It's like he dropped off the face of the earth."

"And nothing's coming in?"

George was getting mad again. "I just told you, Bud: no. Nothing. Here I've got a surveying business that's been doing just fine for better than seventy years, and now all of a sudden it's dying. And I don't know why."

"Neither do I, my friend. Neither do I."

George sighed heavily and gripped his temples between thumb and fingers. He had another thumping headache, like the ones he'd had at Amityville. "I've already laid off everybody but Hank. Hell, I couldn't let him go, he's been here since Dad took over. But if something doesn't happen soon, he'll have to go, too. All we've got on the books is the Wagner job, and even if he pays on time, that won't net us enough to pay the bills."

The voice in his ear tried to sound comforting. "Things are bad all over right now, George."

Don't patronize me, he thought. "Yeah, I know. Bad all over."

"I'm sure it will improve."

"Sure it will. Improve."

There was a long, lifeless silence. George filled it with slow, controlled breathing and a finger tapping on the desk top. Finally, his accountant cleared his throat.

"Well, I'll get back to you on that IRS thing."

Suddenly, George felt a thousand years old. Who cared about the goddamn audit anyway? "Fine," he said. "You do that."

"Right." There was another pause. "Uh, George, I—"

"Yeah? What?" He didn't want to talk anymore. His head hurt too much. And damn it, there was nothing more to say about it. Nothing.

"Never mind. I'll...just talk to you soon. Good-bye."

George let the phone drop without another word. Why am I treating Bud like that? he wondered. He's been good to me. And God knows ol' W. H. Parry, Inc. owes him money, too. Just like everybody else.

Besides, maybe business *will* improve. I don't

know why it's gotten so bad in the first place, so I'm the last person to know when it'll get better again.

He sat in his creaking desk chair and stared dully at the papers on his desk. It *had* to get better. Fast. Or there wouldn't be any business to worry about at all.

The phone rang again, and sent a sharp pain screaming through his temple. He snatched it up, hoping without hope that it would be good news, for a change.

It was Kathy, and the news was terrible.

When it rains, it pours, he thought as he threw the van around the corner and sped up the final block to Joan Conners's house in East Babylon. Just like it says on the Morton's Salt box, and it's God's truth.

Kathy was waiting for him in the driveway. She came up and opened the car door almost before he had stopped the engine and set the brake.

"Is it any better?" he asked.

"No, it's—"

A weird, wolflike howl cut through the late afternoon. It wound around the house, mingled with the sound of the rising wind. It was the saddest, most painful sound that George had ever heard.

"My God," he said, "is that *Harry?*"

"Come look," Kathy said. "Please, come look."

The howling came again, even more chilling the second time. George jumped out of the van and raced to the backyard gate at the side of the house.

While he was fumbling with the latch, the

howling stopped, cut off so abruptly that it sounded as if a bit of recording tape had been snipped in half. George cursed, then kicked his way through the gate—and stopped in amazement at what he saw.

His old friend, Harry, the charcoal black malamute retriever, was standing stiff as a wrought-iron statue at the foot of the oak tree where he was chained. The dog's eyes were glowing—actually glowing, he thought, with a fire of their own. They were focused on something invisible and far away, something George couldn't see. Harry was watching it so intently he was quivering with the strain.

Behind the dog, below the loop of slack chain that was supposed to hold him, the two-foot trunk of the ancient oak had been chewed and scratched away with incredible force. More than a third of the hard, gnarly wood had been gouged out by teeth and claws.

Harry's mouth was dripping with blood.

"My God," George said under his breath. "Did Harry do that?"

Kathy nodded. There was fear and sadness in equal portions, fighting in her eyes.

George took a step toward the dog, and Harry burst into life. He tore his eyes away from whatever he was watching and turned as if he had been stabbed in the haunches. A growling, guttural sound—half yelp and half growl—came out of his throat, and he jumped, high and predatory as a timber wolf.

He landed with his teeth buried deep in the trunk of the oak tree. He tore at it with paws and teeth, again and again. Violent swipes of his claws ripped wood chips loose and sent them flying. The dog whipped his head back and forth in rage, tearing larger and larger chunks free and flinging them into the rising wind.

The growl grew and grew, swelling in the dog's throat as he leaped and tore. When the sound got to be too much, Harry backed away from the tree and howled. He threw his black muzzle straight up, pointing at the sky, and let the ululating, painful, tragic sound escape into the freezing air.

When the howling died away, Harry flinched and turned again—away from the tree, away from his sworn enemy—and looked back to the distant horizon of madness, his lambent brown eyes unfocused. He found the faraway thing again, and watched it, frozen. He was waiting for another attack.

"He's been doing that for hours," Kathy said carefully. George could tell she was trying not to cry. "He's like a robot or something. And he doesn't seem to know we're even here. We tried holding him down, so he wouldn't hurt himself, but we can't. He's too big."

George looked at the trembling dog, at the wounded trunk, at the blood shining on black fur. He couldn't think of anything to say. He couldn't even begin to explain it.

What could possibly make Harry do this? It wasn't like any sort of distemper or rabies he had ever seen. It wasn't like any disease at all. It was like . . . like a hallucination, like a walking nightmare. He knew that dogs could have dreams, but could they actually be driven mad?

"Maybe we should call a vet," he said, not believing it for a minute.

"The local vet's a friend of the family," Kathy

said, sounding oddly disgusted. "He's already been here."

"What did he say?"

Kathy didn't answer. George looked at her for the first time in a long while and asked it again. He didn't like the look on her face. "What did he *say*, Kathy?"

"Oh, George, we know more about animals than he does!"

*"What did he say, damn it?"*

Kathy looked at her clenched fists. The answer was almost a whisper. "He said we should have him put to sleep, before he attacks the children." She looked up and put a hand on his chest. "But, George, you know there's not a chance that Harry would hurt the kids. He loves them, we both know that."

George looked at the dog again. He was still watching, quivering, waiting for something horrible to happen. Put him to sleep? Harry? That would be like executing a member of the family.

They had been through so much together. Through the first uncertain months of marriage; through George's early concerns about the children, and his new fatherhood; through the house—hell, Harrry had lived through Amityville with them, and now they were supposed to kill him? One simple injection, and—

Harry snarled and turned. He bared his teeth and yelped, and the muscular hind legs flexed as he leaped at the tree again. Already the howl was beginning to build—an unearthly, unutterably lonely sound that breathed and built in the poor animal's chest, fighting to free itself.

George bent his head and covered his ears with his hands. He didn't want to hear that sound again. When he looked up, Harry was sitting as he had first been; back was to the tree, eyes blank and afire. His spine was rigid with tension and fear.

George stumbled across the yard and knelt by his old friend. He stroked his dark head and muttered comforting sounds, but Harry didn't seem to notice. Even when he took a fistful of the dog's loose skin in his hands and pulled, Harry didn't move. He just stared and stared, waiting—watching.

Kathy was at his side now. She put a hand on George's shoulder.

"Maybe it's been too much for him, Kathy," he said. "We're not doing all that well with it ourselves, and he's only a dog, you know." He stroked the animal's head again and again. "Only a dog," he whispered.

As if hit by an electric current, Harry suddenly jumped and turned. He vaulted at the tree, and the violence of his movement threw George off his feet. A flailing paw caught him in the shoulder. It cut through his wool shirt in two parallel lines.

Blood oozed through the scratch. George clamped his hand over the wound and looked at the dog in amazement.

He was tearing at the tree again. His own blood was flowing freely from the torn tissue between his teeth.

He didn't even know that George was there.

Kathy stood over the sink and stared blankly out the kitchen window as the daylight faded slowly into the darkness of early evening. George was sitting cross-legged on the lawn, watching

Harry as he howled at the treetops or stared trembling at the blackness. *Please,* she thought as Harry jumped at the tree for the thousandth time. *Please stop it.* Relax, Harry. Be your old self. Like before.

But nothing changed. She saw George adjust the crude bandage at his shoulder and wince at the pain, but he wouldn't leave.

Her mother stood behind her and looked out the window herself. "Is he still out there?" she asked, and Kathy knew she meant George, not the dog. The unholy howling that pierced the evening every few minutes told everyone exactly where poor Harry was.

She nodded. "He hasn't moved for more than two hours," she said. "I think he loves that dog more than the children do."

Or at least as much, she corrected herself. The two boys were out there now, standing a few feet behind their father, and watching with huge, wet eyes as their old friend went mad.

The children already knew what George and Kathy had decided to do. They hadn't been told, but they knew somehow.

Joan Conners put an arm around her daughter's waist and squeezed. "Have you decided yet, Kathy?"

She sighed deeply. It was not a question she wanted to answer. "The vet is coming in the morning to take him away," she said, and she felt tears in her eyes again. She turned away and hurried from the room.

Outside, George patiently cleared bits of bark and loose skin away from the dog's muzzle as Harry stood trembling, watching the invisible thing. "I'm sorry, pal," he whispered. "I wish I knew how to reach you, but you have to understand. I can't stand by and watch you beat yourself to death. I just can't do that."

Harry's glowing eyes didn't flicker. He was beyond hearing.

George put both arms around the dog and squeezed. He didn't care if Harry jumped now; he simply couldn't let go. Not yet.

"What's happening to us?" he whispered. "We got away, Harry, I swear to God, we got away. So why is it still happening?"

The dog didn't move. He was watching. Waiting.

By 7:45 the next morning, a single, slim finger of light had found its way through the living room curtains and touched George Lutz where he slept, fully clothed, in Joan Conners's reading chair. He had stayed awake most of the night, listening to the sound of Harry's unending combat and his painful, ghostly howl. Kathy had stayed with him as long as she could, but now she was asleep only a few feet away.

He was awakened by his children when they burst into the room, shouting. He was on his feet and alert in an instant, his nerves jangling with adrenaline.

"Mom! Dad! Come look at Harry!"

Kathy sat up, still fuzzy with sleep. "What, honey? What is it?"

"Come look at *Harry*," Greg said, happily.

And the dog trotted into the room. His fur was twisted with clumps of matted hair and dried blood. Chips of wood and bark were clinging to his jaws. But his tongue lolled out of his mouth with a casual, good-natured sloppiness, and his tail wagged back and forth in its old, cheerful rhythm.

George looked at the eyes—at the warm, intelligent, *sane* eyes he had seen so often.

"Harry?" he said, barely able to believe it. "Is that you?"

Harry barked and jumped up. George wrapped his arms around the mutt and hugged him so hard he almost lifted him off the ground. Then the dog was gone, squirming away so he could race to Kathy and lick her sleepy face.

She stared at the dog in open wonder. "George, he's all right!" She laughed and hugged him, and his tongue lolloped across her cheeks again. "George, he's *better!*"

"What did you kids do to him?"

"Nothing," Greg said a little defensively. "We just went out to see him, and he was all fixed."

"So we brought him in to show you," Matt said. "Is that all right?"

Harry was bounding happily around the room, greeting each of them as if he hadn't seen them in weeks. "All right?" George said. "It's great! *Great!*"

Amy toddled out of the dog's way, then dodged him again, and came to rest in her mother's lap. She looked up at Kathy with huge, solemn eyes. "He doesn't have to leave now, does he, Mommy? He can stay with us, can't he?"

George laughed. He couldn't help it, he couldn't contain it. Maybe it was just a hideous coincidence, or maybe the force that had followed them from Amityville was more subtle and powerful than they had ever imagined. But he knew—with a certainty that almost stunned him—he *knew* that Harry had been fighting

154

something very real . . . that he had fought it and *won*.

He reached down and swung Amy off her feet and into his arms. "No," he said, "he doesn't have to leave. He's part of the family, isn't he? And we always stick together."

Kathy laughed, Harry barked, the children cheered and ran between his legs, and pure joy flooded through George Lutz.

They *were* a family, and they had been through more danger and fear than any other he knew. Whatever happened next, he prayed that they would be strong enough to face it; to fight it and defeat it, and always stay together. Always stay a family.

# 12

A roaring thunder, loud as the falls at Niagara, filled the air over Father Mancusso's head. He looked up and squinted as the silver belly of a huge jet plane wallowed and rose in the air above him. The thunder slowly faded as the jet turned and disappeared into the smog.

A middle-aged man with deep brown skin jostled his elbow and muttered a few apologetic words in Arabic. The priest smiled wanly and nodded. A young woman in a dress that he thought was far too low-cut joined him at the curb, trying to carry three suitcases in one hand and an impossibly furry coat in the other. He watched as she spotted a recognizable face in the traffic jam before them and waved her coat like a semaphore.

"Willy! Willy, over here!" She frowned when

she couldn't catch his attention, muttering, "son of a bitch." Then she saw Mancusso's clerical collar for the first time, and she blushed a deep red. "Excuse me, Father," she said, and dashed across the street.

The priest smiled genuinely this time, and shook his head in good-natured disbelief. For some strange reason, he actually enjoyed airports like Kennedy International. So many different people, so many different faces with stories to tell. Sometimes waiting at the terminal was more fun than the trip it framed.

But this had been a good visit. He felt stronger and healthier than he had since his first visit to the Lutzes's home in Amityville, so many months before. He had hoped to hear from them during his trip out West, of course, and he had been surprised at the lack of response to his post-cards.

Ah, he thought happily. Here they are now.

A '74 Ford van was weaving through the tangle of traffic, moving slowly toward the curb where Father Mancusso stood. He peered at the windshield, expecting to see the faces of his friends, and the moving silhouettes of their children in the rear.

But he could only see one burly, shadowed form in the driver's seat. No one else seemed to be inside. For reasons he couldn't quite identify, that disturbed him.

The van hit the curb at an acute angle and almost jumped onto the sidewalk. Mancusso took a step back in alarm, but the van straightened with a squeal of rubber against concrete, and he saw inside clearly for the first time.

George was all alone. And he was not the

happy man that Father Mancusso had hoped to see.

His cheeks were hollow and slightly blue. There were dark circles under his eyes, and the creases in his forehead that Father Mancusso had seen at that long-ago Communion had returned, deeper than ever. George hadn't washed or combed his hair in a long time, and his overlong beard was tangled from inattention.

He looked very much as he had at Amityville, in the worst of times.

"Welcome home," George said shortly, and threw open the passenger door without getting out of the car. The priest had to struggle to load the luggage, but George didn't seem to notice. He was glaring at the traffic ahead of him and ignoring Mancusso entirely.

When Mancusso finally climbed into the passenger side, he tried to sound as cheerful as he could. "Thank you for coming to get me, George," he said with a forced lightness. "It's good to see you."

George didn't answer. He jammed the van into gear and shoved his way into traffic without a signal. A car to his rear screeched its brakes and blasted a horn at him.

What had happened? Why was George acting like this? And where were Kathy and the children?

"I thought Kathleen would be with you," Mancusso said gently. "She's well, I trust?"

George only snorted and changed lanes so violently that the van rocked on its wheels. Then he gunned the engine, twisted the wheel, and sped up a freeway onramp, oblivious to the traffic tie-ups in his wake.

"Not exactly," he said curtly.

Mancusso was more than a little taken aback by the driving. He looked at George with confusion, forgetting what he had asked.

George glanced at him for the first time and scowled. "Kathy," he said, annoyed. "She's not exactly well."

"Oh." Father Mancusso swallowed and frowned. "George, what *is* it? What's happening? You look as if you haven't slept in days." The van veered in traffic and nearly clipped the rear end of the car ahead of them, but Mancusso tried not to watch. "And what's this about Kathleen? What do you mean, she's 'not exactly well'?"

"She's about the same as me," he said.

Mancusso put out a hand and touched George on the forearm. The muscles were hard as stone under the shirt-sleeves. "George, I think you should tell me what's been happening. Perhaps I could be of some help."

"It doesn't matter," George snapped. "It never helps. It just keeps happening and happening—"

He stopped himself. The priest could see him physically force himself to calm down. He was slightly awed by the control he saw in this man, and taken aback by the fear that dwelt behind it.

A huge sigh escaped from the bearded man at the wheel. "I'm sorry, Father. I'm really glad you're back. I do need someone to talk to, but I hate putting it all on you. You've helped more than you should have already."

"Nonsense. Just tell me what's going on, George."

It was hard for George to speak, he could see that. The words came slowly at first, and with great difficulty. But after he had begun, he talked quickly, almost impulsively, as if some psychic dam had burst and the fear and relief were rushing to escape.

"A few days after you left for San Francisco, another group of psychics went into the house with Laura Harding and John Davies. I kept telling them I didn't want anything to do with it, that I didn't want to know what happened. I just wanted it *done*. I told you that, didn't I? I just wanted it cleansed, and that was all."

"Yes, you told me."

"But they called me. They went to the house and things—things happened to them there, and they called me in the middle of the night to tell me about it." He shook his head and jammed on the accelerator harder than ever. "They won't go back. They say there's nothing more they can do to help, that the evil is too strong. And maybe it's even stronger than they imagined. Because since that visit, since they called me and told me . . . it's started all over again."

He was hunched over the wheel, driving fast and erratically. Father Mancusso tried not to look at the road at all.

"The headaches are back. And the nightmares. I feel sick, Father, like I did at Amityville. And it's cold, too. It's cold all the time."

"I'm so sorry, George. I—"

George spoke as if he barely knew the priest was there. "Two weeks ago, my grandfather died."

Father Mancusso closed his eyes and said a

silent prayer. He had been a fine, energetic old man, and the priest knew how much George and Kathy had loved him. "Oh, George," he said. "Why didn't you call me?"

"It wouldn't have mattered, Father. He was dead. Away from it. Sometimes, I almost envy that—"

Again, Father Mancusso saw George pull himself short, *force* himself to stop and change direction. He wondered how long the man could survive under this kind of self-imposed pressure.

"Even at the funeral, strange things happened. Like when Kathy drove herself to Granddad's house. All the wheel nuts on the station wagon unscrewed. *All* of them, Father, on both sides, even though we haven't changed a tire for months. The nuts on cars are screwed in opposite directions on each side so the torque can't make that happen. It's impossible, Father, but it happened. When she got to the house, the wheels were wobbling so badly it looked like she was driving some toy car out of the circus. If she'd traveled another two blocks, they would have flown off completely. It could have been a hell of—it could have caused a terrible accident, Father. Terrible."

"But she's all right?"

George smiled bitterly. "She wasn't hurt then, no. Not in that way."

A huge white Lincoln Continental swooped in front of them, only inches from the van. George shouted an obscenity and stood on the brakes, and the van screamed and turned broadside in the traffic. Father Mancusso closed his eyes and tensed for a collision, but George regained control of the wheel and wrestled the van back into the fast lane, still cursing and muttering.

The priest forced himself to take a deep breath. "Stop the car, George," he said solemnly.

"Huh?" he said, still driving.

"*Please* stop the car, George."

After a moment, he nodded. He pulled them to a stop on the gravely soft shoulder and leaned on the steering wheel, breathing heavily. "I'm sorry, Father. I kind of . . . I'm having trouble with things like this right now."

"What else, George? What else has happened?"

The bearded man stared at the lifeless instrument panel for a moment, counting breaths. Finally he blinked and said, "The business. It's collapsing. I don't know what I've done wrong, but there are no new orders, no money coming in at all. Even the old customers have canceled. And the IRS is doing a five-year audit on me for no reason. For no reason at all!"

He breathed again, and Father Mancusso watched the traffic sweep by in a pale blur of color and noise.

"And Kathy and I aren't doing well, either. We're arguing again, over ridiculous things, *stupid* things. But we can't seem to control it. Just like at the house—just like at Amityville, Father."

Mancusso put his hand on George's arm again, and the simple touch seemed to break some final, fragile barrier. George trembled and sobbed, bent over the steering wheel with his fists clenched in anger and frustration.

"It's like an infectious disease!" he said. "Like we carry some sickness with us wherever we go. And it affects everybody, Father. Now Kathy's mother is involved, and the business, and my family, and you. It's some rotten, stinking disease."

He was calmer now, and a little weary. Father Mancusso watched him straighten up and rub his face dry with the heel of a hand. "Sorry," he said. "I've just been under a lot of strain."

"There's nothing to be sorry about, George. You know that."

George nodded and started the engine.

"You're sure you're all right?"

"Yes, I'm sure. Just tired."

"Would you like me to drive?"

George hesitated for a moment, then shook his head. "No, I think I'd rather do it. I'll be more careful this time, I promise."

"All right, then."

There was a long pause while George breathed again, then again. Finally, he calmly pulled out into traffic without a screech or a horn from any direction.

Father Mancusso sat and watched the road, his thoughts spinning. Half an hour ago, he had been a happy middle-aged cleric coming back from a well-deserved vacation. Now it was all changed. He was in the darkness again.

He chose his words carefully. "George," he said, "have you ever heard of Yggdrasil?"

George looked baffled. "Igg-what?"

"Yggdrasil is the Tree of the Universe in Norse mythology. It covers the whole Earth, and its roots go everywhere. Every tree in the world buds from some root of Yggdrasil."

"So?"

Mancusso thought very hard before he spoke. "The force that attacked you, that nearly destroyed you in that house in Amityville, is one small root of an evil tree much like Yggdrasil. It has roots and branches everywhere, all over the Earth. It is too encompassing, too pervasive to truly be understood, but I do know one thing about it: it is evil, George—inherently, totally evil.

"It's not just in Amityville. Its twisted branches cover the Earth. And I know its power first-hand, as you do. I have touched it myself."

Father Mancusso's eyes took on a slightly unfocused, distant look. "It was during one of my trips to San Francisco—not this one, but one I made a few years ago. I was taking a long walk down Market Street, on my way to a mission that an old acquaintance of mine had founded. Market Street is a marvelous place, George—full of odd little shops and bakeries, bookstores and clothing bazaars. I remember I was passing through a block that was chiefly arts and crafts shops, and a young man called out to me.

"He was very blond, I remember, and dressed in a wildly colorful denim outfit. It was clean and rather cheerful, and his long hair was neat and carefully combed. It was all very upstanding, really. He was lounging in the doorway of a store that sold perfumes and oils, gaudy posters and drug paraphernalia—a head shop, I suppose you'd call it—and at first I thought he must be talking to someone else. Then, just as I passed him, he called out again.

"He said, 'I'm talking to you, Pops.'

"You see, George, I was in street clothes—an old pair of painter's pants, a flannel shirt. He had no way of knowing I was a priest.

"'You're about to make a big mistake,' he said to me. 'I've got something in here a man like you could use. Right inside here.'

"I'd been in situations like this before. This wildly dressed young fellow was a barker, a salesman who tries to lure customers into his shop. Normally, of course, I would have ignored him and continued on my way. But there was something strange about him, George. Something I couldn't quite put my finger on. So I hesitated— just for an instant!—and he tried even harder to sell me.

"'What is it you need, Pops?' he said to me. 'You want some postcards? A snapshot of San Francisco? Maybe a handmade scarf, or a nice set of bookends?' He was really very good, George. Quite a salesman. Then he snapped his fingers right in my face and said, 'No, I've got it! Fragrant oil, Pops. A dandy little scent that's just perfect for you!' I remember that very well—'a dandy little scent,' he called it.

"I admit, I was intrigued. And since I wasn't in all that much of a hurry, I decided to play along a bit. 'What kind of oil?' I asked him.

"'An oil the likes of which you've never known. This fragrance sings to you, Pops, and it lasts for days. Your friends will beg you to tell them where it came from, and I guarantee you, this is the only store in the world where you can get it. I personally nurture every single drop. Absolutely unique.'

"As he was talking, he backed into the store, and I, like a fool, followed him in.

"The store looked normal enough inside. I remember there were rough wooden shelves filled with glass and ceramic sculptures. There were natural soaps and body oils, bits of hanging decoration, and one wall and the entire ceiling were covered with those brightly colored art posters that were so popular a few years ago.

"If I'd had any presence of mind at all, I would have left as soon as he moved behind the counter, but I was more than a little mesmerized by the whole experience. This young man was remarkable, George. Quite a charmer. And I didn't even think twice when he put his hands under the counter and brought out a small vial of fragrant oil. He put it right in front of me.

"I remember that bottle very well, George. It was a small cylinder of green-tinted glass, with a black label and gold lettering. There was only one word printed on the label, and that word sent shivers down my spine.

"The oil was named for one of the lesser-known demons of darkness. I myself had only come upon the name accidentally, but I knew that simply speaking it could give the creature power, and spoken often enough, provide a gateway for the demon into our world.

"And I remember that, quite suddenly, I was able to place the strange feeling I had for this young man and his musty old store.

"'You didn't make this,' I told him, and I think he was a little offended at that.

"'I certainly did!' he said indignantly. 'Every precious drop!'

"I shook my head and said, 'Impossible. A man as young as you hasn't the experience or the knowledge to do it.'

"An evil little light came into the young man's

eyes, and I realized that he had misunderstood me. He gave me the most hideous grin I've ever seen and said, 'You're one of us!'

"I must say, George, I was ready to run screaming from that store right at that moment. But I forced myself to smile—it must have been a pale expression, too!—and I reached out and took up that small bottle. It tingled in my palm, George—actually tingled, as if it had some internal energy of its own.

"I turned away then, as if holding the bottle up to the light, and when my back was to the man I clenched the vial tightly in my hand and I recited a prayer. I blessed that wretched oil and touched it to the small silver crucifix that hung about my neck, under the flannel shirt—this crucifix right here." Father Mancusso fingered a small, shining cross on his breast. "Then I turned back and placed the bottle on the counter.

"'I have no need of this,' I said, and I left the store as quickly as I could. I heard the boy behind me cry out—I think he must have been very surprised—and then, in the reflection of the shop's glass door, I saw him begin to pick up the vial.

"He dropped it as if he were burnt. The last sound I heard in that awful place was the sound of the demon's oil crashing to the floor, and a hideous, high-pitched wailing that I didn't think could possibly have come from the polite young man behind the counter.

"I was two storefronts away when I heard the sound again, and—I couldn't help it, George—I actually stopped and turned to see what could make such an awful sound.

"I will never forget what I saw standing in the

door of that modest little perfume shop. Some part of it was the face of the young salesman, but it had been hideously transfigured. The eyes had been drawn closer together and peaked at the far ends. The brow was bloated, swollen large enough to cast a shadow over an impossibly long and sharp nose. And the teeth, George—like some carniverous animal's teeth—were set in a perfectly round mouth. It was screeching obscenities at me. 'You ruined it!' it screamed. 'I'll smash you, I'll squash you like a bug!' There was more to it—much more—but I didn't listen. I forced myself to turn away, and I hurried down Market Street clutching my crucifix with both hands and praying to God Almighty that I would reach my friend's mission alive and safe."

The priest realized that his fingers were tightly wrapped around that same crucifix, even now. George was looking at him very closely, concerned at the strange intensity in the priest's voice. Mancusso forced himself to calm down.

"Evil is a real force, George, as invisible and fundamental as electricity or magnetism. And it is infinitely more powerful than either. That salesman I encountered was an arrogant young fool who was playing at something he simply didn't understand—a minor entity at best—but his master is something else entirely.

"His master is the axis around which all evil things rotate. His master is the most powerful force in the universe, but for God Himself. And the forces you are facing draw their strength from the same source. They are as prevalent as the air itself, as many-fingered as Yggdrasil, and very nearly beyond human understanding."

George was almost overcome. "Father, I—I

**169**

don't know what to say. Are you telling me it's hopeless? That there's nothing I can do?"

"No, no. Good Lord, George, I'm sorry if I made it sound like that. But you must understand the magnitude of the power you face. It *is* limited in our world. Simply by existing at all on this—this plane, I suppose you'd call it—its potency is limited. But if you want my advice—and I know you haven't asked for it, but I'll give it to you nonetheless—if you want my advice, you'll try and get away."

"Get away?"

"Sell the house. Sell the business, if necessary. Drive all thoughts of the evil you found in Amityville from your mind, if you can. Get away, George. Go somewhere—anywhere—where you can start over."

"But you said the evil is all around us, Father. It can find us anywhere we go, can't it?"

"Perhaps. Perhaps finding a new life will only postpone your trouble. I don't know. But staying here, so close to the house where the power first found you only makes you an easy target."

George was thinking fiercely about all his friend had said. It wasn't the first time he had considered leaving New York. Obviously, things weren't working out anymore. There were plenty of good reasons to pull up stakes and resettle somewhere else, and here Father Macusso was giving him the best reason of all. "Father," he said slowly. "I think—"

The priest at his side made a strangled, nauseated sound and clutched at George's arm.

"Father Mancusso! Are you all right?"

The priest bent forward and slipped from his

seat. George gasped at his expression. He was white, almost translucently pale, and trembling as if from intense cold. He asked Mancusso if he was all right a second time, but the priest couldn't answer. He seemed unable to breathe at all.

George pulled the van to the side of the road and set the brake. Then he unfastened the Father's seat belt and supported him with both hands.

"What is it? Father, tell me, what's the matter?"

For one horrible moment, he thought his friend was dead. His eyes seemed frozen in his skull. His hands were tensed, locked as if in rigor mortis. His strangled breathing cut off... and then, in one immense convulsion, he collapsed forward and exhaled with a groan. His hands fluttered at his face.

"Father? Father! What happened?"

"I'm... all right, George. Just... give me a second."

The color was slowly coming back into his face. He straightened and wiped the sweat from his cheeks. George helped him sit up, and adjusted the bucket seat so the priest was almost lying down. There was a wild, unpleasant look in his eyes.

"What *was* that?"

"I imagine our... 'friend' in Amityville didn't like my advice," Mancusso said grimly. "Which makes it all the more valuable to you." He looked at George with exhausted, brimming eyes. "Tell me you'll leave, George. Tell me you'll try and get away."

George didn't want to answer. He wanted to understand this first; he wanted to fight if he could.

"Tell me," the priest said again.

"Kathy and I have discussed going away for good," he said hesitantly. "But it's not that easy, Father."

"Take her and go, George. She may thank you later if you make her go."

George stared at the trembling priest. He looked suddenly old and very tired. Without another word, he nodded to Father Mancusso and started the van. It was a long time before either of them spoke again.

In the late afternoon of the next day, Kathy Lutz finally found herself alone with her mother. The children were down the street, playing with their new friends. George, after a long talk with his wife, had gritted his teeth and gone off on another trip to Syosset.

She forced herself to take another sip of black coffee. Usually she took healthy amounts of cream and sugar, but not now. She had an almost perverse liking for the bitterness. She was even vaguely glad when it burned her tongue.

"It was a huge argument, Mom," she told Joan as she stared into the sludge at the bottom of the cup. "George finally said he was going to leave and take the kids no matter what I said. Can you believe it? No matter what." She shook her head and swirled the dregs of coffee. "I don't know. I've never seen him like this before, not even at the house. He's so damned determined!"

Joan Conners sat at the table and took her daughter's hand. "Maybe it's a good idea to start over."

"Where? In California? We don't know any-one there. I've never even been there! What possible good could it do?"

"It's a fresh start. A chance to—"

"Why are you taking sides against me? I'm your daughter! You don't even *like* George!"

Joan held her temper. She knew the strain that Kathy was under, and she wasn't about to make it any worse. "He's a good man, Kathy. I've known that for a long time. I'm sure he only wants what's best for you."

For a long moment, their eyes locked—Kathy tense and glaring with anger, her mother calm and warm and very strong. Finally, Kathy looked away and sighed. "I'm sorry, Mom. I know I'm acting crazy. My nerves are shot. I can't seem to sleep at all anymore. I . . ."

She looked at her mother again, and there were tears in her eyes. "I think you're probably right," she said. "I think you're *both* right. It's just that—it's just that I'm scared, that's all. I've been scared for so long now, and I hate it, Mom, I just *hate* it."

Joan Conners took her daughter in her arms and held her. They would be leaving soon, she knew. Leaving her behind.

But leaving her, she knew, might be the only thing that could save them.

# 13

George dropped another sheaf of papers in his lap and leaned back in Joan Conners's favorite reading chair. He had been going over the Lutz family records for hours, and now he was fighting an old-fashioned tension headache.

He closed his eyes and tried to relax, tried to forget what he'd put himself through in the last forty-eight hours. First there had been arguments with Kathy—long, drawn-out affairs, as far away from the childen as they dared to get. In the end, she had finally agreed. They would take the kids and go to California. They would run away.

*Run away.* It was strange how empty and bitter those words made him feel. *Getting a new start. Making an important career move.*

Those sounded all right, somehow. But *running away* . . .

He rubbed his face with both hands, but he didn't open his eyes. He was afraid that he would find the stacks of paper had doubled in size while he'd rested.

George was tired—far more tired than he had a right to be. And looking ahead made him even more exhausted. Packing, paperwork, a long jet flight to San Diego. It made him weary just to think about it.

What had happened to the energetic young man he had been such a short time ago? What had become of the boundless energy of childhood?

A smile crossed his face when he thought of his first trip away from home, so long ago. At the feisty age of seven years, he loaded up his red wagon with every precious possession he had—though it didn't begin to fill it—and ran away without warning. He couldn't even remember why he'd done it—probably because his parents had tried to stop him from having his own way, and George always tried to get his own way—but he did remember that they had been forced to come and get him. He didn't give up; he didn't come home. They had to come find him.

But he was glad when they had. He remembered very clearly how cold and lonely it had been out there. Alone.

Where had he found all that energy? When he was barely past ten, he'd shoveled snow, chopped wood, done any odd job available just to save money for his first drum set. And when he'd bought *that*, he did the same for his first real hobby kit. By the time George celebrated his twelfth birthday, he'd finished a full-sized hydroplane and was practicing for three hours a day on the drums.

What drive. What ambition. Where had that boy gone? He had been a fine football player, good at lacrosse. He'd lifted weights every day and still found time to play in a rock group. Nothing could slow him down. Nothing could stop him.

Then came the cars. George almost grinned at the memory of his maroon blacktop '52 Chevy—the two-door coupe. God, that had been a cherry. And he could remember the car after that, and the car after that, in the same loving detail.

He'd slaved at a paper mill. He'd driven a bus. He'd studied air traffic control and handled the pressure with ease while he rebuilt two cars and a motorcycle.

*That* George Lutz would never have given up. He didn't believe in running away. He didn't think it was possible. The years in the U.S. Marines and private training in the martial arts had only strengthened that conviction.

But things were different now. *He* was different. Or was he just making excuses?

No. There was Kathy to consider, and the children. He was happier with them than he'd ever thought possible, especially after the mess that had been made of his first marriage. They were a family now, a single organism, and all that cocky self-importance couldn't stand up to real obligations—and love.

Yes, things were different now, but he was

still a fighter, still a driver. If someone could just show him how to fight the thing from Amityville. If there was just some thing, some physical thing he could beat, he would do it in double time. But Father Mancusso had convinced him. The power he faced was larger than things, larger than any single man, and there was no shame in defeat. No shame in . . .

Running away. There it was again. And if there was no shame there, why did he feel so damn rotten about it?

The doorbell rang, but George didn't move. He heard Kathy pad across the carpet and open the door, and finally, when he heard a familiar voice from the front porch, he straightened up and opened his eyes.

He looked ruefully at the papers in his lap. They did look a little thicker than before.

"Bud! How's the accounting business?"

"Fine, Kathy. How are you?"

"Getting along. George is in the living room."

George cleared off his lap and rose to shake hands with the man who'd been handling his business affairs for almost half a decade. Bud Masters was a spare, wiry fellow with watery blue eyes and short red hair as rough as a wire brush. He liked shaking hands with this man. There was a simplicity and strength in him that he admired more and more as they worked together.

But he didn't think this was going to be one of their better meetings.

Bud Masters, on the other hand, had been nervous since he'd returned the phone call from

George Lutz. Once they'd managed to put the IRS debacle behind them, he'd thought things would return to normal. And a debacle it had been. He was still telling the story about the Internal Revenue claim of $4,000 against his client that ended in a payment of $53.00 and an apology from the government.

But George hadn't been willing to return to business as usual. He was antsy, restless. Bud had talked to him more in the last two months than he had in the previous five years.

Now, talking with George in person for the first time in weeks, he was even less pleased. The man was obviously exhausted. It looked as if he'd gained ten years and lost fifteen pounds since their last meeting, and the mess of personal financial records on the coffee table completed the bleak picture.

They were going to leave.

George frowned. "Bud, I've got some bad news for you. Or maybe good news, I don't know."

"Shoot."

He took a deep breath. "Three things, actually." He ticked them off on his fingers. "We're moving to California. We're selling the business. And we're going to give the house back to the bank."

Bud Masters didn't look surprised, just a little disappointed. George had already told him about the offer for W. H. Parry, and he had been investigating it, but he had never said it straight out like that before.

The accountant rubbed his forehead with one

hand and stared at the papers in his lap. "Well," he said, "I can't say I'm overjoyed with the decision, but if that's what you want..."

"That's what we want."

"But George, if you just *give* the house back to the bank, you'll probably lose all of your twenty-thousand-dollar down payment. If the house is sold for a good price—and that's a pretty big *if* right now—you might get some of that back, but I have to tell you, that's a long shot at best."

"We know that," George said. He felt strangely calm about the whole matter now. He liked the feeling.

Bud Masters shook his head. "I don't get it. Why not place it with a good real estate agent? I can give you a couple of names—"

"We can't do that, Bud," Kathy said. She was perched on the arm of George's reading chair, one hand draped loosely around his shoulders. "Not with all we know about the house."

Bud shrugged. "Anyone who buys the house will be doing it at their own risk. Besides, anyone who makes a bid on it probably won't believe what happened in the first place, so what does it matter?"

"It matters to us. We didn't believe it ourselves, Bud. We didn't care one way or the other. But—"

George cut off the discussion. He didn't want to talk about that—not now. "We just won't take that kind of load on ourselves. That's our decision."

They could see the wheels turning in Bud Masters's mind. He had a set, stubborn expression. He was ready to argue some more. Then he looked at them closely and, seeing the determination in their expressions, he shrugged a second time. "You're the boss," he said, doing an expert job of hiding his annoyance. "What about the contents?"

"I've already spoken with the Salvation Army," George said, fingering the list of phone numbers he had compiled. "They'll take care of all the canned food and clothing. We'd like you to organize an auction for everything else in the house."

Bud smiled deprecatingly. "That's not really my line."

"You can take a percentage for your time."

"That's not the point."

"Please, Bud," Kathy said. "We need someone we can trust."

The accountant blushed from the roots of his red hair downward. "All right," he said softly. "I'll find someone who can handle it." Then he riffled through the papers to hide his embarrassment and said, very businesslike, "Have you heard any more from the prospective buyer for the business?"

"Yes, I'm meeting with him tomorrow."

"George, you know the price he's offering is ridiculously low. It's just an opening bid, so he can feel you out on this. The corporate structure and the equipment alone are worth more than a hundred thousand, and he's only offering forty. Besides, the escrow deal stinks. It could tie you up for months."

George nodded wearily. "You're right, but it's an offer, and that's what I've been looking for. We've got to cut all ties with Am—with New York as quickly as we can. He made an offer; I'll accept it. If you think he'll go for that, that's all there is to it."

Bud's annoyance was getting the better of him. "Look, George, why don't you let *me* handle the negotiations? This guy is expecting a counter-offer. If you come back with a quick acceptance, he's sure to stretch out the escrow as long as he can, because he'll be convinced there's something wrong with the company. There *has* to be, don't you see, or you wouldn't be so blasted eager to sell it."

George just shook his head. Bud was going to have to understand that this was the way they wanted it. Get out now, even at a loss, but get out *now*. "How soon do you think escrow can close?"

"I'm telling you, it's going to be a problem. Just give me a few days with him—*please*. I'll—"

"No, Bud. No. I want this thing locked up tomorrow. We're leaving for California within the week."

Bud Masters pressed his lips together very tightly and shoved his papers back into the briefcase. He was angry, George knew, but this was the way it had to be.

"All right," the accountant said bitterly. "Whatever you say. It's your property. I'll get on it as soon as I see the papers. Maybe there's some way we won't have to lose our shirts on the deal after all, I don't know."

"Thanks, Bud. We appreciate your help."

Bud stood, then sighed heavily and gave them a reluctant, weary smile. "I know you're under tremendous pressure, George, and I don't want to add to it. It's just that I'm frustrated—*very* frustrated—that it has to end this way." He shook George's hand firmly. "Don't worry, I'll organize the auction. And I'll do the best I can to expedite everything else."

"Thanks again, Bud."

"No problem. And...good luck, you two. Really."

George nodded. "We're going to need it."

Father Mancusso walked with his friend through the central courtyard of the rectory, toward the street beyond. It was a crisp, biting spring day, miles away from the soggy, frigid weather of a few weeks earlier.

He was walking far more slowly than usual. The man at his side was just as eager to prolong the moment.

George Lutz had come to say good-bye, and neither of them wanted to begin.

"So the business is sold, is it?" Mancusso said, watching the toes of his shoes. "That should give you some financial security, I would think."

"Not really," George said. "There are some problems with the escrow, but my accountant will have to solve those by himself. We're not waiting any longer."

Father Mancusso nodded. George didn't have to explain. "I'm sure it will all work out," he said, not really knowing what that meant.

George shrugged. "It'll mean a drastic change in life-style when we first get to California, but I've already applied for a job in San Diego as an air traffic controller. I've got a good record; there are a lot of jobs available. It shouldn't be long before we're on our feet."

Mancusso nodded again, vaguely uncomfortable. He knew he should say something comforting and encouraging. These were friends of his, and they deserved a decent send-off.

But he had nothing left to say to the Lutzes. He felt cold and empty when he thought about the house in Amityville, and he hated that feeling. He never wanted to think about it again.

"I realize this has been traumatic for you and Kathy, and especially for the children. But you know what I think. You've made the best possible decision."

George smiled weakly. "Thanks, Father. It's good to hear that right now."

He looked at the priest, and Mancusso saw something in his expression—a solemnity and strength he didn't want to confront. He turned away and tried to lighten the mood.

"What's this Kathleen tells me about you writing a book?"

George looked genuinely surprised. "A book? Oh, the tapes. No, you see, one of the writers we've gotten to know during all the news coverage has come to us about doing a book on . . . on what's happened. We gave him the tapes we made—we told you about these?"

"Yes."

"At first we'd hoped that the tapes might be used to help Ronald DeFeo."

Mancusso was baffled. "DeFeo? The boy who lived in the house before you?"

George nodded. "We thought at first that he might be able to get a new trial. He still believes that the voices from the house told him to—to do what he did—and we thought maybe the tapes of what happened to us might help him somehow."

Father Mancusso put his hand on George's shoulder. "That was a fine thing to do, George."

"It was a longshot at best," he said, shrugging again. "But I suppose it was worth the try."

"That it was."

"Anyway, if a book does get written out of all this, at least we'll finally get our side of the story out in the open. That's a nice thought. So much garbage has been written." He shook his head sadly.

"I know, I know."

They reached the curb outside the church, and the priest saw Kathy climb out of a late-model station wagon. Amy was sitting quietly in the front seat, fascinated by the traffic, and the two boys were in the back, locked in a playful wrestling match.

Kathy kissed Father Mancusso on the cheek. "How are you feeling about the move, Kathleen?" he asked her.

She gave him a wry smile. "Strange, actually. I'm feeling a little strange about the whole thing. But I know it's for the best."

"Well, New York's loss will be California's gain," he said with false cheerfulness.

"I suppose."

The three of them said their final good-byes, and Kathy and George climbed back into the station wagon while the children said their own farewells.

Father Mancusso leaned down to the open window on the passenger side. "What will you do about the car?"

"It's a rental," George said. "We'll just turn it in at the airport."

He reached in and gave Amy a gentle pinch on the nose. She smiled and wriggled in her mother's lap. "You be good now," he said.

"I will," she told him.

He smiled. "What time's your flight, George?"

"Ten-thirty."

Mancusso frowned. "Tonight? Are you stopping somewhere on the way to the airport?"

"No."

"You mean you're going to spend six or seven hours just waiting for your flight at Kennedy? George, why don't you stay here a while longer? Make yourself comfortable; we can spend the afternoon together. I'd be glad to have you."

"Thanks for the invitation, Father, but no. We'd just as soon go out there and wait."

Father Mancusso could see the sadness and discomfort in their expressions. They had made their decisions, he knew, and now they were deathly afraid that the power from the house would do something to stop them. They couldn't let that happen.

And he couldn't blame them for being afraid. Too much had happened already for them to be anything else.

He leaned through the window and kissed Kathy warmly on the cheek. "You have a beautiful family, Kathleen. That's a lot to be thankful for." He reached across her and took George's hand in one final, firm, shake.

"God bless you both," he said, trying to keep his voice from trembling.

"God bless *you*, Father," George said earnestly.

Then the station wagon was underway, and

**186**

Kathy was leaning out of the window, shouting "Thank you! Thank you, we'll write as soon as we're settled!" and he was smiling and waving at the unfamiliar car, and wondering if he would ever see them again.

# 14

Kathy squinted and frowned and reached up to punch off the light that was glaring in her eyes. They had been in the air for more than three hours, and the words in the book she was reading were beginning to blur.

She shifted in the narrow airliner's seat and tried to find a more comfortable position. There wasn't one. Finally she stretched out as far as the space allowed and straightened up.

American Airlines Flight 524 from New York was the classic red-eye—an all-night junket from Kennedy to San Diego International. The lights had been lowered soon after takeoff, and most of the passengers were huddled under blankets, fast asleep.

Kathy envied them. She was wide awake—if anything, she thought, more awake than she'd been when they'd stumbled onto the plane after seven and a half hours of waiting in the terminal.

George was stretched out in the seat next to her, his head back and his mouth slightly open. He was snoring very softly. Amy was in the window seat to her left, curled into a warm little ball. Kathy smiled through her fatigue and drew the thin blanket with the American Airlines monogram closer around her sleeping daughter. She kissed her lightly on the cheek and said, "Sweet dreams, honey." Amy didn't even move.

She stood very carefully and eased her way past George, careful not to wake him. He had had a more difficult time at Kennedy than she, trying to hold down the children, get the dog on board, and keep a cranky wife content. If anyone needed the sleep, he did.

She walked softly down the aisle and checked on the boys. Greg and Matt were two rows behind their parents, and they were asleep, too, huddled together to ward off the jet's air-conditioned chill. Half-read comic books lay open on their laps.

Kathy rubbed her rear end, weary from all the sitting, then stopped it abruptly when she realized someone might be watching.

Oh, the hell with it, she thought, and finished easing the kinks. It serves them right for making such tiny little seats in the coach section. She wished idly for one of the spacious, overpadded, first-class seats, but she knew they had to be careful with what little money they had until they were established in California.

California. The word held promise and problems for Kathy. She was still fighting with herself over their decision to leave New York for good, and though she didn't want to worry unnecessarily about the future, she couldn't be the completely happy-go-lucky Pollyanna type, either. It just wasn't in her.

The important thing, she knew, was being a family. They were still together, that was what mattered, and they would stay that way no matter what.

She asked the sleepy flight attendant for a cup of tea, and two minutes later she was given a half-empty Styrofoam cup with some vaguely brown lukewarm liquid in it. She moved slowly back down the aisle and managed to slip into her seat without waking George or spilling the tea down her dress.

Kathy sighed. Then she pulled a blanket up around her shoulders and put the seat as far back as it would go without crashing into the passenger behind her.

Her last thoughts, before she drifted off a few minutes later, centered on Harry. *He* was getting a good night's sleep, at least, drugged with a huge dose of sedatives and loaded into the animal carrier like a side of beef. She had a fuzzy image of him snoring away in the pressurized baggage compartment, oblivious to the roar of the engines and the chilly artificial air.

Was it noisy in the baggage compartment? she wondered. Was it cold?

A few seconds later, Kathy was asleep.


Amy woke up almost an hour after Kathy drifted off. She looked up with bright blue eyes and saw her mother sleeping soundly, a wisp of brown hair curling on one cheek. She saw her

Daddy in the far seat, leaning back and making a little *rrrrr* sound every time he breathed in.

Very slowly, very carefully, Amy turned in her seat and climbed to her knees. She had to use both hands to lift up the heavy plastic cover over the jet plane's window, so she could look out at the huge metal wing and the night sky beyond.

Her five-year-old eyes moved back and forth across the dark, silvery expanse of the wing. The metal plates glinted in the moonlight. The stars burned more brightly and steadily than they ever had in New York. Multicolored flames as big as her arm danced at the rear of the engines, but Amy barely noticed any of it. She was looking for something special.

Finally she stopped and stared at a very particular spot, ten feet beyond the fuselage and three feet from the leading edge of the wing. For the briefest blink of an eye, something began to form there—a wisp of a figure, a sketchy white form that was swept away by the wind almost before it took shape.

Amy smiled then and closed the cover. She turned away from the window, still smiling, and curled up in the seat with her head in her mother's lap. A few moments later, she had slipped into sleep again . . . and still, she smiled.

The dog was barking. The children were screaming. The disembodied voice of the terminal's announcer boomed and grated time after time.

Kathy Lutz was seriously considering homicide as the only real alternative. She paced around the small mountain of luggage, snapped at the children, and looked at George with growing animosity.

They had arrived at San Diego International Airport more than an hour ago, and they were still waiting for a ride. As·usual, something had gone wrong.

George was a few feet away, shouting into a pay phone. "Look, just get somebody down—" He waited, fuming. "I understand that, I *know* you're sorry, just—all right. *Thank* you. Yes." He slammed down the phone and huffed back to her, shaking his head in disgust.

"Somebody messed up," he said. "They're all *very* sorry, and they'll have a car here in about forty-five minutes. The people at the motel are leaving the key out for us."

Forty-five minutes? Kathy tried not to sound too sharp when she asked, "How far *is* it to the Red Fern?"

"How should I know? I've—" George was as edgy as she was, but she could see that he was doing his best to keep calm. He stopped, took a deep breath, and tried to put on a smile. "About a half hour's drive, I think," he said with false calm.

Kathy wanted to sit down. She felt as if she'd been standing for hours. She looked around for a seat and said, "Maybe picking a motel and a car service from the phone book wasn't such a great idea, huh?"

George shrugged wearily and she was sorry she'd said anything at all. "Okay, okay, I know I really blew it this time. I'm sorry, babe."

"Oh, George," she said, and reached out to squeeze his hand. "It's okay."

He squeezed back, and he smiled, genuinely

this time. Then she sat down on the edge of an upturned suitcase, and it slipped out from under her. She landed on the airport carpet with a resounding *thwack!*

They both laughed until they cried. And the children shrieked, and the dog barked away, still half drugged, and the terminal's announcer boomed and grated. But suddenly it didn't seem all that bad.

Sally Harper, domestic supervisor, took the stairs to the second floor of the Red Fern Motel one at a time. She always took the stairs one at a time. There was no reason to waste precious human energy that she might very well need for more important matters.

Mrs. Harper—everyone called her Mrs. Harper —had been in domestic service for more than fifteen years, first as a private maid in Beverly Hills, then as a supervisor at a small motel, and finally here, at the Red Fern—"one of the finest establishments of its kind," she would tell her friends. Frequently.

Now, after fifteen years of making other people's beds and cleaning up other people's messes, she was about to retire. In another three months, her husband would get the promotion he had been after for so long, and with it would come a raise. At last Mrs. Harper could begin to spend the time with her children.

She paused on the landing and caught her breath. It's about time I retire, at any rate, she thought primly, making sure her steel gray hair was properly in place. After all that's happened this week, I do believe I'm letting the pressure get the better of me.

She pushed open the door to the second floor with a commanding sweep of her hand. Mrs. Harper never used the elevator. The main elevators were for guests, and the day maids could hear her coming if she used the service lift.

Just as she suspected. Halfway down the hall, leaning on their linen carts and oblivious to the time, their duties, and apparently everything else, Mrs. Harper saw two of her employees chattering away.

These new girls, she thought angrily. The way they dawdle at their work, you would think they actually *enjoy* this place.

"Ladies!" she said sharply. Mrs. Harper always called her employees 'ladies' and 'gentlemen.' It was the only proper thing to do. "Ladies, I assume there is some reason for this high-level conference?"

The two women—Molly and Anna—turned and looked at her very casually. They didn't seem terribly upset at being caught unawares.

"Won't you two ever finish this floor?" Mrs. Harper said. She had come to realize that intimidation was as ineffective as everything else with these girls.

Molly smiled as if she hadn't heard the question and jerked a thumb over her shoulder. "They're at it again," she said.

Mrs. Harper looked blank. "Who's at what again?"

"That family in 216. The Lutzes. They're moving again."

"That's the fourth time in three days," Anna said, nodding.

Mrs. Harper did not see any purpose in gossip. It wasted time and invaded other people's privacy, and she had a firm rule to avoid it at all costs. But this, on the other hand, was rather interesting.

"Why, do you think?" she asked, sounding almost friendly.

"They're complainers," Molly said, sneering. "They complain about everything, Mrs. Harper. It smells bad. There's bugs in the room. There's flies in the windows." Molly shook her finger at Mrs. Harper. "Now, I cleaned up some of those rooms after 'em, and I never found nothing like no bugs or flies, I swear!"

"Of course not!" Mrs. Harper said. Good Lord, not at the Red Fern!

Molly shook her head in disbelief. "First they was in 312. Then they was in 126, and then in 216. Now they're up and goin' to 220." She gave a wry little smile. "I wonder what'll be wrong with that one?"

Mrs. Harper barely heard the question. Something that Molly had said earlier had sent a shiver down her spine.

Room 312. So it was the Lutzes who had moved out of there so unexpectedly. That was why *she* had been the one to do the cleanup; the schedules had all been made but Management wanted the room ready for last-minute arrivals.

The moment she had used the master key to let herself in, she had felt . . . strange. While she stripped the bed, emptied the ashtrays (which didn't really need it, but one always emptied the ashtrays), and put the used towels in the linen cart, she tried to ignore the feeling. But it got worse and worse.

It felt as if someone was watching her. She

was sure someone was in the hallway, or the bathroom, or the closet.

Then, when she had looked in the mirror above the bedroom dresser, she had seen something. Well... nothing, really. Some sort of shadow in the glass, or some little flicker of a reflection from the hallway, but—but it had frightened her. Very badly.

Mrs. Harper had thrown the towels unevenly on their rods. She had left the room unstraightened and undusted, and she had even slammed the door on her way out. Ten minutes later, she'd felt fine again, and a little ashamed of her behavior.

It was part of getting older, she supposed. Part of thinking about retirement, of letting the pressures get the better of her. But now...

Room 312.

Anna said something she didn't hear, and Molly laughed loudly. It snapped Mrs. Harper out of her reverie.

"You girls!" she said sharply. "You'll look for any excuse to stop working, won't you?"

Anna grinned at Molly and shrugged her shoulders.

"Back to work now. I want this floor finished in twenty minutes, and no dawdling. Is that understood?"

"Yes, Mrs. Harper," they said in sullen unison, and Mrs. Harper turned and clicked down the hall to the fire exit.

There was work to do. Plenty of work. And no time to worry about that silly family and ... and the strange thing she had seen in Room 312.

# 15

The sky that arched over San Diego was as blue as a ceramic bowl and dusted with clouds. The temperature was in the low eighties, and George rolled down the window to let in the breeze as he drove the family down Highway 101.

"Just another winter's day in California," he said cheerfully, and guided them down an offramp. The Pacific glistened steel blue in the distance.

"Horrible, ain't it?" Kathy said, grinning. They passed a sign that said WILSON KENNELS, NEXT RIGHT.

They had been in San Diego for a little less than two weeks, and so far things hadn't gone very well. First there had been the delays at the airport, then the misunderstandings with room reservations. The only good thing about it all had been keeping Harry for their first night in town. He had simply been forgotten in all the confusion.

But the next day they'd been told to board him, and it took a while to find a suitable place. Then, as soon as they returned to the Red Fern, all the troubles with the rooms began.

George was amazed that no one had put the Health Department onto that fleabag hotel already. Of course, the manager claimed there was nothing wrong, and the maids said they couldn't find anything either. But George knew a foul smell when he smelled one, and bugs were bugs.

He had planned to report them to the Health Department himself, but he didn't want to start their new lives in California with problems like that. Besides, he thought, what if there weren't any smells or flies? That would mean . . .

No. George was doing just as Father Mancusso had told him to. He was starting over. He was trying to forget Amityville and all it encompassed.

Now for the future. Kathy had found a nearly new condominium in La Jolla, a prestigious community just north of San Diego. The building was relatively inexpensive—especially for California—and only a year and a half old. It would be perfect for them until they could afford a small house of their own. And he'd already dropped off his résumé at a couple of different places; he would be getting calls for work very soon, he was sure of that.

Kathy pointed across him, to his left, and George swung the rented car into a wide driveway between two cedar trees. A series of white clapboard structures and a large, old-fashioned

Victorian house were set far back from the drive. He could hear the barking of dogs through the car's open window.

Little Amy was the first one out of the station wagon. She hit the ground running, with Matt and Greg right behind her.

They were speeding toward a tall, spare fellow who looked more like the stereotypical New Englander than a third-generation Californian. He was standing in front of one of the small outbuildings holding a frayed leather leash. The Lutzes' dog, Harry, was at the other end of the tether.

The Lutzes had visited the kennel a number of times, just to keep Harry company. George and Kathy had gotten to know and like the sour-faced old fellow, and Wilson, in turn, knew why they had come today.

As the children ran toward him, Mr. Wilson leaned down and unclipped the leash from Harry's collar. The dog bounded forward and nearly bowled the children over. They screamed and barked and wrestled on the grass in one huge, happy tangle.

The Lutzes joined Mr. Wilson on the lawn near the office and took the leash from him. "Thanks for looking after him so well," Kathy said. "We were a little worried about that, you know. This is the first time we've had to put him in a kennel."

Mr. Wilson twisted his mouth into a shape the Lutzes had come to recognize as a smile. "Well, can't say Harry much cared for it, but we didn't mind at all." He nodded toward the mutt. "A good ol' dog, he is."

"Thanks."

George handed him a check and shook his hand. Then they called to the children and loaded up the car, and everyone waved good-bye.

They were off. It was time to visit their new home.

George had just opened the door to the U-Haul trailer when a huge drop of water, as big as his thumb, fell out of the sky and hit him on the head.

He cursed and squinted into the sky. It was black with storm clouds, as thick and heavy with rain as any he had ever seen in the East.

He glared inside the trailer and tried to decide what to do. He was just about to unload the few pieces of furniture they had been able to buy, along with the few items they had had shipped out from New York State.

Three more raindrops landed on his shoulders, and the rising wind kicked the door of the trailer into his shoulder. He stopped it with his hands and waited a moment longer, to see if the rain would let up or get a good deal worse.

"George!"

He turned to see Kathy running over the small grass-covered hill that separated their condominium from the road. She had his raincoat clutched in one hand, and as she joined him, the wind began to howl like an animal.

"The radio says it's the edge of a tropical storm!" she shouted over the noise. "Heavy rain till morning!"

"Oh, great!" he said, and threw the raincoat over his shoulders. He slammed and locked the trailer doors, then he and Kathy ran over the hillock to their new house. They were soaked to the skin by the time they reached the porch.

Kathy swung open the door and they hurried inside, dripping on the newly cleaned carpet as they shed their coats.

"You'll never guess what they're calling this storm," she said, shaking out her hair.

"I give up."

"Kathleen. Hurricane Kathleen."

He grunted. "Not exactly what you'd call a good omen, is it?" he said sarcastically.

It was the wrong thing to say. A dark look crossed Kathy's face, and George realized what he'd done. He slapped on a grin and started to tickle her. "A joke!" he said. "Only joking!"

She laughed in spite of herself and wriggled away, aiming a playful punch at his shoulder.

"Oh, George! Don't tease me!" She took his hand to stop the tickling and led him into the empty living room.

They stood at the picture window and watched the lightning and the lashing of the rain as it thundered toward them from the Pacific.

By midmorning of the following day, the storm had passed them by. George could see the results of the wind and rain all around him: fallen trees, downed power lines, and mud on every visible surface. It would take weeks for San Diego to clean itself up. But now it was time to unload the truck.

He levered a heavy cedar chest onto his back and hurried toward the house, cursing himself for not moving a chunk of broken palm tree out of the walk when he'd had the chance. It would have made his trip three steps shorter.

He thumped up the porch and through the door, groaning a little more than necessary under the chest's substantial weight. He even tried to wipe his boots before he tracked on the carpet, but there wasn't much point to that. He'd made a mess of it already.

Kathy was standing in the doorway of the kitchen, wiping her hands on a dishcloth.

"Where would you like it, ma'am?" he said, lowering the chest to the carpet. The thing was heavy.

Kathy was frowning. George didn't like that look.

"What is it, babe?"

She started to say something, but she stopped. Then she tried again. "George, I know your great-grandfather made that chest, that the wood is from one of the first ships from England, and all that. And I know the psychics said that cedarwood was... well, *safe*. But..." She paused and glanced nervously at the box. "But it *was* in the house with us for a while—just for those few days before you took it to the office, remember? —and I feel strange about having it here." She looked down at her apron, embarrassed. "I know that sounds crazy, but—"

George smiled and turned away. "It's no problem, babe," he said, and started to pick up the chest. "I'll just put it in the garage."

"Are you sure it's okay?"

He turned back to her, still smiling. "It's fine. Really."

"George, I want to tell you something. I know I was the one who made all the trouble about coming out here. But now that we've been here a while, I have to say... things feel better already." She looked into his eyes, and inexplicably, she felt like crying—a happy sort of crying. "I—it really feels like a fresh start, George. Really it does."

He said, "For me, too, babe," and kissed her. And they stood there among the unpacked cartons and mismatched furniture of their living room, close in each other's arms, for a very long time.

# 16

It was just after eleven o'clock on a sunny weekday morning, and Kathy was checking the mail for the third time that day. She wasn't expecting anything particularly important, and there was plenty to do in the house, but it was as good an excuse as any to get away. As she hurried down the stairs of the porch and up the condominium's driveway, she had to admit, if only to herself, that she had wanted to leave the house all morning—even if only for a few moments each time. If only to catch her breath.

Why is it so cold? she thought as she wrapped herself tightly in her light sweater. The bright sunshine of the California spring should have warmed her through, but she was shivering as she reached the mailbox.

There were four receptacles grouped together

in a cinder-block kiosk across from their home, complete with an inset bin for trash. The mail had finally arrived. Kathy unlocked their box and took out a fistful of envelopes. She sorted through the correspondence before she headed back to the house.

No reason to take this junk mail to the house, she thought idly. More deeply, she knew it was simply another excuse to stay out in the open a moment longer.

She pulled all the mail labeled OCCUPANT or RESIDENT from the stack and flipped it into the bin. There was a supermarket mailer . . . a subscription form for a science magazine . . . a flyer from their senator. She smiled sadly at the other copies of the same brochures that were already waiting for the trash pickup. Such a waste.

As she crossed the street to the house, still fingering the remains of the mail, a car horn *blipped* behind her and tires thumped against the concrete lip of the drive. She glanced up and moved quickly out of the way as George pulled their rented car snugly, if a little too quickly, into the driveway.

She waited for him at the front door, but he stayed in the car for a long moment, staring dully at the hood as if concentrating on something complicated and unpleasant. Kathy was just about to go to him when he pulled the key from the ignition and climbed out of the car. He slammed the door to the station wagon and stalked up the walk, still glaring at nothing in particular.

"Hi, babe," Kathy said gently. "Did—"

He walked past her without a word or a

glance. She followed him into the living room, congratulating herself on her own patience.

"How'd it go?" she asked.

He had already collapsed into the reading chair in the living room. "I didn't get the job," he said grimly, "but I'm damned if I know why."

Kathy laid the stack of mail on the end table and came up behind him. Her hands went to his shoulders and rubbed gently at the knotted muscles of his back.

George's head bowed with fatigue. "I don't get it," he said softly. "I'm qualified—more qualified than most. I've got a good record, and they needed me. But after a minute or two, the guy just sort of froze up. I don't know."

He sat hunched in the chair for a very long moment and enjoyed the touch of his wife's hands. Then he reached up and covered her fingers with a hand of his own. "Thanks, babe," he said in a newer, stronger voice. "That's much better."

She kissed him on the back of the head and said, "Why don't you open the mail? I just picked all the trash out of it."

He nodded and scooped up the stack, and smiled at the first return address he saw. "This should be good news. It's from Bud."

He tore open the envelope, and a long, business-sized check fluttered into his lap. George glanced at it and frowned at the small amount, then scanned the note on Bud Masters's Accounting letterhead that accompanied it.

"Well," he said, more bitter than angry, "the escrow still hasn't closed."

"Then what's the check?"

"A few of the business's uncollected debts came through."

She shrugged and looked at the amount. "Well, it's better than nothing, George. At least this should help keep us going until Bud gets things sorted out."

"If he ever gets it sorted out," he mumbled to himself, and moved on to the next letter.

It was a friendly note from Joan Conners, bringing them up to date on the latest gossip from East Babylon. The simple, chatty, cheerful warmness of the letter put them both in a better frame of mind.

George put the letter aside and smiled at Kathy for the first time. "So how was your day?"

She smiled in return, but it came out a little pale and weak. "Okay, I guess."

George looked at her closely. "What is it, Kath?"

She looked away. "Nothing, George. Just getting a little bored, I suppose, and lonely. I mean, we've been here more than two months now, and I haven't really found many friends yet."

George squeezed her hands and said, "I know, babe. It's hard to start over like this. But . . . are you sure nothing else is bothering you?"

She shrugged and stood up, still unwilling to look directly at her husband. "Oh, it's nothing, really. I just felt strange a couple of times today."

He started to say something, but Kathy waved him off. "It's nothing, George, really. I'm fine. Forget it." She gestured at the letter in his hands, if only to change the subject. "What's that, a bill?"

George looked at the envelope and scowled. "From New York," he grumbled, and ripped it open.

Kathy watched the frown deepen and twist as he read the note. "I don't believe this," he said. "They're still sending us electricity bills from Amityville!"

"Didn't you already write and tell them they'd made a mistake?"

"Twice. I told them that the power was turned off as soon as we left—before they even sent the *first* bill. And I told them that we'd be glad to pay for the charges through the end of January. And I told them I'd appreciate it if they'd please get their records straightened out." He shook the letter at her, and it began to wrinkle in his hands. "But now this comes! Some little bureaucrat is as good as calling me a liar. 'Yes,' they say, 'we discontinued the power on such-and-such a date, but electricity is still being consumed by the residence.'"

"How is that possible?"

"It isn't! I mean, I don't know how. But they say the house is in our name, so we have to pay for it."

"But they said they turned—"

"Kathy, *I don't know*." He crumpled the letter in his fist and threw it on the carpet. Kathy took a deep breath and let him calm down.

Finally she cleared her throat and said, "What are you going to do about it?"

He sniffed and tried to keep his voice clear and steady. "Forget it! I've done everything I'm going to do about the house. They can get the money from whoever or *what*ever is using the power now."

211

He stood up and gave Kathy a long, unexpectedly warm embrace. When they finally pulled apart, he said, "I'm sorry, babe. I'm real edgy today. Think I'll change and go work on the bike for a while, okay?"

Kathy smiled brightly and nodded. "Dinner will be ready in about forty-five minutes."

The cool black Harley Davidson motorcycle that George had shipped out from New York nearly filled the workshop half of their garage. It was his pride and joy—a huge, awesome, midnight black machine with a polished black shell as hard and shiny as the chiton of a monstrous insect. It seemed to glow with a power of its own, and when it ran, George knew, that finely tuned engine could purr like a cat.

He had bought it a month before they moved into Amityville, and when the trouble at the house began, he moved it to a friend's bike shop on the far side of Long Island. *If Kathy hadn't reminded me about it before the move,* he thought, *it might still be there.*

But they had remembered it, and now he found a strange solace in tinkering with the bike. As he worked, he worried over the unpleasant and unexpected problems he had encountered in California.

Today's turn-down had been the fourth—or was it the fifth?—in that many days. Nobody would tell him why they wouldn't give him a job he was fully capable of doing. He hadn't even mentioned the name 'Amityville.' He'd used Joan's address, so it couldn't be that.

Today's interview, with one of the well-appointed private airports outside town, had been particularly disappointing, since it was for an air traffic controller's job. They'd seen his papers, and talked to him on the phone, and the general impression he'd had was that—well, one quick personal interview and the job would be his.

But it went sour. The minute he arrived, something had just...*chilled*. It was as if the memories of Amityville and his own confusion and depression followed him around like some sick cartoon thundercloud and frightened off potential employers.

Oh, hell, he thought, it's probably just bad luck and bad timing. I've got another interview on Monday, with Lindberg Field. I should get that one, and then I can forget all this nonsense about the house.

George flipped the light canvas cover off the bike and looked for a place to put it. He finally shoved the tarp out of the way, on top of the antique cedar chest that Kathy had asked him to store in the garage. Originally, he had intended to cover the chest with packing pads and use it as a counter for his tools, but for some reason that had never seemed quite right to him. It was better just to leave it unused and uncovered in the corner.

The bike really is beautiful, he thought. And in a few days, it'll be in perfect shape. He rubbed his hands and searched through the tools he had left strewn on the concrete slab, deciding what to do. A little tune-up was just the ticket. He would check the timing, clean the points, and maybe even take it down the freeway for a quick spin.

He would need the ratchets, and the tuning

kit, and . . . the timing light. Damn it, he thought, that's still stored away.

George glared at a cardboard box with the air freight company's insignia printed on the side, sitting on a shelf high above his head. He considered giving up on the whole project. Nothing's easy these days, he thought. Nothing. But he shrugged the annoyance away and looked for something to stand on so he could get to the shelf, feeling like the monkey he'd seen on "60 Minutes" that week—the one who had to stack up empty boxes and broken furniture just to get to a bunch of bananas.

He stripped the tangled canvas cover off the cedar chest and moved it under the shelf. Then he stepped up very delicately, careful not to mar the fine old surface with his boots.

As he reached up to take the carton down, a wave of nausea clutched at his stomach. George doubled over and swayed, as if someone had punched him in the stomach. He grabbed at a lower shelf for balance, and a second wave struck him.

Cold sweat smeared his brow. He coughed lightly, like a sick animal, and climbed off the box still bent over. He was fighting to keep his lunch where it belonged.

The wave of nausea relented and he straightened enough to wipe his face and take a deep breath. What was *that* all about? he wondered.

He turned and sat on the cedar chest to catch his breath, and another wave, worse than the first two, slammed into him. George grabbed at his stomach and groaned. Splotches of light and darkness tore at him, and he lurched to his feet, disoriented and slightly panicked.

*The chest.* It happened each time he was in contact with it. Kathy had said it herself, when he'd brought it into the house. It had been with them, if only for a little while. It had been at Amityville. . . .

George stumbled across the garage and nearly tripped over a wrench that was lying in the middle of the floor. He pulled himself up against the hard wooden wall and kept going.

It couldn't be the chest, he thought numbly, and slipped through the side door. It must be some sort of anxiety attack. I've been worrying too much about getting a job—*not* getting a job.

It was bright and clean outside, and cool with the coming sunset. He put his back against the stucco wall of the garage and gasped for breath. Slowly, far too slowly, the sickness drained away.

Kathy thought about electricity and tension and unemployment as she busied herself with the preparations for dinner. The children would be home soon, she knew, hungry as a pack of wolves, and if she knew George half as well as she thought she did, she would have to drag him out of his makeshift workshop to get him to the table. He could get so absorbed in his work, even in his hobbies.

She was cutting a slab of cheese into quick, efficient little cubes when the kitchen door opened. It startled her a bit, and she turned suddenly to see her husband filling the doorframe. He looked strange, she thought. Scared, somehow, and a little pale.

"Did you forget something?" she said carefully.

She saw him swallow and smile weakly. "Forget? Uh, no. I just...decided not to work today, that's all."

He was hiding something, but Kathy let it pass. She knew he was a lot more worried about not finding a job than he let on. She looked back to her preparations, and out of the corner of her eye she saw George shiver and straighten before he came into the kitchen and moved behind her.

"How's the food coming?" he asked.

"It'll be about twenty minutes yet," she said, trying very hard to keep it light.

He put his hands around her waist and squeezed gently, and Kathy smiled in spite of herself. She nudged him but she kept working.

"Something smells good," he said.

"Oh, George, nothing's cooking yet."

"Then it must be you."

She giggled and turned to the side, a little reluctant to leave him. As she reached for one of the cupboards, she suddenly spun back and slapped him lightly on the wrist. He was trying to steal a piece of cheese.

"Honestly, you're worse than the kids. Why don't you go read the paper or watch television or do something constructive before you eat—"

Kathy saw something across the room that made her stop short. Her muscles froze and tightened like wires. Her fingers curled involuntarily, closed into fists and bit at the soft flesh of her palms.

No, she thought numbly. Please no....

A large black fly had buzzed through the open door. It flew lazy circles around the kitchen, its thick hum filling the quiet afternoon.

George saw it moments after Kathy. He looked back at her and, in an instant, he realized what had happened. He jerked open the cabinet under the kitchen sink so violently that cans of cleanser and stacks of rags were upset, and pulled the flyswatter out. The hook from the cupboard door came with it.

The fly was fat and slow, and George crushed it with the plastic swatter the moment it landed on their yellow tablecloth. The *whack* of the swatter shattered the spell. Kathy gasped and rushed to the table. She clutched at the four corners of the cloth, pulled it into a heap—napkins and all—and dragged it out of the kitchen.

Not in this house, she thought over and over. Not here, not in this house. She pushed the tablecloth and napkins and the smeared remains of the insect deep into the trash can and sealed the plastic lid over it.

George was waiting for her in the kitchen. She hid in his arms, trying not to cry, and he stroked her hair slowly, comfortingly.

"I'm sorry, George. I'm sorry."

"It's all right, babe, it's all right. You have a lot of scars—we both do. I guess they'll take a long time to heal, that's all. A lot of time."

It was a penetrating and shadowless blue light that split the familiar walls of the California condominium into threatening planes of flat luminous mist. George walked through the moonlit landscape as if he were walking in slow motion. His feet were trapped in some invisible quicksand. The air itself was charged with a mucky, throat-thickening gas.

He was shirtless and shoeless, dressed only in his pajama bottoms, as he moved down the stairs to the first floor. There was furniture in the house that he didn't remember—pieces they had left behind in Amityville. And there was a smell, a sound, a feeling he'd never wanted to experience again.

George found Kathy in the kitchen, crying as she slashed at the tiny black particles that swooped and buzzed around her. She had a flyswatter in one hand and a rolled newspaper in the other. The newspaper's headline said TERROR-STRICKEN FAMILY FLEES HOME IN NEW YORK SUBURB.

He rushed into the room and took the newspaper away from her. A single fly, as big as his thumb, was watching him from the yellow tablecloth, sucking at its own body and rubbing its legs together in a continuous sawing motion, and he brought the paper down on the insect with all his strength. He smashed the fly flat, crushed it under its own shimmering wings, and he started to smile... until the fly's legs twitched and moved, and the shimmering wings vibrated, and it was on its legs again, looking at him again, rubbing and rubbing its legs together and sucking at its own body.

Kathy dropped the swatter and screamed, and George turned to look at her.

Flies were coming through the kitchen door in one impenetrable black wall. They gushed through the windows, out of the oven, from between the cracks in the tile.

They were all over Kathy. She was buried in flies, covered in a roiling, buzzing cloak of them. She was trying to scream, but no sound reached him. There was nothing but the buzzing.

He turned back, and the flies covered him, too. They swarmed up his hands, his arms, his legs. He felt the tingle of their mandibles, the minute vibrations of their wings, the microscopic kiss of their fluted mouths.

Now Greg and Matt were in the room with him, moving as slowly as George through the invisible muck. He called to them, cried out to them, but there was only the buzzing, the continuous buzzing, and then the flies covered them too—swallowed them, deafened them, drowned them. George tried to beat them away, tried to squeeze them between his fingers, but the room grew even thicker with insects. The light itself was draining away, blocked by millions of tiny bodies.

He stumbled out of the kitchen, past the furniture he had left behind in Amityville, and fell into the flat blue light of the living room. He started up the stairs, twisting under the coating of insects, and tried to clear his eyes . . . and he saw Amy.

She was standing at the top of the stairs, rubbing her sleepy eyes. Then she looked up and saw George—and a black cloud of flies.

"Daddy!" she screamed.

The moving black blanket swarmed toward her, but something was stopping them. An invisible wall seemed to be holding them at bay.

More and more flies joined the assault, and the shape of the invisible force grew sharper, more distinct—etched in the air by a sea of moving darkness.

It was a huge outline, like a giant halo around Amy. It looked like a pig, George thought.

Amy looked around her, as if seeing something for the first time. "Jodie?" she said. "You know you're not supposed to be here! You promised you would leave. Mommy and Daddy will be mad at me. You have to go home, Jodie. Go home!"

George tried to call to her, but it was too late. The protection suddenly disappeared, and in an instant Amy was smothered.

George screamed.

And screamed.

And screamed.

He sat bolt upright in his bed. He was covered with a slick, greasy sweat, and his heart was racing in his chest. The light was normal now. It poured in through the door to the hallway, making golden patterns on the carpet.

No flies. No stench. No horror. It had been a nightmare, another bloody nightmare.

He turned and saw Kathy beside him, upright and knotted with tension. There was sweat on her forehead, too, and a twitching in her hands. When he touched her, she jumped and looked at him, and he saw the same fear and revulsion in her eyes that he knew was lying inside him.

"Flies?" Kathy said.

George clutched at her, held her, and knew that they had been locked together in the same dream, the same nightmare—one that neither of them could control or escape.

"Yes," he said, "yes." They lay in their bed,

clinging to each other for warmth, trembling against the night, and waited for the sound of something thick and tiny to buzz at the screen a few feet from their bed.

It never came.

## 17

The sunshine worked its way deep into Kathy's body. She stretched and smiled, and dug her toes into the warm sand around her feet.

George put down the book he had been reading and turned to look at the ocean. The children were in the shallows to his left, splashing and playing in the tide pools and shrieking gleefully at what they found there.

"What'cha thinking 'bout, babe?" Kathy asked lazily.

George hesitated before he answered. He didn't want to break the languorous, pleasant spell of the afternoon.

"George?" Kathy said again. There was a thin thread of concern in her voice.

He shrugged. "Nothing, really. I was just thinking about the book."

"Why, babe?" Cathy seemed puzzled at his concern. "The new writer's working on it, isn't he?"

"Hell, I don't know. I guess so."

George squinted at the sun and decided it was past time for leaving. He stood up and called to the children, and they grumbled a bit before they shook themselves free of the water.

"Mom and I are going for a short walk," he said, "and when we get back, we're going to head out. Why don't you start packing up?"

"So early?" Greg said. He loved the beach more than the other two combined.

"We'll stop and get something to eat on the way home," George promised. "You can choose the place."

That did exactly what it was supposed to do—it started a small, good-natured argument among the children. Kathy got them to clean up while they argued, and then she and George slipped away, walking down the beach hand in hand.

Some time in the past, George thought, this beach probably had pretty big crowds. After all, it was only seconds from the Coast Road that ran through La Jolla, and the large cliff that towered above the beach cut it off from the worst of the winds. For a long time, there had even been a convenient stone staircase cut into the cliff itself that led straight down to the white, wide strip of sand.

But years ago—George couldn't tell how many—nature had reclaimed this fragment of seashore. A storm or an earth tremor had broken a huge piece of the cliff free, and the steps had been buried in rubble. Farther down the beach, a similar slide had collapsed an over-hang, and cut it off from the easily accessible beach farther north. Now it could only be reached by a long, slightly precarious trip around the rocks, and then only after a careful climb down the steel staircase that adjoined the lifeguard's station. At high tide, the rocks themselves were covered with water, and that cut the beach off from any access at all.

George liked the isolation—had liked it when they'd first stumbled across the beach weeks before—and now the Lutzes claimed this un-named stretch of sand as their own. The few other hardy visitors here were something like trespassers to them.

Kathy leaned into her husband and spoke just loudly enough to be heard over the waves. "Thanks for suggesting we go out to dinner."

"I thought the kids would like it," George said wearily, "and I don't want to go— I mean, I'm having such a good time that it seems a shame to go home. Just yet." He didn't sound the least bit sincere.

They stopped and looked out over the chop-py, whitecapped swells beyond the surf, still holding hands.

"You feel it, too, don't you?" Kathy said.

"Yes," George told her. There was no point in hiding it any longer. "It's not as bad as it was . . . back there. But something's wrong."

"Will it get better?"

"Kathy, I don't know. I just don't know."

"What if it doesn't?"

"Don't ask me that. Please. I just . . . don't . . . know."

They watched the powerful, endless motion

of the waves for a few moments more, and then without another word they turned and headed back up the beach toward their afternoon encampment. The children had nearly finished the packing, but they hadn't decided on a dinner location.

"McDonald's!"

"Jack-a-Box!"

"Burger King! *Burger King!*"

The children were full but no less active when they pulled into their driveway at the La Jolla condominium. George grimaced at the sour taste of fast food, but that was what the children had wanted. And it was cheap.

He had been thinking about employment during their drive home. Now, with the sun fully set and the last light of day draining from the sky, he put it from his mind. He'd worry about it tomorrow. There was always tomorrow for worrying.

Greg and Matt jumped out of the car at the same time and chased each other around the yard. Amy wanted to help Mommy unload, so Kathy gave her a small, difficult-to-break water jug and sent her inside. She and George filled their arms with the remains of the beach picnic and followed her in.

As George struggled to put the key in the door, Greg yelped from the front yard and ran headlong into his father. Towels and suntan lotion went flying. The keys came within an inch of being lost forever in the ivy beside the porch.

"Okay, troops, that's *it!*" George said sharply.

The boys knew that tone of voice. They stopped the game. Fast.

"I want you to wipe your feet out here, on the doormat. Then you will walk inside—quietly—and head straight upstairs to the bathroom to wash off the rest of the sand. And no horseplay. Clear?"

"Clear," Greg said. Matt just nodded.

George finally unlocked the door and pushed inside. He watched with baleful eye while the boys trooped quietly up the stairs, and halfway up the flight, as if on some private signal, they broke into a run, shrieking, "Me first! Me first!"

Kathy simply looked at George and shrugged. He grinned back and shook his head.

Amy put her water jug on the counter and followed the boys upstairs, and Kathy slipped by George as he juggled with his load of blankets and beer cans and dumped the picnic fixings on the kitchen counter.

Something odd caught her attention.

She turned to see George standing in the hallway, staring intently at nothing in particular. "What is it, babe?" she asked.

"Something smells strange," he said. He sniffed the air like a quizzical dog and moved through the archway into the living room. "I think it's coming from in here."

Kathy followed him in, switching on the lights near the door as she entered. It was almost too dark to see.

He was right. There was some hint of a smell. Thin but penetrating, and sickly sweet.

George reached the center of the room and turned to say something, but as he opened his mouth to speak the stench closed around him like a fist.

It didn't drift in, or rise up from the floor. It was simply, devastatingly, *there*, in one massive blow.

Kathy put her hand over her mouth and retched. George stopped breathing and looked around wildly, searching for some clue to the source of the smell.

Never mind, he told himself. His chest began to ache as he staggered to a window and struggled to open it. Fresh air, he thought, that's what we need.

The open window made it only a little better. He gulped at the brackish air beyond the screen and said, "Kathy, I'll open the patio doors. You get some incense."

He turned to move to the patio—and stopped. Stopped. Frozen. He looked down at his legs in disbelief and tried to move.

Nothing. No response. He was suddenly, inexplicably paralyzed, rooted to the spot.

"George!"

He looked up and saw Kathy standing just inside the door. One arm was raised to chest height, the other was held at an unnatural angle at her side.

"I can't even lift my arms!" Her voice was very soft, almost awed, and for some reason that was far more frightening than a shout.

George's mind was racing. He had to keep her quiet, until this—this whatever-it-was—passed. "Try to relax," he said, forcing his voice to remain steady. "I'm sure—"

The light blinked out. It wasn't like a short or the sudden vacancy of a larger power failure. All light—even the last traces of sunset and the illumination of the full moon—simply disappeared.

"George!" There was the cutting edge of real panic in her voice now. George called her name, ordered her to keep quiet, and heard the same frightened sound in his own voice.

His legs were still frozen to the carpet, but at least his arms were free. George twisted on his immobile torso and groped in the blackness for the end table near the window. There was a small lamp on it, a lamp with a switch of its own.

"It's okay, Kath. Just a few seconds more. I've got a light here, right here on the table. Just take it easy. . . ."

He was beginning to babble, but he couldn't help it. His fingers found the tabletop, then the lamp cord, then, finally, clumsily, they fell on the ridged cylinder of the lamp switch.

"Look! Kathy! Look!" he shouted at her as he twisted the post, and light exploded at his side.

Something was still very strange. He could see Kathy across the room, frozen in her unnatural posture. He even caught a glimpse of the kitchen beyond the high archway. But the scene was flat and bleak, almost completely colorless, as if he were watching an old black-and-white film on a dirty screen.

Kathy looked relieved despite her paralysis. "Thank God," she said. "Thank God."

Then the light began to dim.

George looked back at the lamp, at the bulb itself, and it seemed as if it were growing smaller as he watched. The picture shrank and dimmed, and finally in the space of three labored heartbeats, the darkness closed around them again.

He could hear Kathy crying softly on the far side of the room.

"George. Oh, George, there's something in here with us. I can feel it, I can *feel* it!"

"Don't worry, Kathy. I'm coming. Please don't cry."

She sobbed and said, "Please, George, switch the lights on again. Please..."

George tried to force his legs to move, but absolutely nothing happened. They seemed to belong to someone else, to some other body completely apart from his own.

Then, quite suddenly, Kathy stopped crying. His head jerked up and he cocked an ear toward her. He thought he heard a small, secret exhalation.

"Kathy?"

"Oh, thank you, George. Thank you."

"What is it? What is it?"

"Just your hand on my shoulder is enough. I'll be all right now."

"My... hand?"

He had to move. He knew that now; as completely and irrevocably as he'd ever known anything. He had to move.

George used his awareness like a physical thing, like a bludgeon or a probe. He forced it down his arms, along his chest, past his stomach and thighs and legs.

"Take it easy, Kathy. It'll all be over in a minute."

"I'm sorry I was so hysterical, George, but I felt so alone. I know it sounds crazy, but even feeling your hand on my shoulder makes it better. Just keep it there. I'll be okay."

He visualized his leg... his calf... his ankle...

His foot. He would move it. He would take one step, one single step at a time. He had to reach Kathy; he had to.

George felt his hands clench into fists. His head throbbed, worse than ever, and the stench rose up again to close around his throat. Heartbeat. Thunder. Aching jaw. And . . . the foot moved. He took a step. It happened suddenly, so swiftly, he was surprised that it happened at all.

That simple movement shattered the spell. Light gushed back into the room; the smell disappeared; the light beside him flared into life. He grinned and exhaled, his legs moving forward almost on their own accord, as he turned and looked directly at his wife for the first time in what felt like years.

Kathy was far across the room, her right hand clutched at her left shoulder. She looked puzzled, confused . . . and then, suddenly, absolutely horrified.

Her eyes lifted and she stared at George as if he were a demon himself. He was across the room—yards away—and George could see a single, horrible question in her eyes.

If he had been across the room, *what had touched her on the shoulder?*

She made a sound like a frightened animal. "Oh. Oh, George . . ." She sobbed and started to crumple, and he rushed to her side. He caught her before she fell.

Kathy began to scream, and George buried her face in his chest. She clutched at him and he murmured to her, held her closely, tried to say something that would bring her back to him.

"It's over, Kathy. We're okay. Everything's all right, everything's fine."

Suddenly she stiffened, straightening up with a taut snap like a wire drawn tight.

"My God! The children!"

"What?"

"The children!"

She broke away and ran up the stairs, George only half a step behind her. They raced down the hall toward the boys' bedroom and stopped short at the closed door.

"No!" said a young, frightened voice inside. "No!"

George threw open the door, expecting the worst, and found his three stepchildren sitting on the floor, playing Monopoly.

Greg was teasing his sister. He kept trying to steal her token, the little silver terrier, and she was slapping at his hand and saying, "No! No!" He had mistaken her exasperation for fear.

The children looked up at George and Kathy with wide eyes. Greg, the oldest, seemed to understand the expressions on their faces better than his brother and sister.

"What is it, Daddy? Are you all right?"

George swallowed. "I'm fine," he said, feeling a little sick. "Everything all right up here?"

Now Greg smiled lightly. "Sure! I'm winning!"

His brother and sister moaned and they all went back to their game. George turned slowly and looked at his trembling wife. He wondered whether she was shivering with fear or relief.

George had a headache. That almost went without saying these days. He always had a headache, always the same monotonous, piercing *thump* that went from one side of his head to the other and back again.

He put down the draft of the letter he had been trying to write for over an hour and forced himself to stand. What was the point of writing another note to the San Diego Traffic Controller's Office? They'd canceled all his appointments already, and they hadn't even answered his first two letters. He wasn't going to get the job. Not now, not ever.

He held his head in his hands and wandered into the kitchen, following some vague impulse for aspirin. They had never helped before, but maybe now . . .

He arrived just in time to see Kathy shriek at Greg and Matt as she shoved them out into the backyard.

"Get out!" she shouted. "Just get the hell out and play!"

He was dumbfounded. He simply stared at his wife, and after a moment the tension seemed to drain out of her. She collapsed into one of the kitchen chairs so quickly that George thought she probably would have gone straight to the floor if it hadn't already been under her.

"Oh, George," she said, pushing a handful of uncombed hair away from her face, "I think I'm falling apart."

George sat next to his wife and looked at her closely for the first time in days. Things had been very tense at the house since their last trip to the beach almost two weeks ago. They had been avoiding each other, avoiding conversations just as they had at Amityville.

Kathy looked beaten and weary. Her eyes

were dark and sunken. She had lost weight. Her hair hung in limp wings that obscured half her face, and there was a rash from tension and heat marring one side of her neck.

"What's the matter, babe?"

"I don't know. The kids are driving me crazy—I mean *literally* crazy. I guess they're just being normal children, but I swear, if they give me any more trouble today, I'm going to hit them, whether I want to or not. And you know how I feel about hitting the kids, for any reason."

George's headache thundered, worse than before. He didn't want to deal with this. Not when he felt so awful. "Tell me about it," he said, trying to force the pain away and failing.

She rubbed her forehead with one unwashed hand. "It's Amy, mostly."

"Amy?" He'd thought it would be the boys. His stepdaughter was usually the well-behaved one.

"She argues with everything I say. And she's been bugging me about all her toys that we left back in—back in New York. I keep telling her we can't afford new ones, but she keeps asking 'Why, why, why?'" She mimicked her little girl's voice viciously.

George knew he should let the whole thing slide. Kathy was tired, and Amy was taking advantage of that. In a day or two it would all pass, but— Damn it, the pain in his head was making it hard to think. He didn't need a five-year-old girl making it even harder.

He got up and said, "I'll talk to her."

Kathy tried to stop him. "Oh, George, never mind. She's just—"

"I said I'll talk to her! Now!" He stalked into the hall and bellowed up the stairs.

"*Amy!*"

She didn't answer quickly enough for his liking. George leaned on the handrail as if that would help him control the pain in his head and shouted at her again.

"*Amy!*"

Her voice was very small and timid from the upstairs bedroom.

"Yes, Daddy?"

"Get down here! Right now!"

She came as quickly as she could, but she stopped when she saw her father standing at the bottom of the stairs, swaying against the handrail and glaring at her.

"What, Daddy?"

"Come...down...here," he said between clenched teeth. He pointed to a spot right in front of him.

She approached carefully, one step at a time. Her eyes never left his face.

When she was standing only a foot from him, George began to speak—very quietly, very dangerously. "Now, what's this I hear? Are you giving your mother a hard time about toys?"

Amy didn't want to say anything. She looked away and stuck out her lower lip.

George took her roughly by the arm. "Amy, talk to me."

"I just...I don't have any toys, Daddy. All my favorites got left." She pulled away from him very gently, careful not to make him any angrier than he already was.

"We all had to leave things behind, Amy. Didn't we?"

"Yes."

"You don't hear any of us complaining, do

you?" She didn't answer right away. George bent over until his face was only inches from her. "*Do* you?"

She shrugged. "No, but—"

"No 'buts,' young lady. If I hear about this again, you're in trouble. Big trouble. Is that clear?"

Amy started to whine. "But, Daddy—"

He shook her with both hands, unaware of how roughly he was holding her. "*Is that clear?*"

"Yes! Yes! Let me go!"

She pulled away from her father and ran up the stairs sobbing. Her skin was flushed bright red and her tiny hands trembled as she groped for a handhold.

The anger suddenly drained out of him in one devastating rush. All that was left was the thumping pain in his head, and a new guilt and despair.

"Amy?" he said softly. "Amy!" He started to call to her, but the words caught in his throat.

A milky white shadow, as insubstantial as mist, was oozing out of the little girl's body. It rose and coagulated above her head as he watched.

"Amy!"

Kathy was behind him. She saw the milky white thing, too, and the moment she called her daughter's name, the specter clapped out of existence, as if suddenly blocked from view.

Amy didn't seem to hear them. She simply slipped into her own bedroom without a backward glance.

George stood at the foot of the stairs and gazed at the blank wall. He had tried to ignore the fact for weeks. He had hidden from it, and reasoned it away, and made excuses for as long as he could. But there were no excuses left; there were no places left to hide.

They hadn't escaped the power from Amityville. They had only run from it.

And they hadn't run far enough.

# 18

"We have to move, you know. Find a new place."

Kathy smiled faintly and looked out over the ocean. "I know," she said.

"It won't be easy. It means a new school for the kids, and another two weeks of packing and cleaning."

"Don't worry, George. We have to do it, so we'll do it. That's that."

The Lutzes were spending the afternoon at Mount Soledad Park, a flat, grassy area on top of Soledad Mountain near San Diego. To one side was the coastline, clearly visible all the way from Mission Bay to the Scripps Institute of Oceanography and even farther north. A quick turn showed the rest of the spectacular view: all of San Diego was spread out before them.

George had discovered the park late one afternoon while returning from yet another unsuccessful job interview in La Jolla. It had somehow lifted his spirits, buoyed him up, and the next day he had packed up the entire family and shown it to them.

Kathy stood at the edge of the cliff that bounded one edge of the park and looked out over the Pacific. If I raise my hand, she thought, I can point to Antarctica. It was one long, straight southeasterly line across the ocean, past Mission Bay and on for thousands and thousands of miles. She imagined how the water would turn icy and blue as steel; how it would grow thick with the cold, then solid and slick. How snow would cover it, deeper and deeper, and how finally, suddenly, there it would be, invisible and powerful and no less real for its invisibility: the South Pole.

She turned away from the water and looked at George. He was standing only a few feet away from her, and beyond him, stretched out in a building-block puzzle of rooftops and greenery, the entire San Diego basin lay in silent repose. It was a clear, almost luminous day, and far behind him, nearly swallowed by the haze, Kathy could see a ragged finger of stone that was Mexico.

Another country. Another world. Would that be far enough away? she wondered. Would they be safe even if they went there?

She turned again and looked at the fifteen-foot sculpture behind them. It was a white concrete cross—the Mount Soledad Easter Cross—and somehow, standing in its shadow gave Kathy a peace and tranquility she had longed for many times. There was no plaque or sign at the foot of the cross—she didn't even know who had placed it there, or why—but if she could have put a sign of her own at its base, it would have contained a single word; one she had heard many times; one that felt solid and mysterious on her tongue; one she had come to understand only very recently: sanctuary.

There was a thin, distant roar to her right and she looked up to see the tiny silhouette of an airliner weaving through the wispy clouds over Mission Bay. As she watched, it dipped its wing to the sea and soared southward. Part of Kathy wished she were on the plane, that she and George and the children could climb aboard and fly away and never stop flying. And another part of her never wanted to leave the warm embrace of the cross that towered over her head.

George touched her on the arm, and a pleasant chill ran through her. "Beautiful, isn't it?" he said.

She nodded and watched the plane's silhouette until it disappeared into the ceramic blue sky.

"I talked to Bud in New York this morning," he said. "He told me that the escrow is about to clear, so I'll have to go back to New York and sign all the necessary papers. And that writer thinks he's got some sort of deal worked out, too."

Kathy thought briefly of the complications involved in selling the house and their belongings; of the convoluted trade-offs and negotiations that had begun with their halting, incomplete tape recordings. They didn't seem terribly important at the moment.

"I'd feel better if you and the kids stayed in a motel for the week or two that I'll be gone," George said. "What do you think about that?"

Kathy smiled. "I'd like that, George. I can't face that house anymore—especially without you."

George put an arm around her waist, and they walked along the cliff's edge, farther from the children. "Babe, I know we haven't talked much about what's been happening. There doesn't seem to be much point. But we have to hang in together, that's the important thing. If we just hang on, we're going to get through this mess."

Sometimes Kathy doubted that. Sometimes, late at night, after the dreams and the awful smells and the darkness, nothing seemed to make sense. But here, now, in the sunlight and the open air, she believed in George and what he said. "You're right, babe. And don't worry about us, we'll be fine. I bet I even find a new place while you're back in New York."

George grinned. "I just bet you do." He spun her gently to face him and kissed her quickly but with an immense, gentle strength. "So what do you say? Let's go pack our bags."

She nodded and smiled, and they walked slowly down the brick stairs toward the children and the car. Behind them, the huge white cross muttered in the wind, its vast and powerful arms stretching to the sky.

George was sitting in the living room looking over the deed to the Amityville property when Kathy came tiptoeing down the stairs.

"Are they all asleep?" he asked.

"Finally," she said. "I don't think they've ever been this excited about moving, but don't ask me why."

He grinned and finished the last of his tea. "You can't beat those kids down, you know that? They're stronger than both of us put together."

She collapsed into a chair, filled with a pleasant and well-deserved weariness. "You can say that again," she said and poured a cup of tea for herself.

George started to put the documents back in their imitation leather pouch, and a brightly colored slip of paper fell into his lap. He picked it up and scanned it, and a scowl passed briefly over his face.

"What is it?"

"Nothing new," he said, passing it to her.

It was a poorly photocopied half-sheet, decorated with triangles topped by human eyes and signs of the zodiac. The typewritten words in the center were faded and irregular, as if made on an aging manual machine by a typist working very, very slowly. Kathy read only the first few lines:

And SATAN hath the pow'r to take on a PLEASING SHAPE and !!GOD!! need NOT such trickery. Truly, truly I say unto YOU, the POW'R OF !CHRIST!! shall OVERCOME your dark infirmities!!

Kathy's expression echoed George's own displeasure. "Where did this come from?"

"Who knows? It must have gotten put in with these papers by accident." He ripped the half-sheet into four equal parts, then ripped each part into four more parts. "I don't know what all these crazies think we're about, but I tell you, I'm getting mighty tired of them."

Kathy nodded. "I thought when we moved to California, they'd lose track of us, but—"

She stopped and cocked an ear. George looked at her quizzically, recognizing the expression. Her maternal radar had cut in. She was listening to a sound from upstairs that only a mother could hear.

She stood up and walked silently to the foot of the stairs, where she listened a moment longer. Then she called softly, "Amy? Are you awake, honey?"

There was no answer. George joined her at the staircase, and they climbed to the second floor together.

The door to Amy's room was closed, but a bright thread of light shone through the gap at its base. They crept down the thick carpet very quietly. There was the sound of a voice from beyond the door.

Kathy put her mouth to George's ear. "The light was off when I checked on her an hour ago," she whispered.

George nodded and reached for the doorknob. He stopped before he opened the door.

Amy said, "You're such a silly! Why would I do *that*?"

George threw open the door and squinted at the unexpected light. Amy was sitting up in bed, the covers tangled around her waist. She looked up at them, startled, and there was a strange, disquieting movement at the foot of her bed.

It took a moment for George to realize what he saw. There was an indentation in the mattress

—a cavity in the bedclothes, as if something man-sized and very heavy were sitting on the bed. The instant he recognized what he saw, the indentation flexed and disappeared, as if the man-sized thing had decided to stand up.

George stared at his daughter, stunned. "Amy," he said, startled at the harshness of his own voice. "Amy, was that Jodie?"

Amy sat frozen in bed. George saw terror and confession in her eyes. He rushed forward and seized her by the shoulders.

"Tell me, Amy! Tell me! Was that Jodie?"

The little girl tried to pull away. "Daddy, you're hurting me!"

George forced himself to loosen his grip. He wasn't going to have another episode like the one from the week before. He was going to keep control. He had to.

Kathy was at his shoulder. "Amy," she said, trying to sound reasonable and succeeding only in sounding absolutely terrified, "you said that you sent Jodie away."

Amy looked at the bedclothes and thrust out her lower lip.

"Did he leave, Amy? Or is he still here? Were you talking to him?" George slapped the bedclothes with an open hand, and the noise made Amy jump. *"Tell me!"*

"Yes!" she blurted, frightened by her father's anger. "Yes, I was talking to him." She squirmed under the intensity of George's stare. "Jodie's my *friend*, Daddy. We play together."

"When did he get here?" Kathy asked. Her voice was trembling.

"He came with us," Amy said, sounding very reasonable and a little proud. "He sat on the wing of the plane when we flew to California. It was a secret, though. He told me not to tell anyone."

George yanked the sheets off his daughter in one quick, vicious swipe. Amy screamed when he seized her under the arms and swung her in the air, but the screaming stopped when he plopped her down on the edge of the bed.

He pointed one shaking finger at the little girl's innocent face. "You listen to me, young lady, and you listen good. The next time you see Jodie, you tell him to leave here and *never come back*. Do you understand?"

"But Jodie's my—"

"Do you understand me, Amy?"

"Yes, Daddy," she said, pouting.

"And if he ever, ever comes back after that, you are to come and tell your mommy and me right away. Right away, Amy! All right?"

Her lower lip came out farther than ever, but she nodded in agreement.

"Answer me!"

"Yes, Daddy! *Yes*, Daddy!"

George straightened up. His guts felt like a spring, tightly wound, about to explode. He knew that one more provocation, no matter how minor, would send him flying in all directions.

He couldn't let that happen. He turned on his heel and left the little girl's bedroom without another word, and Amy turned to her mother.

"Mommy, it's not fair!" she said. Her eyes were brimming with angry, frustrated tears. "Jodie didn't do anything wrong. He's my friend."

Kathy wasn't angry at her daughter. She was simply, totally, terrified.

"You lied to us, Amy," she said, trying to keep

246

her voice steady. "You don't realize how important that is, but you must never lie to us about Jodie. He could be doing very bad things."

Amy crossed her chubby arms and looked very stubborn. "He wouldn't do anything bad," she insisted.

Kathy sighed and cupped her daughter's small chin in one hand. "There's just no way I can make you understand, honey. I'm sorry, but Jodie has to leave for good. It's really, really important."

Amy started to cry, and Kathy held her gently for a moment. "Come on," she said gently. "Come on now, back into bed."

Amy sniffed and wiped her nose with her forearm. Then she crawled between the covers. Kathy pulled the blankets to her chin and kissed her warmly on the forehead.

"Good night, princess. When you get just a little older, I promise I'll try to explain it."

Kathy walked to the door and switched off the light, but she left the door open a crack behind her.

She could hear Amy crying softly as she walked down the hall.

Exactly one week later Kathy found herself staring into the small, streaked mirror of a Holiday Inn bathroom, crying herself.

George was gone—back in New York, talking with accountants and lawyers and the author. The children were asleep in the other room, tucked into makeshift beds made from comforters and pillows, like the beds they had slept in those first nights away from Amityville.

And Kathy was crying. *I was doing so well,*

too, she thought, scraping at her cheeks and trying to make herself stop. Things had been going so smoothly. All she had done was come into the bathroom to get ready for bed, and when she'd looked in the mirror everything had suddenly jumbled together and fallen in—the trip to California, the horrors at the La Jolla condominium, the troubles with the children and her own fear.

She was glad the children were asleep. She was even glad, in a strange sort of way, that George wasn't around to see this. Leave it to me, she thought bitterly. I do great while things are falling apart, and when they settle down, *I* fall apart.

She grabbed a towel and buried her face in it, weeping like a teenager who had lost a first love. She couldn't stop.

There was a touch of a small hand at her wrist, and she turned suddenly to see her daughter at her side, looking up at her with huge, solemn eyes.

"It's okay, Mommy," Amy said very seriously. Kathy saw a very grown-up concern and understanding in her little girl.

She knelt by Amy's side and wrapped her daughter in her arms. She cried and cried, and Amy stroked her hair and said, "It's okay, Mommy. It's okay," and Kathy realized that it *was* okay. It was perfectly okay to let it go, to free herself of the pent-up tensions and fears she had been storing for weeks.

It felt good. It felt very good.

George yawned and looked at his watch. It was late afternoon, but it felt like early morning to him. He pressed the accelerator of the 1973 maroon T-Bird a little harder, and passed a sign that read SAN DIEGO 60 MILES.

He had mixed feelings about driving the T-Bird from New York to California, but now that the trip was almost over, he decided that it had been worth the effort. It had given him time to think; time to sort out all that had happened.

He glanced nervously at the San Onofre Nuclear Power Plant as it loomed up, blind and rather threatening, on his right. He didn't like that place. Never had.

The escrow on the house had finally closed. Signing the papers, in fact, had been the least of his problems. He'd spent most of his time meeting with Jay Anson, the writer who was working on the story of Amityville now. He'd worked out a deal with a publisher, Anson told him. They were all very excited about the project.

But in all those meetings, in all that talk, the writer had asked him very few questions about their actual experiences in the house. Most of the time, the conversation centered around money, and subsidiary rights, and movie deals. For some reason, that bothered him.

He passed a billboard advertising a San Diego housing development, and thought of the telephone conversation he'd had with Kathy just a few hours earlier. She had located a good prospect for them—a house in the relatively new development called Tierrasanta.

The name, George knew, translated to mean something like "sacred ground." That sounded like a good omen—and they could use a good omen for a change.

He smiled and relaxed a bit as the first brown

smudge of San Diego smog appeared on the horizon. The house is finally gone, he thought. All the ties with New York and the power that lives there are severed. We have a new place to live, a new life to build.

Maybe—just maybe—we can live in peace.

# 19

In the many months that followed, the Lutzes found a peace and normalcy they had almost forgotten existed. There were no apparitions, no hideous smells, no nightmares beyond those that adults are always prone to, and no eerie visitations by things or feelings from somewhere else.

George finally found work—not in his field, but work nonetheless. He and Kathy took the children for sailing trips on Mission Bay, and on camping expeditions into the mountains, and finally, gradually, they made friends and acquaintances—most notably Terri Sullivan, a bright and attractive young woman Kathy met in a continuing education class. Terri often stayed with the children when Kathy and George needed an evening, or even a weekend, to themselves.

The boys seemed taller and more independent every day, and Amy grew into a beautiful, vibrant child, surprising no one by doing so. For a long, healing, joyful time, it looked as if the Lutzes had finally left the world of the supernatural behind.

But during this time, they were slowly, inexorably entering another, newer, no less bizarre world. They were becoming celebrities.

Dear Mr. or Ms. Lutz,
Last week when I saw you on SPEAK OUT on Channel 13, I thought that Mr. Jones was actually hard on you. Personally, I have experienced such a thing just like you yourself, and I am told by many that spiritual training I have had has helped others in positions like ours. Please send me fifty (50) dollars and your address so I can be sure of helping you and yours. . . .

George tossed that one in the trash, along with the others. You'd think I'd be used to it after a while, he grumbled. Here it is almost two years and we're still getting this junk.

Crazy people. Crazy. If he could afford it, he would refuse all the talk shows and radio interviews and the rest, but they needed the money badly. Besides, it might help sell some copies of the book, if the damn thing ever came out.

George sighed and cleared the desk in the Tierrasanta home, preparing himself for a long night. Just as he finished, Kathy came in from the kitchen with two cups of coffee.

"Kids asleep?" he said.

"Like a field full of stones. What are you up to?"

He sighed again. "Now that it's quiet, I thought I'd read this." He pulled a large stack of oversized pages from the manila envelope that had been delivered a few hours earlier. The front page carried the title:

### THE AMITYVILLE HORROR
A True Story

By Jay Anson

---

FIRST GALLEY PROOF

---

"Looks like a couple of hours reading," Kathy said.

"At least." He settled into his chair and flicked it open to the first page.

"In that case," Kathy said, leaving her coffee untouched on the desk, "I'm going to bed." She gave him a peck on the cheek and went upstairs.


Sometime after three o'clock that morning, George woke his wife from a sound sleep. It was the first time in months that she had been awakened at that hour, and when she felt his hand on her shoulder, shaking and shaking, a deep and sinister chill went through her.

She awoke with cruel suddenness. "What is it? What's the matter?"

George looked very serious. "Kathy, I want you to read this." He was carrying the galley proof of the book.

"Now?"

"Now."

"Why on earth—?"

"It's about Father Mancusso." He helped her sit up and switched on the reading lamp by the bed. "I think you should read it."

Until the moment that George and Kathy read Anson's version of the horrors at Amityville, neither of them had guessed the enormity of Father Mancusso's involvement or the depth of his courage. In the weeks that followed, they reestablished close contact with their friend the priest.

Mancusso had long since left New York himself and moved to Portland, Oregon. His parish there was smaller and a good deal less challenging, but as the priest told them in a moment of unusual candor, "I think I've had enough excitement for one life. Frankly, I'm looking forward to growing old and fat and rather dull."

It was a brash, squalling day in San Diego when the book—or, as George and Kathy had come to refer to it, The Book—arrived in the mail. It was an advance copy, without cover design or dust jacket, but it was carefully typeset and corrected. George tore open the padded envelope and started intently to read the advance copy.

"George, did you see this?" Kathy had been sorting through the rest of the mail while he had been reading. A letter from the publisher had arrived with the advance copy.

"What?"

"The publicists in New York think you should go on tour," she said.

"Tour?"

"To promote the book. You know, talk shows, autograph parties, local newspaper interviews . . ."

"More? I thought I was finished with that."

She gave him a world-weary smile. "It looks like it's only the beginning."

The interviewer had a deep tan, a small nose, and too many teeth. George had seen a hundred others like him on the tour—all sleek and experienced, cool, egotistical, and virtually interchangeable.

He was fingering a shiny, obviously unread copy of *The Amityville Horror*. "I understand you have children?" the interviewer said.

"Yes, three," George answered—which you'd bloody well know if you'd read the book, he added silently.

"Do they come with you to these shows?" The interviewer squinted and scanned beyond the camera, as if he could spot them in the crowd.

"No. My wife and I believed they should have as normal a childhood as possible, and we've gone to great lengths to keep them out of and away from publicity or interviews of any kind."

"Ah-hah. Well, you must enjoy the travel yourself, since you obviously don't need the money."

"I don't?"

"I understand the book is selling quite well. And what with the paperback edition coming out soon . . ."

George smiled and tried not to look too condescending. Why did everyone assume they were rich from all this? "We actually don't make much from the book, Frank," he said. That *was* his name, wasn't it? Frank? All these interviewers began to look alike after a while. All the names started to sound the same. "There are publishers to consider, and an author, and a whole series of agents—"

"Of course. And I'll bet there's a sequel in the typewriter right now, isn't there?" The interviewer gave him a broad wink, and there was laughter from the audience. George started to say something, but the four-piece band broke into "That Old Black Magic," and the interviewer turned away.

"We'll be back to talk with George Lutz *and* a special guest, right after this message."

The music swelled and the metallic voice of the director buzzed from the booth at the back of the room: "Sixty seconds!"

A technician lurched onto the dais and tried to attack George with a powder puff. The interviewer stood up and turned his back, and the young wild-eyed woman who had introduced herself to George as the producer brought a trimly dressed, middle-aged man with stark white hair into the light. He blinked at the brightness and shielded his eyes from the glare.

"Frank—"

Thank God, George thought. I had the right name.

"Frank, this is Olson Player, the well-known and respected psychic. He's been on the show before."

Frank seized the man's hand. "You've been on the show before, haven't you?" he said. "Great to see you." He laughed good-naturedly at the man's bewildered expression. "Lights take a little getting used to, don't they?"

"Ten seconds!" the director's voice buzzed.

There was a scramble of technicians and copy people. The music blared from speakers to their right; Frank motioned Olson to the seat closest to him and straightened his tie; large white cards with five-inch block printing on them came up under the camera just as the red light blinked on.

"Welcome back. We've been talking with George Lutz about the strange things that happened to him and his family, as told in *The Amityville Horror,* and in this segment we'd like to continue the discussion by bringing in an expert on the occult—our old friend Olson Player, the well-known and respected psychic."

Scattered applause came from the pit beyond the cameras.

"Olson, the last time you were on the show you made some *remarkably accurate* assessments of the *character* and *life-styles* of some randomly chosen members of our studio audience, simply by *holding* an *object* of *theirs* in your *hand.* Now, you talked about an aura that time. What, exactly *is* an *aura?*"

Olson Player smiled tightly, and George had the distinct impression that his last appearance on this program had been something less than pleasant. "Well, Frank, the aura is an energy field that surrounds every human being. Or, I should say *each* human being. We each have our own aura, as unique and identifiable as a fingerprint."

"Is that so?"

"Ah, yes. Its changing colors or shapes can reflect the changes in physical and mental states of the mind, the body, and the consciousness."

"Well, tell me, Olson, how come we *all* don't see *auras?*"

Olson shrugged easily. "Maybe we all did at some time in the past. Even now, the number of people who see them in one form or another is surprisingly large. And some recent tests show that many, many children can see them at early ages, but for reasons we don't yet understand, they lose the ability as they grow older."

"That's very interesting," the interviewer said, sounding totally uninterested. He leaned forward and plucked the hardcover edition of The Book from his imitation walnut coffee table.

"Now, this here, Olson, is *The Amityville Horror.* You've heard of it."

Player looked wary. "Yes, I've heard of it, but—"

"Have you read it?"

"No, I haven't. I've read some of the accounts in the newspapers, of course, but—"

"Well, tell me, Olson, what do you think of this story about—well, I guess you'd call it a haunted house, wouldn't you? For lack of a better name?"

Olson Player took his time to answer, and George Lutz found himself liking the man in spite of it all. There was a sense of care and integrity about him that was all too rare on the talk show circuit.

"Well, from what I know—which isn't much, mind you—it sounds as if it's well within the bounds of possibility. Things like this have happened to many other people, including psychic investigators I know and respect."

The interviewer let his mouth drop open in a

feigned, comical look of fear. "You mean this sort of thing happens *all* the *time?*"

"Not all the time, Frank," Olson said, matching sarcasm with sarcasm. "But you couldn't call this an isolated case by any means. There are plenty of documented incidents very similar and just as strange as this one. I've had some things like it happen to me, more than a few times."

The interviewer got a look of wide-open cunning. "You know, I'd like to try a little experiment here, if it's all right with everyone," he said, and continued without waiting for permission. "I'd like to know what kind of feelings you, as a psychic, get from this book—or from Mr. Lutz here."

Oh no, George thought. Not this again.

Olson Player looked uncomfortable. "Well, I don't know. . . ."

"What do you say, studio audience? Shall we give it a try?"

The applause and whistles put Player in an awkward position. Finally he nodded and picked up the book with an expression that bordered on dread.

The band played the theme from "The Twilight Zone," and Olson sat very still, holding the book in his hands for a full twenty seconds. He stared at it . . . and then at George.

Finally he put the book back on the coffee table. "These people have been through hell," he said solemnly. "The kind of hell that very few of us, thank God, will ever have to face."

He looked at George very intently. "I'm sorry for that, Mr. Lutz. And I'm sorry that it isn't over yet."

The interviewer's eyebrows went up, and he looked serious for the first time. After all, this wasn't part of the normal scenario. Maybe something important was about to break here. It didn't matter a bit if he believed the story or not; the book was selling in the millions, people were talking about it, buying it—he might have an exclusive.

George was stunned. He had had psychics, real and otherwise, sprung on him from every quarter during this tour, and the one before it. But this was the first time any of them had talked about the recent past—about the problems they'd had since leaving Amityville. What the devil was he supposed to say? After all, he and Kathy had been very closed-mouthed about the problems they'd had, and now . . .

"Well, Mr. Lutz, have you been seeing other things out there in California?"

George swallowed and took it very slowly. "We . . . appreciate Mr. Player's confirmation of our story. What he says—about *that*—is true. We did go through a very private sort of hell. But as for—we would prefer not to talk about anything that may or may not have happened since we left the house."

The band began a quiet vamp into "Bewitched, Bothered, and Bewildered," and a man standing to the left of the camera began making frantic spinning motions.

"Well! We'll pursue this fascinating story of ghosts and haunted houses . . . right after this."

The moment the red light on the camera blinked off, George stood up and put his hand out to Frank the Interviewer. "Thanks for having me," he said quickly, "but I'm afraid I've got a plane to catch."

The interviewer goggled and looked at his producer. "I thought—that is, I—"

"I'd really *love* to stay, really I would," George said. "But you know how these darn promotional tours work!"

He put his hand out to Olson Player. The psychic hesitated a moment, then took it carefully, as if he wasn't quite sure what to expect.

A small charge of energy—something more fundamental than electrical— ran up George's arm as their hands met.

Olson Player smiled a small, secret smile and nodded. "Good luck, Mr. Lutz. The very best of luck."

George left the studio as quickly as he could. Then he went back to his motel and slept for eighteen hours.

George stood awkwardly in the middle of the radio station's reception room and tried to carry on a private conversation with one of the publicists in New York.

"Okay, okay, Maury, I see the problem. So after I finish up here, I'll go off to the TV station, and then have a late dinner with this— what is it, some sort of columnist?" He waited for the answer, looking uncomfortably at the slim receptionist behind the desk. "Okay, Maury. Got it. Give me the address of the TV station."

The receptionist was watching him. He cradled the phone between his shoulder and his ear and made little scribbling motions with one hand on the palm of the other. She gave him a pen and a pad of paper, and he smiled his thanks. Then he wrote down a name and address.

"Great, Maury. Sure, you owe me one. I'll talk to you on . . . What is this, Wednesday already? Great. I'll talk to you on Friday."

He hung up and had a nearly uncontrollable impulse to fall right on the receptionist's desk for a quick nap. He was glad that Kathy and the kids weren't being subjected to this tour. There had been more talking and less sleep than he thought possible in the last week and a half.

"Long day?" the receptionist asked sympathetically.

"Long week," he said. "Long month, long year."

He looked at her dully and tried to clear the fog away. "Say, this may sound really stupid," he said, "but could you tell me what radio station this is?"

She told him the call letters, still smiling.

"Richmond, right?"

She nodded. "In the state of Virginia."

"Thank God." For a moment he hadn't been sure where he was.

There was the squeak of a swinging door behind him, and the receptionist stood up very quickly. George turned and saw a broad-shouldered, barrel-shaped man in a creamy white suit strut into the room.

"Mr. Lutz?" the man said. "I'm Doc Landau. Can I get you a cup of nice, hot coffee?"

George shook his hand and said, "No, thanks." He was already jangling from caffeine and travel.

Doc Landau was an inch shorter and a hundred pounds heavier than George, but the expertly tailored suit made him look as if it were all muscle. His hair was carefully coiffed into a silvery lion's mane that blended smoothly into his beard. The man looks like he has a halo, George thought, and the way he walked, full of the assurance of a small-town celebrity, implied a similar state of mind.

They passed through the swinging glass door and walked down a long hallway decorated with Chamber of Commerce and Merchant Association plaques. George caught glimpses of windowed rooms filled with broadcast equipment, announcers with coffee cups, and stacks of record albums.

"We have a special little room for these interview things," Landau said jovially, and stopped in front of a thick slab of a door with a tiny inset window. "You ready to take me on?"

George smiled uncertainly. "Sure," he said, not sure at all.

Landau ushered him into the strangest broadcast booth George had ever seen—and lately, he had seen plenty. It was thirty-five by twenty feet, with a long, scarred table running down the center and two ten-year-old microphones embedded in opposite ends of it. The walls were padded and stark white, and the room itself, except for two chairs, the two microphones, and a mirrored window along one wall, was completely featureless. Not even a coffee machine, George realized, and there's *always* a coffee machine.

It wasn't a broadcast booth. It was an interrogation room.

Landau gestured to one chair and plopped

himself down in the other. Then he thumbed a button on his microphone and said, "Ready, Charlie?"

A voice buzzed out of a hidden speaker: "Ready, Doc." George looked for the speaker hole, but he couldn't see it anywhere.

"Give me a countdown."

"Three . . . two . . . one. We're rolling."

"Hello, Richmond, Doc Landau here with 'Full Focus,' the program that gets right to the heart of the matter. Today, we're gonna talk a bit about mass marketing and mass hysteria with a man who knows 'em both . . . Mr. George Lutz, author of the allegedly true story of *The Amityville Horror.*"

George jumped. This particular mistake had been passed over too many times before. "I'm not the author," he said quickly. "A man named Jay Anson wrote the book. My family and I are the subjects of his best-seller, and I'm just trying to expand a little on the story, that's all."

Landau waved him away. "Sure, sure. Now, lemme draw the battle lines here for you, Mr. Lutz. I want you to know that I don't believe in UFOs, and I don't believe in ghosts, and the day that some fellah has *real* proof of any of that hooey, I'd like to interview *him*. So I gotta say, I usually don't read books like yours here. It's just not my kind of thing."

George tried to look innocent instead of annoyed. "Then why are you doing this interview?"

"'Cause there are a lotta gullible people out there, Mr. Lutz, who believe in the occult, and I'm just tryin' to keep a few of their hard-earned dollars in their pockets, 'stead of having them go out and buy up the kind of stuff you and your people put out."

Terrific, George thought. A nice, objective interview.

"I figure it's all the same. Your Bermuda Triangle, your Bigfoot, and your haunted house. All the same. It's like the UFO stuff."

UFO stuff? George wondered. *What* UFO stuff?

"So tell me, what do you think of those UFOs?"

Landau stopped talking and looked at George indignantly. He expected an answer. Now.

"Well, ah, I understand that there are plenty of documented sightings, and . . . ah, reliable people who say they've seen . . . things. So I guess I'd say that they may or may not be real. But look, Mr. Landau, what has that got to do with what happened to us? I came here to talk about things in *this* world that we don't understand yet, not about things from *another* world."

"Call me Doc," Landau said by way of explanation. "Everybody does." He reached down into a drawer that George hadn't noticed before and pulled out a dog-eared paperback edition of the book. He opened it to a marked page and began.

"Now, Mr. Lutz, on page fourteen of your work of *fiction*, if you ask me, you say the following. . . ."

He read a long passage and followed it with a question that seemed grossly unimportant to George. But it was only the beginning. The page-by-page interrogation went on for more than three hours, without interruption.

He finally called it to a halt. He was getting

nowhere, saying very little, and feeling like hell. Finally he stood up, said, "That's enough," and walked out of the booth without another word to Doc or his invisible engineer. A moment later he was down the hall, through the reception area, past the desk of the sympathetic secretary, and taking in a huge, grateful breath of night air.

He frowned when the phone back at Tierrasanta had to ring five times. Kathy and he had a specific time for these calls now; usually she answered right away. But the last few calls had been odd, somehow, and now she didn't even seem to be home.

Finally the ringing stopped, but it was a long moment before he heard her voice, distant and weak at the far end of the line.

"Hello?"

"Kathy?"

"George," she said, "is that you?"

"Kathy? Yeah. Of course it's me. I'm in Atlanta, between places. I thought I'd give you a call."

Another long pause. "That's nice," she said faintly. "It's good to hear from you."

George didn't know what to say. She sounded so small and tired. "Hey, you remember that guy in Richmond? Doc Landau? I got a letter from his boss today. Said he got canned for pulling that same stunt once too often. He's been doing it for years now, with—"

"George, come home!"

Just like that. It came over the line strongly, almost brutally, as if Kathy had suddenly shouted a warning.

"What? What did you say, babe?"

"Cancel the rest of the tour. Come home, George. *Please*."

"Is something wrong with the kids?"

"No, no, they're fine. I just..."

George felt a cold wire coiling through his stomach—an old, familiar fear. He tried to ignore it.

"You're not sick, are you, babe?"

"No, I'm not sick. But, George, please, please come home!"

"Why, Kathy?"

It took her a long time to answer, and when she did, it was an answer that George had never wanted to hear.

"It's starting again," she told him. "Just like before."

# 20

Much later, George realized that it had begun earlier than that—weeks earlier—with an incident that had seemed frightening, even appalling, but far from abnormal.

He was home between tours, recuperating from the strenuous schedule and struggling with the tangle of his personal business affairs, and still, there had been public obligations. *The Amityville Horror* was doing very well in paperback, and calls for phone interviews came almost every day.

He was finishing one interview when it began.

"Right, thanks. What were those call letters again? Uh-huh... Well, Ms. Lawicki, best of luck. Right. Good-bye." George hung up and rubbed the back of his neck.

"That sounded pretty good."

It was Kathy, leaning casually in the archway to the kitchen. She had been eavesdropping on the interview.

"Practice makes perfect, I guess," George said, yawning. "At least this woman asked sensible questions. Usually, it's the same old stuff over and over. As if talking intelligently about it would make it seem more real, and God knows that's the last thing they want."

George turned to say something else, but he saw that Kathy wasn't listening. She was leaning more heavily against the doorpost, frowning deeply and clutching her temples between thumb and fingers.

"Are you okay, babe?" he asked, a little alarmed. There was something oddly familiar about the look on her face.

She looked up, surprised and a little guilty. "What? Oh, I'm fine, hon. Just a little slow today." She forced herself to smile and said, "Would you like a cup of coffee?"

"Sure, but—"

The back door banged and Greg ran into the room. His face was flushed and sweaty. There was a new tear in his shirt, and his hair was limp and twisted by the wind.

"Come quick!" he shrilled, all the growing-boy sophistication gone from his voice. "A snake's got Matt!"

George was on his feet in an instant. "Where?"

"In the gully!"

He was out of the house, across the lawn, and standing at the edge of the gully behind the house in seconds. He stopped at the edge of the ridge and looked down, searching for any sign of Matt.

Nothing. The dead brown grass whispered and waved at him. Something scuttled along the dry creekbed at the bottom of the slope. But no Matt.

Greg caught up to him, panting. "He's down in the deeper part," he said, pointing off to the right. "Over there." To the north, the ravine ran off their property, and the dirt walls grew more steep.

George was running again, staring into the deepening canyon as he trotted along its edge.

"Here!" Greg shouted. "Down here!"

He doubled back and scrambled down a well-worn path to the floor of the gully. He could see Matt now, a splash of red Windbreaker against the weathered brown granite. He was on his knees, staring at something George couldn't see. His back was straight, his hands raised away from his side, but motionless.

George rounded a large bush and stopped short. Five feet from his son, no more than four yards from George himself, a rattlesnake lay coiled and ready to strike. Its rattle burred in the still afternoon. Its cold, tattooed hide glittered in the sun.

The snake's mouth was open and hissing. Its head swayed on the end of more than a foot of rippling muscle.

It was pointing directly at Matt.

George didn't move. "Take it easy, son," he said softly, calmly. "Stay perfectly still."

Matt began to turn toward the sound of his father's voice, and the rattle whirred furiously.

"No!" George said, trying to keep his voice low. "Just... stay calm. Stay cool. And please, Matt, don't move."

Matt looked at the snake and said "Daddy?" very softly.

"Hang on, son. I'll figure something out."

George was off to the snake's right, not out of his line of vision but farther away and therefore less important than the boy. George eased forward, a step at a time, until he was ten feet from his son. A large, smooth stone was next to his foot now, and cautiously, as slowly as he could, he bent his knees and put his hand on the rock.

Adrenaline was making him shiver. Sweat was soaking his shirt, and the sound of the breeze seemed unnaturally loud and painful to him. What's it like for the boy? he wondered, as his fingers closed around the stone.

He had considered crushing the snake with the rock, but he knew he wasn't nearly fast enough to do it. He thought of jumping toward it, trying to make himself the target so Matt could escape, but he couldn't risk it. The boy was simply too close.

Now he had a plan. It wasn't a good one, but it was the only one he could think of.

"Matt, listen to me very carefully. In a few seconds, I'm going to say *go*, and when I do I want you to get up and run to me, quick as you can. Got it?"

Matt started to nod, and the rattlesnake twitched.

"No, son! Don't move! I know you understand."

George straightened very slowly. The rock

was warm and rough in his hand. "Okay, Matt. One . . . two . . . three . . . *go!*"

As he shouted he threw the stone, fast and straight. It hit the hard brown dirt less than a foot from the rattler, and the motion made the snake twitch and turn in its direction.

For one instant, the scales seemed balanced. The snake was up and ready to strike, poised between the closer movement of the stone and the larger, louder scrambling of the boy. It was a fraction of a moment, less than an instant, and in the next second the snake had flexed and struck, and Matt was screaming.

The rattler hissed and hit the stone a second time. George had lunged forward as he shouted, and now he had the frightened, screaming boy firmly under the arms. He pulled him off the ground and ran, even as the snake hit the stone a third and final time. Less than a heartbeat later, they were halfway up the gully's wall, far out of range.

Kathy and Greg were at the crest of the ridge, watching them. "Are you all right?" Kathy called frantically.

"Yeah," Matt panted. "I'm okay."

Greg was jumping up and down with excitement. "You were great, Dad! How'd you do that?"

George gathered both of his boys in his arms and hugged them fiercely. "I don't know, son. I really don't know."

For Kathy, it began in earnest while George was on his tour of the South—Florida, Georgia, the Virginias and the Carolinas, and all points between. In the first week of his absence, the headaches came back—incessant, thumping, inescapable headaches, as bad as any she could remember.

She had tried to tell herself they were different from the other ones. She changed her diet. She dropped one of her night classes and got more sleep.

The sleep only made it worse. With sleep came the nightmares.

The creatures and forces from Amityville returned in her dreams. Hooded things. Evil clouds. Images of her children with fingers smashed and swallowed by monstrous flies. But even in the worst of it, she fought to forget, to put Amityville behind her, to devalue the memories and avoid the pain. She wouldn't—she couldn't—admit that the power had found them again.

When George made his frequent calls from the South, she had done her best to pretend all was well. It had worked at first, but as the headaches got worse and the nightmares increased in potency, it became harder and harder for her to maintain the fantasy of a normal life and a happy home.

Finally, one bright and peculiar Wednesday afternoon, it all came crashing down on her.

She was doing her best to clean the house, but the pain in her head was making her clumsy and stupid. She swiped at the counter and upset a ceramic jar that held small knives and cooking spoons, and as its contents sprayed across the counter and clattered to the floor, Kathy felt herself falling into tears.

It was too much. Too much.

She left the cooking utensils where they fell and started for the living room. There were aspirins in the front hall bathroom. Maybe this time they would help her get rid of the headaches. The pounding between her temples made splotches appear in front of her. Her stomach flopped and gurgled, her skin felt hot and tight.

But she stopped just inside the living room archway and gasped. The contents of her stomach jumped and started into her mouth, and Kathy clapped a hand to her lips to keep from throwing up.

The smell was back—the same wretched, putrescent stench that had followed them across a continent. Finally, horribly, it had found them in Tierrasanta.

Kathy cried out from behind her hand and lurched into the kitchen. It was like walking through a wall or a curtain. Here, there was no smell at all. The air was clear and fresh from the open window. But she knew that a few feet behind her, in the dimness of the living room it was waiting for her—waiting to choke her and sicken her all over again.

She stumbled to the utility closet and scrabbled for incense. It had helped them at La Jolla, and even at the motel before that. Father Mancusso had said that incense was special, somehow, that it could make it more difficult for the—the—

Where is it? she thought frantically, scrabbling in the drawer. Where is it?

A box on a high shelf teetered and fell. The sound exploded in Kathy's head like a bomb, and aluminum cookie cutters and broken tools spewed across the floor.

No more, she pleaded, sinking to her knees and trying to hold the pain between her hands. *No more*.

The door to the kitchen opened very slowly, and Greg eased his head into view. His eyes searched the kitchen and found his mother kneeling on the floor in front of the broom closet.

"Hi, Mom," he said very carefully. Even through the thudding in her head, Kathy knew there was something wrong.

"What's the matter?"

Greg came into the room, and she could see the shadow of her other son behind him, still hidden by the door. "Nothin'," he said sullenly.

She forced herself to get up. Cooking utensils and junk from the cardboard box were scattered around the kitchen. It looked as if a windstorm had thrown debris around the room. "Matt?" she said. "Come in here for a second. Let me see you."

Matt shuffled into the kitchen. He had scrapes on both his elbows, and a blue black bruise discolored one eye. His shirt was ripped, and his hair was mussed, and there was a streak of dirt ground into the knees of his new jeans.

"You've been fighting," she said. It was more a statement than a question.

Matt looked embarrassed, and Kathy didn't blame him. George had spent a lot of time with the boys, teaching them to defend themselves, and he'd spent almost as much time warning them to stay out of trouble and away from any fight they could avoid.

"It wasn't my fault," Matt mumbled.

"Really, Mom, he didn't start it," Greg told her.

"Were you there?"

Greg's eyes grew wide. Now *he* was in trouble, too. "There—there were three of them," he said, and looked away from his mother. "It was all over by the time I got there."

"He didn't help me," Matt said defensively.

Greg shrugged. "He didn't need it."

The pain in her head was making Kathy groggy, but she did her best to ignore it. "What happened, boys?" she said wearily, rubbing her head. She had nearly forgotten the stink in the living room. "Start at the beginning."

"They started it!" Matt said.

"Why would they do that?"

Matt didn't want to say. He looked around the room, as if someone else would appear and get him out of trouble. "They—they—" It came out all at once. "They said that our story wasn't true and that we were all liars!" he blurted. "They said we never lived in Amityville, and that there was no such things as ghosts, and that Daddy is a liar!"

Oh.

My God, Kathy thought, in all this time, with all this publicity, it never occurred to me that the boys might be going through as much pressure as we are.

"He had to fight 'em, Mom. What else could he do?"

The pounding was worse than ever. "I don't know," Kathy said. "I honestly don't know."

The phone rang, and Greg and Matt saw it as a chance to escape. As she turned to answer it, they started to slink into the living room, and Kathy suddenly remembered the stench she had found there.

"Wait!" she said, and the boys pulled up short. "Wait, now, I'm not going to yell at you. But I—just cleaned the living room, and I don't want it all tracked up." The phone was still ringing. She felt herself shouting to close out the sound. The pounding was worse and worse. "Go outside!" she shouted, hating the harsh sound of her own voice. "Just go outside and wait for me!"

Greg and Matt scurried into the backyard, and Kathy lunged for the phone. She didn't care who it was. She only wanted to make the noise stop. It was like a hot needle piercing her temples.

She held the receiver in her hand for a long moment before she said anything. Then she took a deep breath, and another, and when the room stopped jumping she said, "Hello?" It came out soft and weak.

She heard her husband very far away. He was saying her name.

"George, is that you?"

"Kathy? Yeah. Of course it's me." He told her he was in Atlanta, between interviews. She mumbled something back to him, but the pain and the nausea were rising up again. She could barely hear him.

It was too much for her, too much for anyone. She clutched the phone in her hand and forced the words out of her mouth. "George!" she said. "Come home. It's starting again. Just like before."

George was sick of it—sick to death. Two weeks had passed since Kathy had told him to

**278**

come home, and here he was. He had barely left the house since his return, and what good had it done? The smells kept coming. The awful dreams plucked at him night after night. And the headaches—those pounding, thudding, nauseating headaches—were back and worse than ever before.

Away from the house, outside Tierrasanta, it was no better. The world just kept picking away at him. Picking and picking.

"Eric, don't give me that. And don't take any crap from those Hollywood people, either. It's a simple request—simple, damn it. I don't want the children's real names used in the movie, and that's that."

Eric Hill, his lawyer on the West Coast, made some comforting sounds about contracts and technical advising fees, but George cut him off.

"I don't care about that right now. Just make sure the kids are out of it, all right? And no pictures of the real house. *None*. I don't want any more trouble from the new owners."

Eric buzzed in his ear some more, but George was too tired to listen. "Fine," he said. "Great, great. I'll talk to you later." He hung up without another word.

The pain and the pressure were combining, like a huge open hand pressing down on him. Every time we think we get away, it comes back, he thought. Every time things start to get better, something turns against us. It's been years now—*years* since we first saw that damn ugly house, but the hassles just keep dragging on and on and on.

George forced himself out of the chair and

stomped into the kitchen. Kathy was there, playing listlessly at making dinner. He didn't care. He didn't care about anything anymore.

"I'm gonna go work on the bike," he said, and slammed out of the house. Kathy started to say something, but he didn't wait to hear it.

He kicked open the side door to the garage and slammed on the light. He hadn't worked on the bike in weeks—not since he'd started the tours and the interviews and all that talk, talk, talk.

He tugged the canvas cover free with one vicious swipe, and a wrench someone had laid on top of it flew up and banged him in the shoulder. George kicked the damn thing across the room, and it hit the wall with a sound like a gunshot.

A small, separate, serene part of his mind pricked him. What's going on here? he asked himself. What are you so mad about?

Okay, okay, he thought. Settle down. You're letting it get to you. You can't let that happen.

He crouched down on his haunches and looked at the Harley, breathing deep and slow.

It was a beautiful bike. Clean, polished, as heavy as he was at rest, but as light and responsive as a thoroughbred on the open road.

He ran a hand over the chitonous black fanning and remembered the rides he had taken. Cool wind. Empty highway. Blank, endless afternoons on the back roads of New York State.

He stood up easily now, and gripped the handlebars. It was a good feeling, healthy somehow. He put his weight under it and lifted the bike off its blocks. He'd turn it on its side, very carefully, and—

George froze with the motorcycle six inches off the ground. His muscles screamed at the weight. Sweat sprouted on his forehead, and his teeth clenched so tightly that he could hear them scraping against each other.

But he didn't move. He didn't dare. Because on a shelf less than four feet from him, on a horizontal plank anchored into the pegboard at shoulder height, a coiled rattlesnake was hissing and swaying, its tail burring madly in the dusk. *How the hell did it get there?*

The bike's weight shifted in George's hands, but he refused to let go. One movement, one breath, and the rattler would be on him. He could see the snake's fangs only inches from his trembling forearm, gleaming in the light of the single overhead bulb.

His eyes moved in his head, sweeping the shadows for some chance, some minor possibility of escape. The trembling was almost out of control. In another ten seconds he would drop the bike and the rattler would strike at him.

There was a shovel on the floor less than a foot from the motorcycle's front tire. It must have fallen off the wall, George realized. I have to put those pegs in better, I wouldn't want anything to rust—

*Stop it*. He was wandering, panicking. He knew that shovel couldn't help him; it was too far away.

He could feel the bike slipping from his hands. The shaking was uncontrollable now. One finger slipped . . . and another . . . and in one burst of speed and desperation, he moved.

It all happened at once. The bike dropped and hit the concrete with a crash. The snake snapped forward, jaws gaping, and struck at George as he threw himself down, scooped up the shovel with one hand and brought it between him and the snake like a shield.

Something hit him square in the chest and he fell back. The bike twisted to the side and hit him in the shins, and he fell on top of it—and on top of the snake, glowing like copper wire on the concrete. He brought the shovel down with all his strength as he fell, and for an instant he thought of the horror of a live rattler trapped beneath his body.

A moment after he hit the floor, he hoisted himself up on his elbows and rolled. The rattlers body was twitching on the cement, its head smashed flat by the shovel. And there was a bruised, remote throbbing in George's chest.

He stumbled to his feet and lurched out of the garage. He called Kathy's name as he crashed into the kitchen, and she ran into the room, hair flying.

"George! What is it?"

"Call the paramedics," he said, his heart racing. "Rattlesnake bite."

He fell into a chair and leaned back, panting. The throbbing in his chest joined with the thumping of his heart, and he tried to calm down. It had only been one strike, one bite before he had killed it, but it was so near the heart. He had to be careful. He had to stay calm if he wanted to survive.

He heard her on the phone, talking high and shrill to the operator. George forced himself to unbutton his shirt and look at his chest. At least he could see how bad the wound was. Maybe there was something he could do.

He frowned and opened the shirt wider. He had expected the worst—a purple swelling around a bleeding cut, an open slash of skin, at least a bruise.

There was nothing there. He could still feel the ghost of a sharp pain, rapidly fading now, but he couldn't find a bite or a bruise of any kind. There was no wound at all.

He pulled the chain that held his St. Michael's medal out of the way and looked a third time. How could he miss it? Had the snake hit him on the side somehow?

No. There was nothing there, either—at least nothing he could see.

Kathy slammed down the phone and ran to him. He had his shirt off now, and he was straining to look over his shoulder.

"What is it, babe? Are you all right?"

"I can't find where it hit me. I know it did—it *had* to, it was too close not to, but . . ."

His fingers probed at the parts of his back he couldn't see.

"Do you see anything, Kathy?"

"Should I?"

They looked again, and George sat quietly, trying to locate the pain. It was strangely diffused now, more a general ache than an injury. Five minutes after Kathy's telephone call, sirens sounded in the driveway and a team of paramedics rushed into the kitchen.

One of the medics had the look of a veteran—a solidly built, bearded man with tired gray eyes. After a rapid, economical examination of George's chest and back, he frowned. He checked George's eyes and measured his pulse.

"I don't know, Mr. Lutz," he said slowly. "I guess it must've missed you."

"But it was right next to me," George said. He felt hazy, somehow, as if it was all part of a dream.

"Well, they don't miss very often, that's true, but you seem fine to me." He gestured to his partner to put the equipment away and gave George a small white card. "Look, if you feel anything strange in the next forty-eight hours—a tightness in the chest, maybe, or any unusual lethargy—be sure to give us a call. It looks like you've had a pretty good shock, so you'll feel a little nauseated after the adrenaline wears off, but even if *that* feels weird, don't be shy. Call 911. Okay?"

"Okay." George stared dully at the card. It had the medics' names and the emergency telephone numbers on it.

The medic picked up his black leather case and said, "Take care," and a moment later he was gone. George stared after him for a long time, and after a few moments he wasn't sure if the man had ever really been there at all.

Kathy sat in the other chair at the kitchen table and looked intently at something in her hand. "George," she said slowly. When he didn't respond, she said it again: "George?"

He turned and looked at her. "Huh?"

"Do you think the snake could have hit *this*, instead of *you*?"

She held up a small golden disc. It was the St. Michael's medal that he had been wearing for months.

He looked at it dumbly, and for some reason he thought of Father Mancusso... and of that warm, faceless being of light he had seen in his dream, so long ago. The one who had saved him, who had locked the demons out of his dreams.

He took the medal and examined it closely. "I don't think so," he decided. "It's too small, and there aren't any tooth-marks or scratches on it."

Father Mancusso had told him that St. Michael was considered the patron saint of all those who battle evil. "He is the Great Protector," the priest had said.

George kept staring at the medal. It was warm and solid in the palm of his hand.

Maybe he *had* been protected, and maybe this wasn't the first time.

It was tall as a house, as black as night. It made a sound like the squealing of a tortured pig.

The legs were thick and brown, like the stumps of rotting trees, and the matted hair of its chest was bristled and filthy.

It had the head of a boar—the huge, leaking snout squashed flat against the face, squinting eyes, fleshy jowls, a slick, watery coating of fat and sweat.

It smelled like something dying.

The talons of the pig-thing shot out at George. He dodged instinctively, and another claw swiped at him. He threw himself forward and rolled out of range, and the impact against the concrete stunned him.

He scrambled to his knees and thought, No, not concrete. The ground seemed to be made of some blue rock, tough and featureless as shale.

He got to his feet and backed away from the pig-thing, but it still approached. Where am I? he thought. How did I get here?

The beast squealed louder than ever and lunged at him, and George turned and ran. Fight, he ordered himself. Stand and fight. When he had gained some ground, he turned to set his feet wide apart and throw up his hands. The pig-thing was there, only a few yards away, and one word echoed through his brain like a hammer against his skull.

*Jodie!* the echo said.

Something hit him with tremendous force, and he fell back against the ground. He opened his eyes and expected to see blood, but there wasn't any. He was whole and unhurt.

The pig-thing approached and he scrambled to his feet. Something hit him again and he was down, and he knew even before he opened his eyes that, visible wounds or not, he couldn't be hit again and survive.

Another word entered his brain. It was huge and warm, more solid than the pounding of the pig-thing's name.

*Protector,* it said. *Protector.*

Now, when George stood, he knew he wouldn't fall again. Light blossomed over his head, and the pig-thing squealed and retreated. He threw a kick and connected with a satisfying *thud*, and the light lanced down with a physical strength.

"You can't hurt me!" he shouted, and the pig-thing turned and ran. "I'm protected! *Protected!*"

He looked into the light and smiled. It was a woman in white, a bright cloud of power, some-

thing almost too vast and good to be compre-
hended. And slowly, as he watched, it grew and
grew and enclosed him in its brilliance.

George awoke slowly from the dream. The
brutality of the pig-thing was still with him.
Sweat had stained his pajamas and the sheets on
his bed, and the fear was like a cold, dying
thing inside him.

But an idea was there, too. A hope. A possibility.

Kathy was awake beside him, and without a
word between them, she knew that he'd had
another nightmare. He kissed her and said,
"Kathy, we have to leave here."

Kathy said, "I know that."

"And maybe next time," George said, "it'll be
different. Maybe next time, we'll have help."

## 21

George screamed and sat up in bed. His head was pounding. His hands were greasy with sweat. His heart was thumping in his chest like a runaway machine.

He breathed harshly, rapidly, waiting for a second sound, listening for disaster. Nothing came. He blinked his eyes, gulped in another breath, and watched as the nameless shapes of horror that had haunted his dreams slowly, slowly receded.

He was alone.

It had been a week since the dream about the pig-thing, since the light had returned to help him. But now the blackness had swallowed him all over again. Now, night after night, beasts came and tore at his dreams.

He turned to look at Kathy, and found her

sitting next to him, her eyes wide and dry, her lips pulled back from her teeth in a silent gasp. She looked oddly inhuman in the moonlight, almost canine, and when George put a hand on her arm he found her skin was as cool and stiff as the surface of an artificial limb.

"No more," she said, and the trembling began. "George! George . . . no more."

She was cracking open. The trembling was like something outside her that shook her, pounded at her, and the sobs came from her mouth in short, vicious cuts. "No! More!" she gasped, clinging to him. "No! More!"

George held her tightly until the trembling stopped and she slept again. But he didn't close his eyes. He was awake hours later, when the sun rose.


"We can't go on like this, babe," he told her the next morning. The coffee cup in front of him was crusted with some brown, fibrous matter around the lip. It made him sick to look at it. "We have to do something."

"Like what?" The weakness of the night before had been replaced by a fragile brittleness. George knew that a single word could shatter Kathy all over again.

"I'll go down to Saint Pat's and see if I can get some holy water."

"No," she said flatly. "You tried that last time, and things got worse."

"I know, Kathy, but maybe we *do* have help now."

Kathy threw her dishtowel into the sink. It landed with a loud slap against the ceramic. "Where was your protection last night, George?

Where has it been night after night after night when the headaches and the dreams and the flies are here?"

He shook his head and looked at his dirty cup. "I don't know, Kathy. Sometimes it's there, sometime's it's not. I think we have to believe in—"

"I wish I could believe that! I really *want* to," she whispered.

George went to her and she turned away. She put her weight against the kitchen counter and let her hair fall forward to obscure her face. Kathy's voice was calm and quiet now, as if it were coming from very far away.

"I'm sorry," she said, "I'm just tired. If you think it will help, let's do it." Her voice was so soft that George could hardly hear it. "I doubt if it can get any worse," she whispered.

He stepped through the front door of his home in Tierrasanta, listening intently. The glass vial was warm and solid in his hand.

He uncorked the spout. He raised the bottle over his head and brought it down in a swift, smooth motion. Droplets sprayed from the perforated cap of the vial and spattered on the carpet at his feet.

"In the name of the Father, the Son, the Holy Ghost, bless this house and all who are in it."

Nothing happened. No sounds, no groaning, no hideous smells.

He moved to the archway between kitchen and living room, and brought his arm down again. The droplets of holy water formed a random pattern where the wall met the linoleum floor.

"In the name of the Father, the Son, and the Holy Ghost, bless this house and all who are in it."

Still nothing. He moved to the hallway, to the pantry, up the stairs to the second floor. At the juncture of each room, at every place where he had smelled the stench, seen a fly, felt the cold, he laid down a pattern of sacred water.

"In the name of the Father, the Son, and the Holy Ghost, bless this house and all who are in it."

George ended at the foot of the bed where he and Kathy slept, looking down at the rumpled cover, the twisted pillows, the sheets stained with his own sweat. His arm came down once in a vertical line, then raised again and swept from left to right. The water tattooed a huge, pointillistic cross on the bed beneath him.

"In the name of the Father, the Son, and the Holy Ghost," he said, and now it was almost a plea. "Bless this house and all who are in it."

The water was gone. He capped the empty vial and joined Kathy in the car, where she waited with the children. He was exhausted, drained, dulled by the effort. And buried deep within him, there was hope.

He awoke at 3:15 that morning in the middle of a scream. A thing as black as night with red eyes that stood out from its skull had been chasing him through the empty rooms of the Amityville house. He imagined he could see the tiny stains of the holy water on the spread that was crumpled in his fists, and it made him angry—very angry.

Kathy was asleep so solid it approached coma. George cursed and threw himself out of bed, seething with frustration. Maybe it wasn't the force from Amityville at all. Maybe he was just warped, just cracking up from too much traveling and too much publicity.

But he knew that was rubbish. He knew.

The blessing hadn't worked. The thing from Amityville was still with them.

George sat at Kathy's side while she picked up the phone and dialed 503, the area code for the state of Oregon. He watched her as she nodded to him—the phone was ringing. He saw her face tighten when someone picked up the receiver over a thousand miles away, then blossom into a smile when she recognized the sound of the voice.

He heard her say, "Father Mancusso? This is Kathy Lutz. Father, we need your help."

Father Mancusso arranged the wafers of the Holy Eucharist on the simple silver plate before him. He was in his snugly fitting cassock, concentrating on the preparation for the Mass, and waiting for something—*anything*—to happen.

He smiled grimly. What do I expect? he asked himself. A clap of thunder? A bolt of black lightning from the kitchen ceiling? Or maybe he was preparing himself for something less spectacular but no less horrifying—like an attack of the hideous, debilitating sickness he remembered so vividly from New York.

In the months since his move to the Pacific Northwest, the priest had done his best to follow his own advice. He had tried to put the memories of Amityville behind him, to hide them in a special, protected part of his mind.

The sickness had not followed him. The dreams and the fear had drained out of him. Even the frequent, friendly telephone calls from Kathy and George Lutz had not rekindled the old horror, and he was glad of that. These people were his friends, and he had not wanted to desert them.

That was why the call from Kathy had surprised him so. In the weeks before he heard from her, he had felt a new lightness, an ease of movement and thought that was far greater than anything he had experienced since the months before Kathy and George ever heard of Amityville. At first, he had no clue to the origin of his new energy, until a cheerful, untroubled letter from the Lutzes made him wonder if finally, finally the thing from Amityville had grown tired of them and moved on.

He pulled his outer vestments over his shoulders and straightened them meticulously, concentrating on the details of the preparation. He did not want to become caught up in the tensions of the couple that stood a few feet away. He couldn't afford that now.

So what am I to think? he wondered. His friends George and Kathy did not look as horrid as they had during the trial at Amityville, but there was a—a force around them, an atmosphere of evil that clung to them like a thick, adhesive fog. They were stronger now—he could see that in the steady gaze that Kathy offered him, feel it in the grip of George's hand. They were his allies now, not his fellow victims. They trusted him, but they didn't expect miracles, and that feeling, that sense of hope could explain the greatest difference of all.

Because Father Mancusso had been in the Tierrasanta home for almost an hour, and nothing had happened. No smells, no voices, and—thank God, he thought—no sickness.

George Lutz took his wife's hand and said, "Why a Mass, Father, and not a blessing?"

"The Mass is very powerful, George. It is the central ritual and miracle of the Catholic Church. That in itself should be enough."

He had thought long and hard about his decision to help the Lutzes. It hadn't been easy. They were already looking for another house. Kathy said she'd found one in Rancho Santa Fe, wherever that was, and they were negotiating for it now. They would be in Tierrasanta only a few more weeks, so why risk everything to cleanse this place?

Mancusso looked on another battle with the demons from New York with unmitigated horror. Quite frankly, he told himself, I don't know if I could survive another illness like the last. But the thought of allowing an innocent to become caught up in the struggle—innocents like the next owners of Tierrasanta, or a fellow priest—was even more horrifying than the recurrence of his own troubles.

So he came. He packed his vestments and his phylacteries, and he boarded a plane to San Diego.

Now the children were safely tucked away at the home of the Lutzs' young friend Terri. The house was closed up against the bright afternoon sun, and their dog was chained in the backyard, whimpering at his leash and fascinated with the activity in the house.

"Stand before me, George, Kathy," Father

Mancusso said gently. "When I ask you to kneel, please do so." He saw the young woman nod, and he smiled at her. "You know how it works, don't you, Kathleen? I'd almost forgotten." She smiled even wider and Father Mancusso turned and raised his arms to the sanctified cross he had mounted on the living room wall. "In the name of the Father, the Son, and the Holy Ghost . . ." And the Mass began.

Mancusso moved through the familiar, powerful ritual with a practiced grace, alert for the slightest feeling. Nothing came. Nothing happened. He expected a rumble at the mention of God's name, some bolt of cold or nausea when the Host was laid upon the tongue, some rattling gasp or thunder at the Benediction. But the house stayed quiet and warm and unchanged around him.

He made the final sign of the cross, said, "Go with God," and it was over. George and Kathy looked up at him, eyes wide, and for an instant they all held their breaths, expecting the worst.

George's face split into a grin. It was the most open, most joyful expression the priest had ever seen on his old friend. "Thank you, Father!" he said, almost laughing. "Thank you, *thank* you!"

Father Mancusso looked a little blank and shrugged his shoulders. "You're welcome," he said, and they all laughed together.

The farewells, later that day, were very emotional. The children clung to the priest like a long-lost relative. Kathy had to force herself to let him out of her own tight embrace, and George asked him again and again to stay an extra day or two—a week, if he could.

"I'm sorry," he said, shaking his head. "It's a

small parish in Portland, but there is plenty to do—almost too much, at times." He ruffled Greg's hair, and the boy grinned at him. "I promise, my friends, the moment I can get away for a real vacation, I'll be back."

Amy went "Yaaaa!" and the boys joined the cheer, and there was one last quick set of hugs all around as the public address system blared the boarding call for his flight.

"God bless you," he said to his friends.

"Thanks again, Father," George said for the hundredth time. "I think it'll be all right now."

He boarded the plane filled with hope and good cheer.


And that night, it began again.

George screamed and sat up in bed. His head was pounding. His hands were greasy with sweat. His heart was thumping in his chest like a runaway machine.

Kathy sat next to him, sobbing. He felt tears on his own cheeks, oddly hot and sticky, and he apologized to her, over and over.

"I'm sorry, Kathy. I'm really sorry. I guess—I guess we'll have to leave after all."

"I'm sorry."

# 22

"Okay, I think you've got everything now," Kathy said, surveying the pile of boxes and suitcases with a mixture of satisfaction and weariness. "These are the clothes, these are the toys, this is the stuff for the beach, if you go . . . and here." She took a piece of notebook paper from her back pocket. "This is a list of phone numbers and addresses, including all the places we'll be during the European tour."

Terri Sullivan took the paper and read through it carefully. Then she smiled brightly and put the note in the pocket of her work shirt. "I'll keep it close to my heart," she said, grinning.

George came in with one boy under each arm. They screamed gleefully when he dumped them on their feet. "Late delivery ma'am," he said, and glanced at the clock in Terri's living room. "I think we'd better get going."

"Next stop Amsterdam, eh?"

"The land of Little Dutch Boys and chocolate candy," George said, and turned to his wife. "You ready, babe?"

Kathy was looking fondly at her children. They were both happy that the tour had come up, especially now. Getting away from Tierrasanta was a relief. But George could see the reluctance in her, and he didn't begrudge her a moment's regret. Europe was a long way off. It was the farthest she would have gone without the kids in tow.

Terri saw the mood changing and worked to keep it light. "I wish I were the one flying off," she said. "I've never been any farther away than Las Vegas, and here you are going over to put your fingers in the dykes."

"What's a dyke?" Amy asked.

"It's like a dam," George told her.

"You're supposed to say *darn*," Amy corrected solemnly, and when George laughed the little girl looked annoyed. "Well, that's what you always told us!"

The good-byes were long and difficult for Kathy and George, but eventually they found themselves in the T-Bird with the engine running.

"Fifteen days is a long time," Kathy said as Terri ducked down to the window.

"Look on the bright side, Kath. You'll probably be able to move into that new house in Rancho Santa Fe as soon as you get back."

"We'd better," George growled good-naturedly.

Terri grinned. "And think of the great time

we'll have decorating with all that new furniture you ordered."

Kathy smiled wanly. "Sure. Take good care of the kids!"

"The best. I promise."

"I know you will, Terri. It's just that—"

George didn't want to let this get any more maudlin than it already was. He put the car in gear and said, " 'Bye, Terri! Thanks again!"

The children waved good-bye from the porch, and Kathy leaned out of her window to shout her final farewells. For one crazed instant, George thought she was going to jump out of the moving car and run back to them. Then Terri and Greg and Matt and Amy turned to specks in his rearview mirror. A moment later, they were gone.

"It's only fifteen days," he said. He hated to see Kathy look so desolate.

"Only fifteen days," she repeated, giving a whole new emphasis to the words.

When she says it, George thought, it sounds like a century.


The KLM jet eased downward and made a hard turn to the right as it approached Amsterdam's Schipol Airport. George looked out his window at the city below and saw a series of small, silvery inland lakes decorating the green and gray city. The lakes were connected by an infinitely complex series of canals and locks that ran back and forth from one body of water to another. It looked as if there were more canals than roads, and the waterways seemed as crowded with traffic as the highways.

"Amazing," he said.

"Beautiful," Kathy said. They held hands as the plane touched down.

A distinguished middle-aged man with streaks of gray in his trim Van Dyke was waiting for them at Customs. "Mr. Lutz? Mrs. Lutz?" he asked, and when they nodded he offered his hand. "Hans Vander, with the Dutch Book Publishing. I'm to be your host during the stay in Amsterdam."

George shook his hand and complimented Vander on his English. It was clear and smooth, and the accent made it even more charming.

"How nice of you to say," Vander replied, smiling with real pleasure. "Shall we acquire your luggage?"

Time spent in airports, George thought later, is always one long blur to me. Even in the clean, modern, relatively small Dutch airport of Schipol, the noise and the struggle with schedules and the long lines at Customs dulled his senses.

The first real impression he had of Amsterdam was canals. It seemed impossible to go far in any direction without crossing one.

"Is Amsterdam built between canals?" Kathy asked.

"Oh, yes. This, in point of fact, is the most famous one—the dam for which Amsterdam is named." They were driving a roundabout route to their hotel, and Vander was giving them a short, friendly lecture on his city as he drove. "Amsterdam is still many meters below the level of the sea, you know. Every week, every month, we reclaim more land. You saw, perhaps, from the air, how we use landfilling to build new land in the bay?" They nodded, remembering the circular excavations in the shallow water near the airport. "We are very crowded here, even so. Three places for every four people, which means overpopulation. But you should be very comfortable."

They pulled to a stop at the Sonesta Hotel, not far from the original dam itself. "A nice hotel," Vander told them, "and most quiet. I think you will find it quaint."

George and Kathy smiled together. A good, clean cheerful little country, George decided. Just what the doctor ordered.

The first public appearance in Holland was scheduled to take place at a venerable Dutch clubhouse in the center of the Old City. But when Hans Vander ushered them into the hall on the day after their arrival in Amsterdam, Kathy didn't think of Holland. She was immediately reminded of the old-fashioned German beer cellars she'd seen in a hundred different movies.

There was thick, dark wood everywhere, and tremendous wooden beams that looked as if they could support tons of snow. A fireplace dominated one wall, and antique firearms and the heads of animals covered another over a long, tall set of bookcases.

Today, the room was crowded with reporters, including radio broadcasters with microphones in hand and two or three television film crews.

"The interview will be seen all over Holland," Vander told them. "And other parts of Europe, perhaps. This is why we have reporters here from many countries." He led them to a

303

stout platform with a podium and microphone, then gestured to two chairs at the rear of the stage.

"My introduction," he said proudly, and they sat.

"Greetings, ladies and gentlemen," Vander said in careful English, brushing nonexistent lint from the lapels of his trim gray suit. "I am Hans Vander, of the—"

Shouts went up in the hall. Vander looked blankly at the crowd of reporters waving note pads in his direction. He shrugged and began again. "Today we shall be speaking with— What *is* it?"

A nervous, bespectacled man trotted on stage and whispered in his ear. Vander said something in Dutch under his breath, and George wondered if it was entirely polite. Then their host turned to them and smiled apologetically.

"There is some problem with the public address," he said. "We shall have it cleared up within a minute."

The minute stretched to fill twenty minutes. Finally, Vander apologized to the irate reporters. "All is now well," he said, and the conference began.

He gave a short summary of the Lutzes' experiences in the house in Amityville, and shamelessly hyped the edition of the book his group was publishing. After five minutes of effusive compliments and a narration that was supposed to engross the audience and tingle an occasional spine, he finally turned and introduced "the people to whom the adventure occurred—Mr. and Mrs. George Lutz."

"George and Kathy Lutz," George said, glancing guiltily at his wife. She smiled tolerantly. They were still a hair old-fashioned here, she thought ruefully, but it wasn't all that bad.

"Come on, honey," George said as he stood. Kathy resisted his arm and said, "No, babe, you go ahead. Call me if you need me." She stayed seated and folded her arms.

George hadn't expected applause, and when it rose in scattered fragments from the assemblage, he was vaguely embarrassed by it. What had he done to deserve it? Simply arrived? He smiled and shrugged a little shyly and said, "I am ready to answer any questions you may have."

The first one came from a reporter with a clipped English accent. "Sir. All this... *experience* of yours that you say you've had. Don't you think it might have been mass hallucination or some other purely aberrant disorder?"

There were mumbles from the group as some reporters tried to translate 'mass hallucination' and 'aberrant.' Most of them could speak excellent English, but these weren't the sorts of terms they heard every day.

George shook his head. "No, sir. There is simply too mu—"

The public address system cut out. George trailed off when he realized that no one could hear him, and turned to look helplessly at Vander. His host simply shrugged and waved at him to continue.

George tapped the microphone and it cut in again. "Hmm. I said I believe too much happened to us for such a simple explanation to apply. Another question?"

A woman waved a hand at him, and George

smiled and nodded. "Sir, we would love to know how much money you've actually made from this alleged haunting of yours."

George sighed. "Not nearly as much as y—"

The mike cut out again and he sighed heavily, tapping it back to life. As he began to answer, another reporter rose and interrupted.

"Mr. Lutz! Sir! These events of yours are all so incredible, don't you think? Tell us, why do you think they happened to you, a simple American, and yet not to so many other people?"

There it was again, Kathy fumed. A thinly veiled implication that they weren't quite telling the truth. She found herself hating the questions, and hating the answers they had to give over and over. Why were so many people intent on calling them liars? Oh, they were very nice— they never came out and said it directly—but they said it very clearly just the same. What in heaven's name did they think could have been gained by making up a story like theirs? Did they think it was some sort of game?

George tried to answer the question without anger, and once again the mike cut out. This time it took a good deal more fiddling about to get it working.

Another man stood up and said, "I don't think you answered that last question at all completely, Mr. Lutz. Exactly what *have* you gained from all this notoriety? And why should we be expected to believe your story?"

No one's forcing you to believe *anything*, Kathy groaned inwardly.

George tried not to be annoyed. "I . . . oo . . . know wh . . . if, I'd . . . d—"

"*Damn* it!" he said, and whacked the microphone with the flat of his hand. It let out a loud electronic moan that grew louder and louder, and when members of the audience crowed at him and covered their ears, he reached to the back of the mike and pulled the cord loose. The whine cut off abruptly.

Reporters continued to call out questions, but George couldn't answer above the din. He said, "Please! Please, one at a time!" but everyone wanted to be first. Finally he shrugged his shoulders and put the useless microphone on the podium.

Kathy was fed up. They had come all this way, spent all this time and money, to try and tell their story, and now they had a group of virtually hostile interrogators shouting at them, and no way to answer their questions.

George turned to her and put out his hands in a gesture of frustration and futility. She stood up and walked past him.

"Kathy?" he said, astonished. "Where are you going?"

She walked to the edge of the platform and shouted at the reporters. "Quiet! Let me have quiet!"

Gradually, but more swiftly than George thought possible, the noise subsided.

"We have no idea why these things have happened to us," Kathy shouted, loudly enough to be heard in the back of the hall. "But they *did* happen. My husband and I know, without any doubt, that evil *does* exist in the world, and the fact that people argue over its possibility or its impossibility—well, that's totally academic to us. We have been through it. We have lived it, and we know it exists. If you don't believe that, there is nothing we can possibly say that will change your minds, and if you *can't* believe it, if you simply won't allow yourself to admit that the safe little world you think you live in, the world of answered questions and comfortable surroundings, isn't quite so safe or simple as you thought—that there are mysteries out there and danger that you can't understand or predict—then *you're* the one with the problem, not us.

"So believe what you want. We will continue to tell our story—our *true* story—either way."

Without a backward glance, Kathy stepped down from the stage and walked to the exit at the back of the hall. She was surprised and a little pleased at the encouraging smiles and nods from members of the audience. After all the diplomacy and tolerance, she thought, maybe a little straight talk wasn't such a bad idea.

She paused at the exit and turned to look at her husband. George was standing on the stage looking a little stunned, but when she caught his eye he grinned, whispered something to Vander, and hurried down the aisle to join her.

"C'mon," she said, taking his hand. "Let's go see Amsterdam."

He laughed, and they left together.

For the rest of the day, George and Kathy Lutz were indistinguishable from any other North American tourist exploring the wonders of the capital city of Holland. They walked hand in hand through narrow streets and alleys; they crossed bridges over canal after canal; they rode on trams, dodged people on bicycles who zipped down the cobbled streets at hair-raising speeds, and on three separate occasions they sat in quaint Dutch cafes and discussed nothing in particular while they ate cheese and drank espresso.

Kathy was astonished by the huge number of people who were walking. After all the automobiles of New York and California, the determined pedestrianism of the Dutch was rather charming, and, she decided, it was the only way to see a city—any city. Especially one as beautiful as Amsterdam.

They were strolling along one of the major waterways and nibbling on Dutch chocolate when she saw a tour boat—a long, low, futuristic launch with windows from stem to stern that slid silently down the canal. It was filled with wide-eyed tourists.

"George!" she said excitedly. "Let's take a tour!"

He was happy to oblige. George hadn't seen his wife this happy and carefree in years, and he would have done anything to prolong it. After a few quick questions and friendly answers from Dutch natives, they found one of the large, colorful docks where they boarded a launch that was just about to leave. Soon they were winding through the endless waterways and soaking up the history of Amsterdam, courtesy of an invisible guide whose words came to them in four different languages from tiny speakers set in the side of the launch itself.

As the sun sank low, they stopped at a small food stand in the Centrum, the center of Old Amsterdam, and bought some french fries in a long paper cone. "What do you call these?"

Kathy asked the vendor. He told them they were *patat frittes*. She asked about the unusual foods he was preparing, and the plump man behind the counter was so pleased at her interest that he gave her samples free of charge. He didn't know much English, but he knew one word: "Enjoy," he said, waving away George's money. "Enjoy, enjoy."

Enjoy they did. They walked through the narrow streets well into the evening, marveling at the clean, almost scrubbed quality of the city, and rather pleased at how easily they found their way around. They talked about the tour, the talk shows, and most important, what they wanted to do that evening.

They wandered past a cinema that was showing an American film, and Kathy made an idle comment about the widespread use of English in the city. Many of the films they had seen advertised were shown without subtitles or dubbing.

"You want to see a movie?" George asked.

Kathy considered it and said, "Yes, I do. I don't think we've been to the movies together in years."

George bought the tickets and went off to hunt up refreshments. Kathy moved into the theater to find seats.

It was a small, tidy theater with only a few hundred seats, and Kathy was once again reminded of the grace and economy of Amsterdam architecture. They couldn't afford to waste a square inch of space.

An English couple behind her was holding hands and babbling about all they had seen that day. "Oh, Teddy," the young girl said—young enough to be my daughter, Kathy thought ruefully—"this is a smashing honeymoon!"

Honeymoon? Now, that's nice, Kathy thought. She and George had been married for years, and somehow this trip felt a little like a honeymoon for them, too. It had that same sense of ease and simplicity, of... hope? That was it: hope.

She leaned back in the padded theater seat and thought of her own marriage. It hadn't been an easy decision to make. After all, they had both been married and divorced already, and the Church hadn't made it any easier on them. Finally, to avoid problems with her friends and the clergy she respected, they had been married in a Presbyterian church, and since they had both been through the traditional ceremony before, they decided to do exactly what they liked, instead of what was expected ot them.

A week before the wedding, they sat down and wrote their own vows. They said everything they wanted to say—what they felt about each other, what they expected from the marriage, why this one, unlike so many others, would last. They must have said it well, Kathy remembered. Half the people there had asked for copies— including the minister.

She remembered how she had cooked for weeks to prepare for the party. There had been chickens and hams, salads and homemade ice cream, and more appetizers than she could count. The reception had been a beautiful, bizarre experience. They had invited everyone they knew—everyone—and it was weird and a little wonderful to see their business friends in conservative three-piece suits mingling with George's old biker friends in their leather jackets and levis. Clean levis, of course; it had been a wedding, after all.

George cut two fifty-gallon drums in half and converted them into one-time-only barbecues. Anything and everything, from pork to beef to marshmallows, was roasted in those monsters. They'd even hired a crazy one-man band. The dancing had continued far into the night, and George's grandfather—that abrasive, enticing, immensely attractive old man—had arrived early and stayed late. He'd outdanced, outdrunk, and outpartied everyone else in sight. At the tender age of ninety-three.

George's grandfather was gone now, of course. They had attended the funeral more than a year before. But it was memories like that that kept him from really dying, memories that convinced Kathy that nothing could ever completely die—especially the good in people.

George plopped into the chair next to her just as the lights began to dim. "Couldn't find any popcorn," he said.

"Heathens," Kathy grumbled jokingly.

"But here's more chocolate."

"And there goes my figure." She took a chunk of candy and bit into it, then slipped her arm through George's and squeezed tightly as the credits began to roll.

This is the way it should be, she thought. Just like this, all the time.

It was 1:00 A.M. before they unlocked the door to their hotel room, laughing at some silly joke George had made, and decided to get some sleep. There was a message waiting for them—Mr. Vander had called repeatedly, more than a little distressed. They agreed to let the poor man sleep through the night. They would patch things up and start fresh in the morning. He was a good man, after all, and the people of Amsterdam had been terrific. It was just the reporters and the publicity that was getting to them.

George collapsed on the bed and stretched out on his back to stare at the ceiling, while Kathy wandered into the bathroom and changed her clothes.

"Why am I so wide awake?" she called into the other room. "I thought I'd be dead on my feet from jet lag by now."

"Eight cups of espresso coffee might have something to do with it," George laughed.

"Whatever it is, I love it. I wish I could feel like this all the time." She washed the makeup from her face, slipped into a comfortable old quilted robe, and strolled back into the bedroom to join George on the bed. She felt more relaxed and at peace with herself than she had in years.

"George," she said, trailing a hand over his chest, "I—"

It fell on her like a wave of icy water. An intuition, a certainty, a feeling that something was horribly wrong.

The warmth of the long and happy day rushed out of her in an instant. She felt her muscles tense and her stomach churn with a familiar old fear, and beside her George sat up quickly and shivering at the invisible impact.

"What is it?" he said, rubbing his arms for warmth.

"I don't—I don't know," she said, exploring the sensation timidly, as if probing an old wound. It felt familiar, somehow, as if they had gone through something very much like it before. Like it, but not identical.

"La Jolla," she said. "Like the time we were trapped in the living room."

George nodded. "That's it, that's it. But something's different. It's . . . weaker, somehow. As if we're not at the center of it, as if . . ." He couldn't quite place it. Realization seemed just beyond his grasp; there was a secret scurrying at the edges of thought.

Kathy felt a new wave, more brutal than the first, and quite suddenly she was sure what was happening. She sat bolt upright and clutched at his arm. "George!" she hissed. *"It's after the kids!"*

He turned to her, astonished. "The kids? But how would we . . ."

He stopped. It was a stupid question. They had been through so much in the last few years, working together as a family and as something more than that. They were a single unit, somehow, almost a single organism, and if one of them was hurt, if two of them were in danger, if three of them were terrified, it affected them all.

He knew she was right. The powerful bond between parents and children was telling them that something was happening, thousands of miles away.

The children were in danger.

It took fifteen minutes to complete the transatlantic call, and it took that short a time only because George insisted that it was an emergency. After all, it was the middle of the night. Terri's mother Abigail answered the phone in San Diego on the second ring.

"Abby? This is George Lutz."

She sounded delighted. "George! You're home so soon?"

"No, no, we're calling from Holland—Amsterdam."

"My, that must be expensive."

"Abby, are the kids all right?"

There was a short silence, and George held his breath. "All right?" the woman echoed. "Of course they're all right. Amy's right here with me, playing very happily with her dolls, and Terri's taken the boys to the beach. That Greg of yours just loves the beach."

"Then they're all right? No problems?"

"No, George. None. Honey, are you all right yourself?"

George laughed without humor. "Of course. Let me talk to Amy."

Four hours later, an hour before the sun was to rise over Holland, the phone in the Lutzes' room rang. They answered it before the ringing stopped and heard the whole story. Neither of them had slept—they couldn't, the feeling wouldn't let them. So it was in the depths of a gray European dawn that they learned the origin and final effects of their cold, uncommon certainty.

An hour before the Lutzes returned to their hotel room, in a place ten time zones and half a world away, Terri Sullivan had finally given up. She could handle the boys singly, no matter how insistent they became, but together she was no match for them.

"Okay, okay," she said, surrendering. "If you want to go to the beach, we'll go to the beach."

Amy was sleeping upstairs, buried in blankets and dress-up dolls. Terri didn't have the heart to wake her. She asked her mother if she would mind staying home with the little girl, and Abby had been delighted to have the chance to play mother again.

"Yes, I know," Terri teased her. "I'm too old for my own good."

"Truer words were never spoken," her mother agreed. "Now you'd better get those boys to the beach before they tear the house down."

They packed up sandwiches and lemonade and piled into Terri's Volkswagen for the short trip to La Jolla Shores.

The stretch of beach they chose was a long, smooth, narrow expanse of sand and shallow water bordered by a strip of tough bermuda grass, date palms, and gray-painted picnic tables. The weather was even warmer than Terri had expected it to be, and she was secretly glad that the boys had talked her—pestered her, actually—into making the trip, though she would never dream of telling them that. She was too easy a mark as it was.

The beach was nearly deserted this early on a weekday afternoon, and the trio had a choice of places to lay their blankets. They decided to walk quite a distance from the parking lot and the picnic tables and keep to themselves. Terri arranged the blankets and broke out the thermos while the boys raced to see who could undress first. Greg won by a hair, and the two of them were about to make a mad dash for the water when Terri pulled them up short.

"Whoa, there, fellahs!" she called, and they paused very reluctantly. "Let me get some sun tan oil on you."

Matt went "Aww," and Greg went, "Come on," but Terri insisted. She smeared their backs while they worked over their own arms and legs, chests and faces. "If your parents came back and found you guys burnt to a crisp, we'd all get skinned alive," Terri told them.

Her hand brushed against a chain around Greg's neck, and he said "Ouch!" and squirmed peevishly.

"What is that, Greg?"

"That's my St. Michael's medal."

Terri frowned. "Maybe you should take it off. You might lose it out there, you know, and you don't want it to rust or anything."

Greg squirmed again. "Nah, my Dad said I should always wear it." He jumped to his feet and started backing toward the ocean. "Can I go now?"

Terri laughed and said, "Yes, you can go," and the boys were off like twin shots from a cannon. She laughed again and watched them splash into the shallows, spraying each other with water as they ran.

"Don't go out too far!" she called, but she doubted if they heard her. It didn't really matter. They were smart boys and good swimmers. She didn't have to worry too much about them—no more so than about any young whirl-winds.

She rubbed a little oil on her own arms and winced at the whiteness of her skin. I've got to get to the beach more often, she thought. I look like the bottom of a fish. She straightened the towel beneath her with every intention of lying down, and glanced one last time at the boys. They were jumping up and over the small break-ers near shore, looking more like seals than human children.

As she began to lean back, the overwhelming blueness of the sea and sky seemed to reach out and take her firmly in hand. She sat up fully once more and looked at the cobalt sea scattered with luminous whitecaps, at the shimmering green underside of the waves, at the deep pearl gray of a sea gull's wings as it soared above the breakers.

Terri put her arms around her knees and stared into the sea, fascinated.

The boys, meanwhile, swam through the waves farther from shore, paddling happily among the mild currents of the sea.

"Terri, lookit me!" Matt turned up his tail and dove straight down, so only his legs were visi-ble, riding high out of the water. It was a new trick he'd just learned, and he was proud of it.

He surfaced closer to shore than he'd expected to, and turned in the water to see if Terri was watching.

She was sitting hunched up in a little ball, staring out to sea. "Terri!" he called. "Hey, *Terri!*"

She didn't move.

Matt turned in the water and looked beyond

the waves to his brother Greg. Greg was the best swimmer he knew. He could just go and go, and never get tired.

But he couldn't see his brother—not at all. He kicked his feet harder and rose as high as he could, and then, very suddenly, he saw him.

He was way too far out and splashing around a lot. If their dad had been around, Matt knew, Greg would be in big trouble.

"Hey!" he shouted. "Hey, Greg, you better get back here!"

Greg raised an arm high out of the water, and his head dipped below the surface. It was a long time before he came up again—a *long* time— and when he did he was even further out to sea.

"Hey, Greg! Greg, are you okay?"

He heard his brother give a strangled shout— not words, just a shout—and his head ducked under the water again.

"Greg! Greg, get *back* here!"

The splashing was worse, and he was still drifting away from shore.

Matt had heard all about riptides. His Dad had told them what they were, and how they could drag you way out into the ocean. You were supposed to swim sideways, he said, in the same direction as the shore, and pretty soon you'd be out of the riptide and you could swim in.

"Greg!" he shouted. "Swim this way! *This* way!"

He heard Greg scream again. He was still drifting farther and farther away.

It was too great a distance for him to help. He knew he wasn't strong enough to make it.

Matt paddled frantically until the water was

shallow enough for his toes to touch the bottom. Then he turned and shouted for his mom's friend as loud as he could.

"Terri! Terri, c'mere, Greg's in trouble!"

Terri was still rolled up in a ball, her arms locked around her knees, staring out to sea. Just staring and staring.

"Terri, come *on!* Help!"

Terri didn't move.

The little boy struggled to get to shore, and an unexpected wave knocked him down. He felt the water rush over him, gush up his nose, and for a second he thought *he* was the one who was in trouble.

He fought his way to the surface and found himself surrounded by seaweed and foam, but the water only came to his knees now.

He couldn't see his brother at all.

There was no one else on the beach but him and Terri. He looked up and down, and the only other people were way down by the parking lot.

"Terri, help! Come on, you gotta *help!*"

He splashed out of the water and ran to her, but Terri was still staring into the sea like he wasn't even there. "Come on, *help!*" he shouted as he ran. "Help! *Help!*"

When Terri thought about it later—and she thought about it many times—she remembered best the sea and the sky and the keening cry of the gull. It went on forever and ever, she knew, and there was nothing else but the blue water and the blue sky and the gray wings, and very far off, very quiet, a small cry in the wind.

Matt had to take her by the arm and pull as hard as he could before she turned to him.

"Terri, *help* me! Greg's in trouble! He's in *trouble!*"

She looked at him with a dreamy, confused expression.

"What?"

"Greg's in *trouble*, Terri!"

Now she sat upright, suddenly aware, and said, "What? *What* is it?"

He turned and pointed into the water, past the breakers. They could both see him now: Greg was splashing frantically, throwing up sea foam and gouts of water as the riptide dragged him out to sea.

"Couldn't you hear me? I called you and called you!"

"I'm sorry, Matt. I—I—" She jumped to her feet and stared at the drowning boy. "I must have fallen asleep. . . ."

There was a thin, distant cry—a scream that was something less than a word, half-strangled by seawater. Terri ran to the water's edge and called Greg's name, ignoring the sting of the cold water as it slapped at her ankles.

She could swim, but not that well. The boy was too far away for her to get to him.

She turned and looked up and down the beach, desperate for help, but no one was in sight. She turned back to the ocean and called, "Greg! Greg, stay calm! I'll get you, just *stay calm!*"

The thin distant cry came again.

"Can I help?"

The deep, friendly voice was right at her ear. Terri jumped and spun around, and found a tall, handsome blond man in swimming trunks and a sweat-shirt standing right behind her.

"Where—what—" She was sure the beach had been deserted.

"Do you need help?" he said, smiling.

The cry came again, and she looked back into the water. "There's a boy in trouble out there. I can't— I'm not sure I'm a strong enough swimmer—"

"I'll get him," the blond man said, and stripped off his sweat shirt as he ran into the water. Foam sprayed around him in two white wings, and a moment later he dived through a five-foot wave with a clean, precise cut.

"Somebody's coming, Greg!" she shouted to the boy. "Somebody's coming!"

The man's strokes were strong and steady. He reached the boy in an amazingly short time, and looped a muscled brown arm around him. The swells obscured Terri's view, she could only catch glimpses of what was happening. But she was sure they were coming closer to shore, coming right through the riptide as if it weren't there.

"Matt, go find somebody to help. A doctor or a lifeguard. *Somebody!*" The boy nodded and raced down the beach, shouting to anyone who would listen. The blond man was just coming to shore when he returned with a small crowd of people at his back.

The blond man had Greg over his shoulder in a fireman's carry. He was unconscious, or nearly so, and for one horrible instant Terri was sure he had stopped breathing. "Is he all right?" she cried as he brought the boy toward her. "Is he alive?"

The man didn't answer her. He was concentrating on Greg as he laid the boy on the dry land.

"The paramedics are on their way," a woman from the crowd said, and the blond man nodded.

"Wow, you saved him. You *saved* him!" Matt was jumping up and down with excitement.

The blond man didn't answer. A moment later a white jeep with knobby tires roared down the hard wet sand and two lifeguards jumped out. The crowd moved back as they bent over the boy and began mouth-to-mouth resuscitation.

"Oh God, oh *God*, he can't be hurt. He can't, he just *can't!*" Terri was trying desperately not to cry—she didn't want to scare Matt. But what would she tell Amy and her mother? What would Kathy say? How would she *ever* tell Kathy?

A strong hand touched her on the shoulder.

"Don't worry. He'll be all right."

It was the blond man, still soaked from his swim but dressed in his gray sweat shirt again.

"Are you sure?"

He smiled. "I'm positive," he said.

Terri was relieved. She didn't know why, exactly—the man was a total stranger, and obviously not a doctor or a paramedic. But she knew he was right, somehow. Everything would be okay. "I . . . I don't know how to thank you," she said, still fighting tears. "I'm supposed to be taking care of the boys, and if anything happened to them, I—I—"

"No thanks are necessary."

"Oh, but they are. They— I mean, I—I don't even know your name." She glanced nervously at Greg as the two lifeguards worked on him. How was he? Was he breathing on his own?

"My name is Michael," the man said softly.

Greg coughed and spit up half a pint of seawater. Terri turned and cried out his name and fell on her knees at his side.

The lifeguard straightened up and the crowd at his back applauded.

"Oh, come on," he said, blushing like a fourteen-year-old.

Terri looked up and said, "Thank you. Thank you."

He nodded. "He'll be fine now. Just swallowed a little too much seawater."

The other lifeguard was standing and looking out to sea. "Weird place for a riptide," he said, more to himself than his partner. "Never had any trouble out this way before."

Greg coughed again and sat up, wiping water and sand from his eyes. "Boy," he said weakly. "Boy, oh *boy*."

Terri put her arms around him and wouldn't let go.

The first lifeguard said, "Exactly what happened, anyway?" and Terri managed to stand up and tell him what she could about the riptide, and Greg, and the blond man who had saved him.

She turned to introduce the man to the lifeguards . . . but he wasn't standing behind her anymore. She turned again and looked at the crowd, but he wasn't there, either.

The blond man wasn't anywhere.

"He was here just a second ago," she said, puzzled. She shaded her eyes and looked up and down the beach, but he was nowhere in sight. "I really wanted you to meet him."

The lifeguard shrugged. "Guess he's shy," he

said. "Still, you were lucky he happened to be around when you needed him."

"Yes, we were," she said slowly. "Very lucky." Some vague thought—something about the emptiness of the beach—nagged at her for a moment. Then Greg stood up and said very weakly, "Can we go home now?" and the crowd laughed and helped them to the car.

# 23

There was a crack in the ceiling.

George was lying on his back, too exhausted to sleep, staring at the dimly lit walls of his new bedroom. The only illumination came from a small reading lamp to his left. To his right, Kathy lay curled in a ball, snoring very softly.

A crack in the ceiling. In a brand-new house. A lot of places had them; it probably didn't mean a damn thing. But in that crack, in that unexpected flaw that had no right to be there, he saw a pathetic encapsulation of his recent life.

He and Kathy had returned from Holland with high spirits and higher hopes. A beautiful house in Rancho Sante Fe was as good as theirs. They simply had to sign the loan papers that were supposed to be waiting for them, and the deed would be safely in hand. But in their absence, for reasons that were never made clear, the bank had decided to refuse their loan. No money, no house. No house . . . back to Tierra-santa.

An unexpected flaw in his life that had no right to be there. One of so many.

The furniture suppliers had screamed at the canceled orders. The carpeting people and the drapes manufacturers had kept their deposits. For a while, George was as low as he thought he could be, until they found another house that was almost as nice as the one they had lost. It was in La Costa, a modest and attractive district even farther from the city of San Diego.

"We lucked out finding this one," George said when they signed the lease with an option to buy. He remembered that now, as he stared at the spider-web crack over his head and winced at the pounding between his temples. We were lucky, yes. That's what we thought at the time. A split-level condominium on a hill that over-looked the famous La Costa Country Club; a premium view at discount prices; what more could they ask for?

Then Amy had been hurt—not seriously, but enough to throw a bad scare into them. And that jolt of fear and surprise seemed to burst open some badly repaired dam that had held back misfortune.

It all began again. The nightmares. The un-bearable cold. The queasiness. He was smoking two packs a day and drinking endless amounts of coffee, and his temper grew so short that he found himself snapping at everyone. Everything. And always, always there were the headaches.

Three, four, even five times a day, they pierced and jolted and pounded in his head, so often he almost forgot how to think.

He was cracking up. The moment George thought it, he smiled grimly. Cracking up. Crack in the ceiling. Wisecracking. Going crackers. Crack in the ceiling. . . .

He slept, but not without dreams.

George was floating—at least, it felt like floating. There was no weight in him at all, just a strange and delightful lightness, a mobility and grace that he had never experienced before.

He turned in the . . . air? . . . to explore the sensation, and abruptly, incredibly, in the single blink of an eye, it was dark. The instant it happened, he couldn't remember if it had ever really been light to begin with. Light didn't enter into it; there had been *something*, and now there was *not-something*. That was what he . . . saw? . . . now. Not darkness, or blackness, or even blindness. It was an absence of color, a negation of everything.

He tried to reach out, to explore it, and quite suddenly the weightlessness was a problem. The familiar signals that went from head to arm to hand seemed to be missing. There was no sensation of touch, no feedback pressure to tell him where he was, what he was feeling. No temperature. No sound. No anything.

I'm not in my body, he realized. I am away from it, somehow. Separated.

At the moment of realization, a vast, directionless voice, like simultaneous thunder from twin horizons, roared around him.

*"You are not where you're supposed to be,"* it said.

He looked into the darkness, but there was nothing to see. He was an edgeless patch of gray in an indistinguishable ocean of sameness. If it was a voice he heard, he was hearing it without ears.

"What do you mean, I'm not where I'm supposed to be?" He could hear the words in his mind, but he wondered if anyone—or any-*thing*—else could.

*"You are not where you're supposed to be,"* the voice told him again.

He was getting angry now. He wanted his body back. He missed the feelings, the weight, the sense of being somewhere. "Where am I supposed to be?" he said. "How do I get there?"

*"You are not where you're supposed to be,"* the voice insisted, its intonation unchanged.

Until that moment, the nonspace in which George floated was as devoid of emotion as it was lightless. Then, as the voice thundered a third time, he flinched at the sudden perception of fear—fear as a physical object, coursing through him like the crack of a whip.

*"You are not where—"*

"Who are you?" he shouted. "What am I doing here?"

It's a dream, he told himself. Another nightmare, that's all. Different from the others, but still all in my head. I'll wake up any second now.

But he didn't wake. He still floated in the non-place while the fear rippled over him in waves. It grew in intensity with each crack of the whip.

Run, he ordered, but there were no legs to run with. Move, he demanded, but he was not in a place to move from—he was not in a place at all.

Help will come, he told himself, trying to find some fragment of his earlier calm. It always has before; it's sure to come.

A figure in white appeared before him, slipping into the nothingness like an actor slipping through a slit in a dull black curtain. The solidity dazzled him. It took a moment for the alien qualities of weight and movement to resolve themselves into something he could recognize.

It was Kathy, dressed in white. She wandered in the darkness, walking on nothing, blind and desolate, moving back and forth with her arms outstretched.

"Where's my George?" she said.

"I'm here, Kathy," he called, and relief surged through him.

She didn't respond. She simply turned again, turned away from him, repeating, "Where's my George?"

"I'm here, Kathy! Here!"

She was growing smaller, dimmer. She was moving away from him, and he couldn't follow. Wandering, deaf, arms outstretched and plaintively crying: "Where's my George?"

"Kathy! Kathy!"

Gone.

"What am I doing here?" he cried, angry and frightened by the disappearance of his wife. I'll never get out on my own. I'm trapped out of my body, lost in—in nothing. Where are these beings who are supposed to be helping us?

Nobody cares. Nothing matters. I'll float here

forever, and no one will miss me. To hell with it. To hell with them all.

"Why won't you help me?" He tried to make it a shout. He strained to make a sound, even to hear a sound. "You know that I need you! Why aren't you here? *Now?*"

*"You are not where you're supposed to be,"* the voice reminded him. It was louder now. Power thundered in every syllable.

Some fragment of the grayness was curdling around him. Waves of fear buffeted him, vibrations beyond feeling touched and touched again.

Something's out there, he realized. Something's coming to get me.

"Come on, come on, I know you can hear me! You've helped me before, you've protected me all along. I need you, I need you!

"Where the hell is my protection?

"Why won't you help me?"

A spark of awareness flickered in his mind. Some small and distant part of him awoke and called for attention. It wavered, then brightened. It spoke to him: *You haven't asked.*

George was indignant at his own thought. Of course I've asked, he told himself. I've been asking since I first came to this place.

No, you haven't. You've complained, you've demanded, you've wondered and whined. But *you haven't asked.*

The thing out of nothingness was still there, stalking him. He could feel it coming closer, reaching toward him. He could feel the insubstantial vibration of pure power roaring around him.

The darkness has seeped inside, he told himself. You've become infected with the true arrogance of evil. You expect, you demand, you question, you grow angry at your disappointment. But still, you do not ask.

"But it's coming to get me! It's coming now!"

*You know what to do.*

George tried to calm himself, to clear his mind. It wasn't easy. The malevolence was all around him now, unencumbered by physical laws.

"Why hasn't anyone helped me? Why—"

No! He pushed the frustration and fear aside. Think of Saint Michael, he told himself. Mancusso had called him the Protector. He was the patron saint of those who battle evil. And when he had purchased the St. Michael's medals for his sons to wear, the woman at the religious supply shop had given him a plastic card with the archangel's prayer on it. A prayer, an entreaty.

To hell with it, he thought bitterly. It's nonsense, all of it. No one cares what I do, what I think. It—

*Just ask.*

Desperate, panicking, terrified to the core, George shut out the storm of evil that thrashed just beyond him. He began the prayer of St. Michael.

"Be our protection against the wickedness and snares of the devil."

Now, he thought, shuddering at the forces that touched him. Please, now.

"May God rebuke him, we humbly pray. . . ."

He could feel something. Feel it, with the tips of his fingers: the cool, smooth surface of a wall.

"And do thou, O Prince of the Heavenly Host, by the power of God, thrust into hell Satan and all evil spirits. . . ."

There was light now—physical light, real light, flowing from the reading lamp at his bedside.

"All evil spirits who wander through the world for the ruin of souls."

Weight was back. Warmth had returned. The sensation of *being* flowed through him again.

The ruin of souls, he thought again. Amen. Amen.

There was a crack in the ceiling. He could see it again, thin as a pencil line on fine white paper, shadowed in the glow of the reading lamp. He could see it, he could feel the bed, he could hear the slow and steady breathing of his wife beside him.

A dream? he wondered. A nightmare, a hallucination? Or a vision?

He turned to look at Kathy and touched her on the shoulder, joyful at the warmth, the feeling that came from her. He kissed her lightly on the cheek and she moved in her sleep. A smile crossed her face as she dreamed; a dream, he prayed, that was less horrendous than his own.

She had tried to help him, even in his nightmare. It was as if the bond they had forged from love and devotion—what a trite and powerful phrase, "love and devotion"—was far too strong to be broken now.

He put his head on the pillow and closed his eyes. She was part of it, yes, and the power of light that had balanced the blackness of Amityville—that was part of it, too.

He wouldn't take it for granted again. He

would watch for the arrogance of evil when it rose another time, and if the blackness came again, if the fear returned and threatened him as it has so many times before, he would know what to do.

He would ask.

He said a short prayer of thanks and drifted into a peaceful, dreamless sleep.

# 24

"George, she's getting worse."

George adjusted his rearview mirror to capture the image of his stepdaughter. He found her huddled in her mother's arms, whimpering and breathing far too rapidly. She was the color of old oatmeal.

"I think we should go back."

He looked at her again and said, "Kath, we've got appointments all over town today. There's that lie detector thing for the studio, and 'The Merv Griffin Show'—"

"She was fine at home," Kathy said a little petulantly. "It wasn't until we got on the freeway to Los Angeles that she started to feel bad." She didn't know quite what to say about Amy's sudden illness. There was no fever and no chills; her lungs were clear and her heartbeat was steady. But she was complaining bitterly about how awful she felt.

"Mommy," she said, burying her head in her mother's lap. "Mommy, I'm sick."

Kathy sighed and looked at George through the rearview mirror. "Maybe she just needs some sleep. Can't we at least go back and get the recreational vehicle?"

George didn't say a word. He simply shifted to the right lane and took the next offramp. A few minutes later they were heading south toward La Costa again.

"We're going to be late," he said as he reversed directions.

Kathy didn't say anything.

Chris Gugas stopped at the corner of Hollywood and Vine and looked at himself in the window of the Howard Johnson's. He could see the dim reflection of the city street behind him—the rush of cars, the strange amalgam of street people, businessmen, hookers, and bookworms that roamed the infamous intersection.

It might have been the crossroads of the world once, long ago. Now it seemed to get a little dirtier, a little more tired and sad, every time he saw it.

And Chris Gugas saw it every day. The offices of his security company were only steps from Hollywood and Vine, and passing by the HoJo's to check his suit and tie had become a daily ritual.

He looked fine. He smoothed his dark hair back, straightened his colorful tie, bought a copy of the Los Angeles *Times* from a vending machine and read the headlines as he followed the familiar route to the Taft Building.

Chris Gugas had been a polygraph expert for thirty years, using the machine and his own insight to separate truth from fiction in over twenty thousand cases. This afternoon, one of those cases would change his life.

As he took the elevator to the fourth floor, he pulled a letter from the breast pocket of his suit coat. It was from a press agent with a major Hollywood studio, requesting his help once again, as they had so often in the past. This time, however, it was a little different. They were about to release a new movie based on *The Amityville Horror*, and they were nervous. They wanted additional proof—the support of a respected polygraph expert—to use in a major release to the wire services. Naturally, his name had come up.

Just as he stepped off the elevator, he saw Mike Brown, a fellow polygraphist, opening the door to his own office. He thwacked him lightly on the shoulder with the folded studio correspondence and said, "Are you ready for today?"

Mike turned and looked at him blankly, then brightened. "Oh, the Lutzes. I assume you still want me to take one of them?"

He nodded. "We don't want any talk about payoffs to the guys with the lie detector," he said, dripping sarcasm. He didn't like that term at all. It reminded him of the suspicions and superstitions that still plagued the polygraph, even fifty years after its invention. "Anyway," he said, shrugging, "two heads are better than one."

Mike nodded and said, "I'll take the wife, if you want. Kathy Lutz."

"Sounds good to me."

Mike started to go into his office, and Chris was turning away when his friend stopped him.

"Chris, do you believe in all this stuff?"

Gugas thought about it for a moment. "Well, I've done these kinds of things before, you know. People in haunted houses, that is."

Mike was surprised. "You have?"

Chris smiled. He was fifty-five years old and one of the most experienced and respected men in his field. He had polygraphed Robert Vesco when he was accused of embezzling 224 million dollars, and Terry Moore, who claimed to be the wife of Howard Hughes, and even James Earl Ray, when he was charged with the murder of Martin Luther King. And still, his younger associate was surprised.

"Yes, quite a few times, actually."

"And you believe them?"

He shrugged. "The people I interviewed were telling the truth. That much I know for certain."

Mike Brown took the keys out of his door and stared at them intently, as if they could give him some clue to the mystery. "Yeah," he said, "but this one's weird."

Chris nodded. That it was. That it was.


"Look, Dad! It's the house! *Our* house!"

George came within a heartbeat of slamming on the brakes. High above them, towering over the recreational vehicle from its perch on the side of a Los Angeles office building, a billboard was glaring. Three bloodred words were emblazoned on the sign in letters more than three feet high: THE AMITYVILLE HORROR. Behind the letters, beyond them, was a likeness of the house in Amityville, New York.

It felt as if someone had dumped a bucket of ice water over his head. Even here, even driving through the crowded streets of Hollywood, he couldn't escape that awful place.

"Damn it," he said. For a moment, he was sorry that the movie had ever been made. He wasn't looking forward to its premiere in the next few weeks, either. If only they had let him on the set, so he could have seen what had been shot, and how. It seemed ridiculous to pay him a fee as a technical advisor, and then bar him from the set.

He stepped on the accelerator and looked for the turn that would take them to the baby-sitter's house. Never mind, he told himself. There would be plenty of time to worry about the movie later. Plenty of time.


Chris Gugas greeted his client at the door of his office. The blue suitcoat had been exchanged in favor of a lab coat; his tie was loosened and he wore an easy, sincere smile.

Rule Number One of a polygraph examination: make your subject as comfortable as possible.

George looked a little wary of the short, rather thickly built man with the receding hairline and the ample nose. He had not wanted to give Kathy over to the younger polygraphist either. He was liking this whole idea less and less.

Chris showed him to a seat, and plopped himself down in his own leather chair behind the desk. He saw George's eyes move nervously past the wall-to-wall bookshelf, his complete set of California Laws of Jurisprudence below the windows, the plaques and certificates decorating the walls, and finally come to rest on the mysterious-looking mass of wires and dials set in a metal tabletop at one side of the room. This man would be difficult to put at ease, he knew.

"Why did you split us up?" George wanted to know.

Chris explained his reasons. He wanted the test to be as accurate and indisputable as possible, and this was one of the ways he could make sure of that.

George glanced at the machine again. "Look, do these things actually work? I mean, can't a lot of people fool lie detectors these days?"

Chris smiled. The same old question. "George, I've been doing this for better than thirty years, and no one I've ever interviewed has ever fooled the polygraph."

"Never?"

He took out the standard preexamination test and showed it to George. "First," he said, "we give them this form to fill out. It has questions like, 'Have you taken any drugs today?' 'Have you undergone hypnosis?' 'Are you in any physical discomfort that might interfere with the results?' Questions like that. You'd be surprised at how many people never get past this to begin with.

"Then we give them the test three times. Once, so the subject can just get the feel of it, and a few more times to make sure that the reactions are consistent. Believe me, even the real hard cases I've had in here can't keep lying and get away with it time after time."

George wasn't convinced. "Well, can't you make it look like they're lying? I mean, you're the one that decides. You could make the reactions come out wrong, somehow."

He shook his head *no*. "For one thing, we always tape-record the session, so I can't change the order of the questions on my report, and make it look like you were lying when you were telling the truth. For another, I'll go over all the questions with you before we begin, so you'll know exactly what to expect. I'll even ask them in the same order and in the same way each time. Fair enough?"

George didn't answer. He glanced at the clock on Chris's desk. "How long is this going to take?"

"About three hours, if all goes well."

George had plenty of other questions, too, and when Chris had answered them all, they went over the list of questions Chris planned to ask George during the test. Chris had put the list together after a careful reading of *The Amityville Horror*. When they completed the list, he gave George a copy of the preexamination test to fill out. "You see?" he said when George had finished filling out the test. "No surprises. I won't change a word or even change my inflection when I ask you the questions. I'll simply intersperse them with normal, everyday queries —you know, about the weather, what you had for breakfast, what your name is, et cetera—so I can monitor your reactions at rest."

George couldn't help glancing at the machine

again. "Okay," he said. There was still an element of hesitation in his voice and his facial expression—even in the way he sat in his chair. Chris had been trained to watch for evidence of just such tension. He figured he just about had this one licked.

"Would you like to look at the machine?"

George shrugged. "Sure," he said, trying to sound casual. Still, he approached the polygraph with caution.

The polygraph was a thick silver plate with a series of dials and gauges set into a blond wood table. On one side of it was a small swivel chair where Gugas sat; on the other side was a larger, more comfortable black leather armchair with a variety of attachments hanging from it, sitting parallel rather than perpendicular to the machine itself. A wide paper roll appeared from a slit near the center of the polygraph and ran off the desk to Gugas's left. When the machine was running, the subject would be unable to see the paper tape and the marks it held.

Carefully, casually, he explained where the different sensors would go, and what they would measure. First there were two large corrugated rubber tubes. "One will go around your body at chest level—right about this high," he said, indicating the level of his heart. "The other goes lower, here on your stomach. They measure your respiration. Then there's this," he said, holding up an inflatable cuff with velcro along one edge, "which measures your blood pressure. It goes on your bicep, just like the one at the doctor's office. And finally there are these." He pointed to two small white clips that trailed thick wires of their own. "These go on your first and third fingers. They measure your galvanic skin response—that is, how well the surface of your skin is conducting electricity. We use all three to determine your physical state during the test."

George decided he was just about as relaxed as he was going to get. He took a deep breath and said, "Okay, let's do it."

It took five minutes to wire him up to the machine. As Gugas worked, he told George how often he'd done it in the past. He even mentioned some of his more unusual and important cases. But George was thinking about Kathy.

Was she going through the same ritual down the hall, with the other polygraphist—what was his name? Was she as nervous as he was? What would happen if the results of their two tests didn't match up?

"All right," Chris Gugas said as he took his seat behind the machine and set the paper tape rolling. "Let's run through the questions once."

It didn't take long—twenty minutes at best. Despite Gugas's assurances, George still half expected to feel tiny electric shocks or see blinking red lights—something to indicate what was happening. But the machine simply hummed very quietly and spit out a long, steady stream of paper with marks he couldn't see while he was answering the questions. Gugas himself was gentle and impartial. The questions came out in a comforting monotone. He wasn't trying to prove a thing.

After the first test, Chris came around the desk and said, "Let's try a little test." He took a handful of coins from his pocket and showed them to George. "See?" he said. "A whole assortment. Pennies, quarters—a couple of every kind." He put the coins in the pocket of his jacket and turned away. "Now I want you to put your hand into my pocket and steal one of the coins."

"Steal it?"

"Right. Just take any one of them and hold it in your hand so I can't see it."

George hesitated for a moment. He felt a little like the magician's assistant in a sideshow, but eventually he did as he was told. Nothing up my sleeve, he thought. Pick a card, any card.

When he had the coin out of sight, Chris said, "Fine," and walked back to his place on the far side of the polygraph. "Now, we're going to do a special run here, and I want you to lie."

"To lie?" George was beginning to feel like Little Sir Echo; this was all so new to him.

"That's right. Answer 'no' to every question I ask, whether that's an accurate answer or not."

George shrugged. "Okay."

Gugas cleared his throat, and the paper tape began to roll again. "Did you steal a penny?" he asked.

"No."

"Did you steal a nickel?"

"No."

"Did you steal a dime?"

"No."

"Did you steal a quarter?"

"No."

"Did you steal a half-dollar?"

"No."

There was a pause while Gugas looked over the tape. Usually, he ran a second quick test like this, but in this case there was no reason. He looked up and smiled and said, "You took the dime."

George was astonished. He held up his hand with the palm open and showed Chris the coin he had taken.

A nice, shiny new dime.

"That's amazing," he said.

"Nothing to it. It's just a standard test we do to see how susceptible you are to the polygraph. It gives us a sort of baseline from which to operate."

George nodded. "You want to do the other questions again?" He was almost eager to see the results now.

Chris smiled to himself. It often happened this way. Once the subjects got past their first suspicions about the lie detector, they were more than just cooperative—they were absolute fans.

"All right. We'll probably do it two or three times more, actually, to get a whole series of responses."

George settled himself in the chair. "Whenever you're ready," he said.

Chris nodded and looked at his reference sheet. "I'll ask you the same questions in the same order, George. You know the system works now. The truth will come out."

The results of the second test duplicated those of the first, with even greater certainty. George was as close to a perfect subject for polygraph as anyone Chris had ever recorded. There was no doubt in his mind that the man was telling the truth.

And frankly, he thought, that scares me to death. This wasn't a case of robbery or embezzlement, or even rape or murder. This man was talking about something far worse—about the invasion of the comfortable, modern-day world by forces beyond comprehension.

Chris Gugas didn't like it. He didn't like it at all.

"Okay, George," he said, "let's do it one last time for good measure. We don't want anybody saying we didn't do a thorough job, do we?"

"Sure don't," George agreed. "Just give me the questions."

Gugas wiped a drop of sweat from his high forehead and looked at it in confusion. He really was nervous. Much more so than usual. He shook the strange feeling away and looked back at his reference sheet.

"During your twenty-eight days in Amityville," he said in his practiced, professional monotone, "did you experience unexplained flies and disturbing odors on several occasions?"

"Yes," George answered truthfully.

"At the Amityville house, did you hear what sounded like a marching band tuning up in the middle of the night?"

"Yes," George answered truthfully.

"When you fled your Amityville house, were you in fear for your life and the well-being of your family?"

"Yes," George answered truthfully.

"Are the details you gave me of your frightening experiences at the Amityville house true?"

"Yes," George answered truthfully.

"And after leaving Amityville, did Kathy levitate at your mother-in-law's house?"

"Yes," George answered truthfully.

For once in his long career, Chris Gugas was thankful for the fifteen-second pause he had to take between questions. Normally, it was only to allow the various body functions to return to normal, but this time it was his own heart that was racing, his own respiration that was accelerated. He needed the fifteen seconds just to keep his voice steady.

There was something very strange happening here. Very strange.

He went on, questioning George in greater detail, interjecting everyday questions—"Did you have breakfast this morning?" "Is your name George Lutz?"—whenever his subject's readings became agitated or unclear. But he knew from the beginning that the readings were accurate.

George Lutz was telling the truth. It had all happened just as he had said—as he had been saying all along.

"So what did he ask you?"

George and Kathy were waiting backstage at the Hollywood Palace, where "The Merv Griffin Show" was being taped. Their sessions had taken longer than they had planned, and in the mad dash to make it across Hollywood on time, they simply hadn't had the time to talk about the results.

"Me?" Kathy said. "Oh, they asked if I'd actually seen myself as an old woman at the house . . . whether some invisible being had embraced me there. Things like that."

"Did you pass?"

She smiled shyly. "I guess so. Mike Brown certainly looked shaken up by the time I was finished."

"So did Chris Gugas."

One of the stage managers rushed by and tapped them on the shoulder. "He's introducing you now," he whispered. "Follow me."

They trotted along the back of the sets toward the entrance to the stage. "Remember, babe, we're not supposed to mention the tests."

"I know. That's the deal with the wire services, right?"

"Right. The studio's supposed to release the results when the movie premieres."

"Okay, but—"

They heard a familiar voice from the far side of the set. "And now, ladies and gentlemen, please welcome George and Kathy Lutz."

"We'll talk about it later," George said, and they walked into the bright lights onstage.

That evening, Chris Gugas talked about the session with his wife. He had some vague hope that sharing his anxiety would somehow dissipate it, but it didn't work that way. He didn't sleep at all that night.

The next evening, he awoke at 3:15 A.M. No matter how hard he tried, he couldn't get back to sleep.

The next night, he did the same.

And the night after that.

Finally, a full week after his session with George Lutz, he called Mike Brown into his office. Their schedules had been offset in the last few days, and except for a quick conference together on the day they had interviewed the Lutzes, he hadn't seen his young friend at all.

Mike looked as bad as Chris felt. There were bags under his eyes and new lines of age and weariness in his face.

"Mike, has anything... unusual been happening with you in the last few days?"

Mike snorted. "'Unusual'? Heck, no. Unless you call losing things and forgetting important appointments and snapping at my wife like a wild man 'unusual.'"

Chris felt a cold spot grow in the middle of his stomach. He had been doing the same thing.

Mike rubbed his eyes with the heel of one hand. "I'm probably just tired," he sighed. "For some reason, I'm just not sleeping well. Every night for a week now, I've been waking up at three in the morning, for no reason at all."

"Three in the morning?"

Mike looked up at the strange sound in Chris's voice. "Yeah. Why?"

Chris told him what had been happening to him. Halfway through the story, his hand stole inside his lab coat and across the vest underneath, searching for something.

"I've been reading more of the Bible," Chris said, trying not to sound embarrassed by the admission. It wasn't anything to be ashamed of, he thought. He should have been doing it anyway. "Mike, there are a lot of things in there—and out in the world—that we just don't understand. A lot of questions that only God knows the answer to."

Mike nodded. He was beginning to agree with his old friend, even if he didn't like what conclusions the agreement led to.

351

"I even . . ." Chris frowned and looked down at his vest. "I've even started wearing a . . . a crucifix." He opened the lab coat wide and reached under his vest.

"It's gone," he said, sounding a little stunned.

"What, the crucifix?"

Chris nodded. "I had it on this morning. I had it on when I came in here. I remember seeing it when I put on the lab coat. It's given me a lot of comfort, Mike. I know that sounds strange, but—"

"Chris, nothing sounds strange to me these days."

Chris was more upset by the disappearance of the cross than he wanted to admit. "Where did it go?" he asked. "Where could it have gone?"

Mike stood up. "I'll help you look for it," he said. For some reason, he was just as anxious to locate the crucifix as Chris was.

They looked for most of the day, and during every spare moment in the days that followed.

They never found the crucifix. And Chris Gugas never stopped reading his Bible, or stopped believing in the strange and inexplicable things his polygraph had told him the day that George Lutz came to call.

## 25

"TWA's Flight Five-Fourteen has just arrived from Los Angeles, California. Those wishing to meet arriving passengers, please go to Gate Six. . . ."

Janie Carlton covered one ear with her hand, trying to block out the noise and commotion of Heathrow Airport. That was the flight she had to meet, but she still had a few minutes while the passengers cleared Customs, and she hadn't quite finished her call to her office.

"To be perfectly honest, Bobby, I *was* surprised. Weren't you? I mean, everybody wants to interview them. And just because they *say* they lived in a haunted house for a month."

She listened, smiling lightly, as her co-worker reminded her once again that this was her job.

A job she freely chose to do—and that she did well, he added nicely.

"I know. I know." She couldn't help smiling again. She and Bobby went through this ritual regularly. "And, you know me. I'll do my usual fabulous job of hype. But, if anyone wants my opinion—which nobody seems to, mind you—I think the entire thing is a scheme somebody dreamed up to make money."

Bobby began to go into his standard humorous oratory explaining how it didn't make any difference one way or the other, until, as usual, Janie cut him off.

"I've got to go, professor," she said, with their normal amount of blatant sarcasm. "Keep up your normal hard-working routine. I'll ring you later."

Janie hung up the phone and adjusted her outfit. She was a tall, thin woman who prided herself on her taste in clothes, and all in all, she very much liked her job as press officer for one of the largest book publishers in Europe. She had been called on to handle hundreds of authors and celebrities from all over the world, and it was a very interesting adventure—most of the time.

But there are days, she thought, when I have my doubts.

She patted her hair and hurried across the terminal to Gate Six, doing her best to remember the faces of the couple she was scheduled to meet. She'd seen pictures of them back at the office; they shouldn't be all that difficult to recognize.

She got her first glimpse of them as they

entered the green NOTHING TO DECLARE Customs area. The Customs official waved them through and as they wheeled their luggage carrier forward, she finally approached them.

"Mr. and Mrs. Lutz? George and Kathy? I'm Janie Carlton, with Pan. Welcome to England!"

The Lutzes smiled wanly and said hello, but Janie was a bit put off right at the outset by their cool response. Perhaps I'm more accustomed to the braggadocio of real authors, she conceded, but they needn't be quite so snooty.

It took a surprisingly short time to gather their luggage and haul it to the minicab she had waiting. Soon they had weaved through the mad tangle of automobiles that surrounded the airport terminal, swept under a large overpass, and found their way to the M4 Motorway.

As they rode through the countryside, Janie told them about the tour she had managed to put together. "Well," she said, "the big news is your appearance on 'The BBC Tonight.' It's the most highly regarded chat-show in Great Britain, you know, and it's not all that simple to get guests on." She was rather proud of it, actually. "You'll be appearing there two nights from now, and that alone should get things rolling. You know, I've only managed to get one other guest on the program in all the years I've been with Pan, and *he* was a convicted murderer."

She saw Kathy Lutz blanch, and felt a little wicked for saying it the way she had. "Oh, not to worry, he was innocent—wrongly convicted, you know."

Kathy didn't seem to notice. She was whispering something to her husband.

355

Janie waited for the whispering to stop, then began to list some of the other highlights of the tour—the autograph parties, the interviews on "BBC Radio 4," appearances on the television in Leeds and Manchester both, with some local monsignors in those areas. "I must say, I was rather surprised at their ready acceptance. I thought a monsignor would be a bit reluctant to get involved in all the controversy."

George Lutz allowed that he was sure it would work out fine, and went back to looking out the window of the mini at the rolling hills and country houses. A few minutes later, the rural landscape gave way to the suburbs of London, then to the council houses that ran in long rows on both sides of the streets.

They hit a patch of heavy traffic, and Kathy pointed ahead of them. "What's that up there?" she asked.

Janie smiled. "Haven't you those in the States? That's a roundabout. A sort of circular crossroad for getting you wherever it is you want to be going."

The lemon yellow mini zipped into the stream of traffic that turned in a narrow circle on a grassy area rimmed with concrete. Janie smiled at the Americans as they watched the cars enter the roundabout on all sides, and peel off at the entrance they required like fighter planes leaving a wing formation. Kathy Lutz even smiled at the hodgepodge. It was a pretty smile, Janie decided, if all too rare. George sat staring vaguely out the window as if he'd seen it all before.

Janie was more than a little relieved when they reached Park Lane, near Hyde Park. The cab came to a halt at the entrance of the London Hilton, and an eminently bored doorman helped them with the luggage.

Less than an hour later, the Lutzes were safely ensconced in their suite. "Sleep well," she told them as she handed over carefully typed copies of their itinerary. "We'll be getting an early start tomorrow." She smiled as sweetly as she knew how. "Though I don't doubt you've been through all this rigmarole plenty of times before, eh?" They nodded and George said yes, they had, and thanks for the help, and Janie was ushered summarily to the door.

So much for the fine effects of British hospitality, she thought, and bade them good-night. She felt a little put out as she made her way back to the lobby.

Well, perhaps they were simply tired. It was a long trip from America to England—she'd done it herself. They would probably be good as new, and a bit more friendly, in the morning.

Ten hours later, Janie Carlton was back in the lobby of the London Hilton, and feeling absolutely awful. First her car had refused to start—just *refused*, with no opportunity for debate and no alternative offered. Then she had been caught in the rain the only time in the year when she hadn't an umbrella with her—left in the crippled car, of course—and now, in treading across the threshold of the Hilton, a heel had snapped off her finest pair of shoes.

She thumped down the hall to the Lutzes' door, fuming at herself. On top of everything else, she was half an hour late, and that was far from the best impression to make when it came to difficult clients. But when she reached their door, she forced herself to straighten up and calm down. She made the lines of her face smooth out, and patted her hair back into place.

All is well, she told herself as she tapped on the door. All is well.

Kathy answered the door in her bathrobe.

"George isn't feeling too well this morning," she said without a hello. "We're running late."

No apology. No excuses. Not even an offer of a cup of tea. She was made to wait in the sitting room for a very long time, while the Lutzes fiddled and whispered in their room.

All this whispering, Janie thought, feeling her temper rise again. What the devil is so secret to be whispering so?

After her tenth glance at the clock she strode to their closed bedroom door and knocked firmly. "I do hope everything's going well," she said, doing her best to sound cheerful despite it all. "We really must be going."

The door opened and the Lutzes came out, looking ready for the day, if a little sullen.

"Where to first?" George said desultorily, as if he were off on a quick trip to the gallows rather than a radio station. She reminded them of the schedule for the morning—or what was left of it—and George shrugged. "Let's get it over with," he said.

She pressed her lips together very tightly and led the way to the car, thinking, marvelous, bloody marvelous. This is going to be an absolute joy, I can see.

* * *

Two days later, by the evening of their appearance on "The BBC Tonight," Janie's affection for the Lutzes had grown not at all. They were terribly secretive, extremely quiet people, and though she had come to appreciate the strain under which they were operating, it certainly didn't make it easy for her. Not in the least.

But Janie put on her best face when they entered the studio's green room, where they were to wait for their segment of the program to be taped. This, after all, was the big time, as the Americans would say, and something of a feather in her cap.

The assistant producer who had been charged with keeping them entertained got them cups of coffee or tea and introduced the Lutzes to a fellow guest on the evening's show: Dr. Sarah Whitehouse, a noted psychologist and an expert on parapsychology.

Dr. Whitehouse was a spare, thin-faced woman with brilliant white hair and a winning smile. "So nice to meet you," she said to the Lutzes, absolutely beaming, and they, in turn, were unaccountably warm to her as well. "Of course," the psychologist said, "I've heard a great deal of your story, you know."

"Dr. Whitehouse is something of a celebrity in Great Britain," Janie volunteered. "I believe you've been on 'Tonight' quite a few times?"

"Oh, yes, quite a few, I suppose." She flashed her winning smile again.

"Of course," Janie said, "you Americans have a famous Whitehouse of your own." The Lutzes looked at her blankly, and she said, "The White House. Where the President lives."

George gave her a weak, barely perceptible smirk, and Kathy continued to look blank. Janie felt roughly ten inches tall.

Why me? she thought miserably, and sat back while the Lutzes and Dr. Whitehouse had a jolly little conversation without her. George was polite but distant. Always, Janie thought, he seems to be somewhere else.

Ten minutes later, the assistant producer came back and led them down a narrow hall and into the backstage shadows. A raucous buzzer sounded over their heads, and a voice burred from a loudspeaker: "All right, boys and girls. Let's take one!"

They were led onstage and introduced to their host. He greeted Dr. Whitehouse with particular warmth, and as soon as Kathy and George were seated, Janie was led briskly out of the light and into a small observation area behind the cameras.

One of the technicians sauntered over just as the theme music began and looked her up and down. "'Oo you wif?" he asked.

Janie looked at him with great disappointment. This was exactly what she didn't need at the moment. "Pan," she said shortly.

"Peter? Fly a couple'a quick ones 'round the room."

She sighed heavily and turned her attention to the show. She'd already missed the introductions.

"So tell me, Dr. Whitehouse," the host was saying. "You've had the opportunity to read the book now. What have you to say?"

360

The psychologist's beatific smile had disappeared backstage. In its place, she wore a stern, rather nasty look in the eyes, grouped around a severe frown. "It's rubbish," she said. "Absolute rubbish."

Janie watched George open his mouth in astonishment. Dr. Whitehouse continued without pause.

"I am particularly offended by this so-called 'priest' of theirs. This Father Mancusso, I believe?"

George tried to jump in. "Yes, he—"

"A complete fabrication," she declared. "No man of the cloth, here or abroad, would act in any way remotely similar to this—this figment. Frankly, the creation of such an obviously fictional character in the midst of a book that some claim as fact throws the entire enterprise into question."

Once again, George tried to step in. "Doctor—"

Something thumped behind the set.

"What the devil?" the technician said, and scurried away from Janie's side. The thumping came again, continuously this time, and Janie knew she had never been more pleased with a technical foul-up in her life.

George stopped and began to turn toward the noise, but the host said, "I believe you have some response?"

George turned back again. "I don't—" he began, and a tremendous crashing and ripping exploded backstage.

The floor director, his headset still attached and trailing a long black wire like a rat's tail, jumped onto the dais and made vicious slashing motions at his own throat. "Cut it, cut it!" he

361

shouted. "We'll have to start the whole bloody thing over!"

The noise had stopped now, and once again the cameras rolled. The introductions went smoothly, and once again the host turned to Dr. Whitehouse first, his smile as fresh as it had been on the first go-round. "Now, Dr. Whitehouse, you've had an opportunity to—"

"Excuse me," George said. The host, astonished, turned to look at him. "Dr. Whitehouse seems like a fine woman. She and I had a nice talk backstage just before the program, didn't we, Doctor?"

The woman's severe frown faltered a bit, and she nodded uncertainly.

"Yes, we did," George continued smoothly. "But for some reason, she seems to have a real problem with the Catholic Church. I don't know what her particular grudge is, and what she thinks that has to do with our story, but I'd really like to know why she feels it's necessary to criticize the clergy, even in a private conversation, when they're not around to respond."

The host looked slightly stunned. After a moment of pure, blank puzzlement, he turned again, moving like a poorly worked puppet, and said, "Dr. Whitehouse?"

The psychologist spluttered and mumbled, and quite suddenly, Janie realized, *she* was the one on the defensive, and George and Kathy were simply concerned innocents.

Bravo, she thought. George and I may have some friction of our own, but he does know how to handle these vultures in close combat.

The overattentive technician came back to her, wearing a broad hangdog expression.

"Weren't my fault," he said grudgingly.

"What?" The man was terribly annoying.

"I heard the thumpin' just like everybody else, so's I went to check. Didn't find nothin'. Musta been those old pipes back there, though they've never given us a moment's worry before. And how was I supposed to know they had old set pieces stored back there? It's bloody dark, back there!"

"*You* made that awful crash?"

He looked indignant. "Wha' if I did?" he demanded.

Janie laughed so loud that the floor director shot her a filthy look. She stifled another giggle, but the technician was permanently devastated. That was the last she heard from him.


A few days later, on another chat show in a studio far from London, Janie had another pleasant surprise.

They were in Leeds, attending what she had come to regard as one of the landmarks of the tour: an interview that included a local monsignor.

They had arrived late, after having trouble with their rented car, and so hadn't had a chance to speak with the monsignor before the program began. She had no idea what he might have to say.

George had extricated himself rather tidily from the debacle with Dr. Whitehouse—Janie had to admit that. But how would he fare against a man of the cloth?

As she waited for the introductions to end, her mind wandered back to a time when she had discussed a bit of the occult with her own clergyman. She had been little more than a teenager, but for a time she'd been rather addicted to the Ouija Board. Some frightening things had happened—some things she had seen and felt, but couldn't quite explain—so she went to talk with her local vicar.

She had expected him to scoff at the whole silly idea, to call her an impressionable young girl and send her on her way. And it had surprised her, and frightened her a bit, when he had ordered her—*ordered* her—not to play with the Ouija or anything like it, ever again. "This is very serious business," the vicar had said. "It could be quite dangerous to you, and I want you to stop."

She had stopped.

Suddenly she heard the monsignor clear his throat, and she snapped rather abruptly from her reverie. He was a round, cheerful fellow who looked as if he were smiling even when he was deadly serious. In spite of the jolly demeanor, however, Janie found herself holding her breath when the chat-show host turned from George and Kathy and said, "So, Monsignor, you've heard the details now. Do you believe something like this could actually happen?"

"Mr. Linnington," the priest said, "I've known for a very long while that such things are possible. There are forces beyond human understanding, forces with which only God himself may grapple." He cast an eye at the Lutzes, who were listening intently. "Now that I have heard the story of these young people firsthand," he said, leaning forward and folding his hands before him, "now that I have spoken with them

364

myself, there is no doubt in my mind. Their story is true."

Janie grinned and resisted the urge to applaud.

Perhaps all is not lost after all, she thought. I may, in fact, surprise myself and make it through this tour in one piece.

"We're canceling the rest of the tour."

The voice of Bobby, her co-worker at Pan, sounded slightly pained. "Now, don't be flyin' off the handle again, Janie. I'm sure we can smooth out whatever—"

"I'm not flying off the handle, Bobby. Don't be ridiculous! I simply said we were canceling the rest of the tour, and we're *canceling the rest of the tour*. Have you some difficulty with that?"

Bobby sighed. "All right, Janie. Whatever you say."

She was still angry with him. What business did he have, telling her how to handle this? "It was the Lutzes who suggested it in the first place, Bobby, and we've finished most of it already. We've been all over Manchester and the north counties; I arranged for that interview with Diane Aldous at the *Evening Star;* I even went off to Glasgow with them, and I think that's quite enough."

He was trying to be patient. "All right, Janie, if—"

"Bobby, they're absolutely impossible. Every blessed time we go on a train, they huddle in the corner like nine-year-olds and whisper to each other—just *whisper-whisper-whisper*. It's driving me batty!"

"You told me," Bobby said.

"Don't be so bloody patronizing, Bobby! You don't know what it's been like these last few weeks. Besides, I'm only canceling the last few days of the tour, the parts down in Wales, and quite frankly I'm glad as I could be. I don't think I could stand another train ride with them. Whisper-whisper-*whisper!*"

"Believe me, love, I'm twice as glad as you are."

Janie pulled short at that. Now *Bobby* was the one who sounded angry. She glanced about the lobby of the Hilton as if she were afraid someone would hear his outburst. "Whatever do you mean?" she said icily.

Bobby sighed again. He seemed to be doing a great deal of sighing these days, she thought. "Janie, you know I love you. We've worked together for years and rather nicely, too, thank you. But these last few weeks, you have been an absolute hellion."

"Me?" She was dumbstruck at the thought.

"Yes, you. Snapping about like a damn field commander or some such, squawking at every little problem with these Lutz people. It's not as if you haven't had difficult ones before, but you've gone absolutely 'round the bend over these two."

"I have not!"

"You have too, and don't start any silly little schoolgirl battles with me, because I won't have it!"

She swallowed her anger. Bobby never fought with her—never—and this conversation was unnerving her badly. Maybe he was right. She had been feeling rotten the last few days. Sick at the stomach, for some reason, with a small, persistent knocking in the head as well. "I'm sorry," she said softly, but it was a long time before Bobby said anything at all.

When he did, he sounded a bit sorry himself. "You better pop off," he said gently. "Haven't you one last meeting with the Great Horned Lutzes before you bid them adieu?"

"Yes, just now, in fact. I'm to give them their plane tickets and pack them off. They're leaving on Thursday, and since the cancellation's come through, they'll have a bit of a holiday now."

"Well, good for them."

"And good for me."

"Now, don't start up again," he said, only half joking.

"I'm not. Promise."

She said good-bye as gently as she could and went through the familiar straighten-and-comb ritual as she walked across the Hilton's wide, overmodern lobby and waited for the lift. Could she have been all that awful—not just to Bobby, but to George and Kathy Lutz as well? Now that she thought on it, she did seem to be having more than her usual share of rows with producers, reporters, interviewers and such. Normally, she could go weeks without a battle of some sort, but now they seemed to be daily affairs.

It was all rather spooky, actually. Maybe the business of running about for the sake of selling a few books was finally beginning to affect her, and all for the worse.

But some odd things had been happening. Like that affair with the film cans.

One of the producers had been making a huge effort to get some news footage from America on the Amityville house itself. It took far too many intercontinental telephone calls, far too much aggravation, but finally one station had agreed to send them a small reel—but only in a special package, and only by special messenger.

The package from New York had arrived very quickly. But when the sealed film cans had been opened, the reels inside had disappeared. They weren't there. They had been put on a plane in New York, flown all alone to London, and somehow, some way, had simply vanished.

Janie was still absorbed in her own thoughts when she reached the Lutzes' apartment. She knocked a little harder than she had intended, and as the door began to swing open, she felt the old tension rush back in on her. She set her teeth and fixed a small, highly artificial smile in place. Just this one last time, she told herself, and I'm free.

George was the one who answered the door, and the moment she saw him, Janie knew that something was terribly, terribly wrong. Or... right, actually. Too right.

George was smiling, big as life. Smiling at her.

"Janie! Come in, come in. Can I get you a cup of coffee? Tea, maybe?"

She allowed herself to be led in, feeling completely at sea. "I suppose. Tea, please."

George sat her down on the divan and went to a silver tea set that the hotel must have only just delivered. "Did you order that for me?" she asked, still lost in astonishment.

George shrugged good-naturedly. "For all of us. Kathy and I just wanted to sit down and talk to you for a while. Seems like we never had the chance to do that before."

Sit? Talk? With her? She accepted the cup of tea with a distant nod and a blank expression. She couldn't recall that George had ever fetched her a cup of tea before, and here he was beaming like an old friend. He even had a plate of biscuits waiting.

"Cracker? Muffin? What do you call these things, anyway?"

"Biscuits," she said.

"Right. Would you like one?"

"No, thank you. Perhaps later."

Kathy came sweeping into the room in a sun dress she must have brought with her from California. It was a light, summery color, and it flowed around her like water. From the smile on her face, the speed and grace of her movement, Janie thought she looked a full five years younger.

Kathy said, "Janie! You're here!" and gave her a kiss on the cheek.

A kiss on the cheek!

"Look," she said, "we just wanted to apologize."

Janie was beginning to recover. "Not to me, I hope."

"Oh, especially to you. See, this tour came up very suddenly for us, and we've been having— well, we've been having a lot of problems with it. Stuff we haven't wanted to bother you about."

She swallowed carefully. "I see," she said, not sure she wanted to see at all.

"I know it's been hard on you. All this traveling and setting up and getting us there on time." She shot a wry look at George and grinned. "Especially getting us there on time."

George jumped in. He had already said more to her in five minutes than he'd said in a week, but apparently he wasn't quite finished. "What we're trying to say, I guess, is thank you. Thank you for all your help, and thank you for letting us cancel the last part of the tour. We miss our kids like hell, Janie. We really want to get back. The whole tour has been a real strain, and we're glad to put that behind us. And if we've been hard to deal with—well, we're sorry."

Janie didn't know what to say. She opened her mouth to protest—or perhaps to accept their apology, she wasn't sure which—but George cut her off. He seized the teapot and filled her cup again. "Drink up," he said, "and then we want to take you out to dinner. Wherever you want to go. Our treat."

Janie looked dumbly at the cup of tea, then at the bright, sincere faces before her. She still wasn't sure what had wrought such a tremendous change in them. Simply canceling the tour? Giving them a holiday? Or was it something more?

"Thank you," she said, sipping her tea. She was grateful for the moment it gave her to order her thoughts. "That is, thank you for the concern, as unnecessary as that may have been. And thank you for the tea, and for the invitation to dinner. I . . ."

No. She wasn't about to get maudlin about it. The tour was behind them, and they were being just as warm and generous as they could be. She wasn't going to spoil that with silly questions. "And I think I know just the place."

They smiled even wider and joined her in another cup of tea.

The restaurant she had chosen was only a few blocks from the Hilton, and they had all elected to walk the distance. Kathy had done a bit of fussing about the wardrobe, but finally she had decided to stay in the summer dress from California that she had been wearing all afternoon.

It was an uncommonly bright and warm day in London, and Janie thought that Kathy looked like some sort of summer flower—a daisy, perhaps—as she flounced down Park Lane toward Piccadilly with her arm threaded through her husband's.

"Oh, Janie," Kathy said, remembering something, "we wanted to especially thank you for that interview with Diane Aldous."

"My pleasure," she said, smiling. The columnist with the *Evening Star* was an old chum. It had been one of the easiest arrangements she'd made.

"She told us about a—a man that we thought we would meet," Kathy said, and now the look at her husband had a trace of hesitation in it.

"What sort of man?"

"His name's Timothy Johnstone. He's an Anglican priest, Diane told us, and an—" Another wary glance at George. "An exorcist."

George snorted. "Exorcist! My God!" Janie

saw a shadow of the old, surly, uncommunicative George Lutz she had lived with for the past few weeks. "I don't know why she thinks anyone would help us, even if they could."

Kathy forged ahead, squeezing her husband's arm more tightly in her own. "Diane said that Reverend Johnstone has helped a lot of people with problems like ours."

"We've heard that before, too," George grumbled mildly.

"And that he would certainly understand what we've been going through." Kathy looked at her husband and smiled. "Besides, we've got a few days off here in England before the plane leaves . . . so why not, right?"

George didn't say anything, and she nudged him. "Why not?" she said again.

He shrugged. "Sure," he muttered. "We'll go and see him."

Janie did a little shrugging of her own. "Well, I can't say I've heard of this fellow myself, Kathy, but Diane Aldous is a good friend— not to mention one of the most widely read columnists in the country. If she think's he's worth meeting, I expect he's very much worth meeting,"

Kathy nodded. "All right, then," she said. "We'll give it a try." She broke away from her husband and ran a few steps, and Janie marveled once more at the change in these people. "Come on, George!" she said, laughing. "Let's eat!"

Janie saw George grin and shrug away the darkness that was building up behind his eyes. He ran to his wife, caught her up in his arms, and gave her a good, sound kiss, unmindful of the strangers who watched them, smiling.

Strange people, Janie thought. Strange, good people. And I think we may be friends after all.

## 26

Reverend Timothy Johnstone smiled and said, "All right, then, Ryan. I'll talk with you soon," and hung up the phone. It had been a long, pleasant conversation with an old friend—a doctor he had helped some months before.

He poured himself another cup of tea and thought about the case. Not so unusual. The man had been doing things, saying things, even thinking things that he simply did not understand. He had been quite sure that he was going mad. And it had been very difficult for him to look beyond the boundaries of modern medicine and into the more volatile and uncertain realm of God.

Still, he had come—slowly, reluctantly, and far later than he should have—but he had come. And Timothy had helped him.

He looked out the window of the vicarage into the thick green hedge at the boundary of the churchyard. Today he had a different problem altogether—a rather special one, in fact. An acquaintance of his, Diane Aldous, had interviewed an American couple who had been through quite a horrid time of it back in the States, and she was convinced he could help.

He picked up the book she had given him and flipped through the pages again. He'd read it through the night before, and even allowing for the embellishments and liberties often taken by authors, there was no question that something very powerful had happened to the Lutzes—something very powerful and very real.

Strange, he thought, how the need for my services seems to be growing. No doubt some part of it had to do with his growing notoriety. For years, people had found him only indirectly —through personal recommendation or happy accident. But since that American movie, *The Exorcist*, had been released, he had participated in hundreds of interviews and television programs, and his address and name had been noised about in the most unusual places. Now, troubled people from England, from the Continent—even from as far afield as Australia and the Americas—were searching him out and asking for his help.

Was it just because he was slightly more accessible than others in his profession . . . or were there more cases to contend with than ever before?

Whatever the reason, he knew there was much more work to be done. He had performed literally thousands of exorcisms, great and small, and others had done the same. Yet untold numbers of people were walking through the world feeling plagued and impotent and alone—people that could be helped if only they could find him.

Timothy Johnstone sighed and finished his cup of tea. At least the Lutzes found me, he thought. And with God's help, some good may come of it.

George first saw St. John's Church in North London through the window of Diane Aldous's Citroën. She had volunteered to take them to Timothy Johnstone herself, and to make the introductions. But he knew that, from here on in, it was up to him and Kathy.

He didn't like this idea, not at all. Even the thought of exorcism made him a little queasy. It smacked of cheap theatrics and special effects—all sorts of fakery. Besides, so many others had talked about the same sort of things—those wretched ghost hunters and vampire-slayers and all the other crackpots. Exorcism fell into the same ridiculous category, as far as he was concerned.

Still, it was a beautiful old church, he thought. He took Kathy's hand and squeezed it, and together they climbed out of the car and gazed up at the classic lines of the solid stone cathedral. The large stained-glass windows glinted, even in the overcast, and the huge spire of the church seemed to pierce the gray, bulging clouds of the English sky.

George could see that it had been there for centuries. He tried to picture the changes the building had seen in all those years—the wars and ruin, the triumph and challenge. It was almost more than he could take in. Imagine centuries, he thought. Centuries.

To the left of the drive, a newer section had been built on to the church. Diane had told them that it was the vicarage, where they would meet the Reverend Johnstone.

George held back a sigh of resignation and thought Okay, what the hell, let's give it a try. He didn't believe for a moment that a simple Anglican cleric could help them, but at least he was a learned man. Maybe he would believe what they had to say; he might even have some good advice. After all the reporters and the skeptical questions, it would be nice to have a sympathetic ear for a change.

And who knows? he told himself. Maybe he can help. Maybe.

Reverend Johnstone greeted the three of them at the door of the vicarage and they shook hands all around. George judged him to be fifty-five or sixty. His nose was small and aquiline; his hair was thinning; and he wore a standard cleric costume: black pants, a black coat, and a white collar, all a little shabby. He had an old, comfortable-looking sweater under his jacket, and there were small white flecks of dandruff on his shoulders. For no particular reason, George liked that. It made the man a bit more human.

Reverend Johnstone kept up a steady stream of polite conversation as he led them to his study. George glanced at the large bookcases and saw an abundance of titles on the occult and black magic. The reverend's desk was covered with papers, and the small-paned window in one wall looked across the manicured lawns of the church to the bushes and brownstone buildings beyond. The room felt right, somehow. Warm, solid, filled with a quiet strength.

He offered them all some coffee or tea, and when it had been served the reverend settled himself in a large, exceedingly comfortable leather chair behind his desk and smiled warmly at the trio.

"Now, what can I do for you?" he asked.

George shrugged. "Frankly, sir, I don't know. Diane tells us you're an 'exorcist.'" Skepticism dripped from the word.

Reverend Johnstone shrugged back at him. "I've helped quite a lot of people, Mr. Lutz. Politicians, for instance, from England and your own country. Entertainers, housewives, businessmen—even other members of the clergy. They have all derived some benefit from what I prefer to call 'clearing.' Two Hell's Angels who were in serious trouble came to me. Even a witch—a high priestess of the order who was in fear for her life and her immortal soul—was helped."

Reverend Johnstone's eyes lit up as he remembered a specific case. "There was a barrister recently—just as an example. He was at his wit's end. Strange things had been happening to him all at once. His entire practice—his entire life—was in jeopardy when he came to me. We went into the church, and I cleared the problems that were plaguing him. He returned to his work, and his home life, and hasn't been bothered since."

George couldn't help scowling. Barristers? Bikers? Black magic? It was just too much to swallow. "And all these people," he said, trying to sound polite despite his doubts, "all these clients of yours were affected by the same thing?"

Timothy Johnstone let the cynicism pass him by. "Not exactly, no. There are three major forms of psychic attack: oppression, possession, and witchcraft." He leaned forward, looking intently at George and Kathy. "Black magic is not the problem here, that much I can see immediately. Oppression and possession, however . . ."

Kathy had been listening very closely. "Oppression?" she said, frowning.

"When one is attacked by an outside force of some kind, I call it 'oppression.' When one is taken over from within, by a spirit or a presence, wholly or in part, that is possession."

A chill ran through George Lutz. He thought about the house in Amityville—about the things that had happened to him, about the things he had felt compelled to do. He thought about the night in East Babylon when Kathy had attacked him. Could they be the victims of both oppression and possession?

"And exorcism works against all three?" Kathy asked.

Reverend Johnstone nodded. "Yes, it does. Psychic forces take hold of one—or, if you will, they open a connection to one in an almost physical sense. That connection must be severed." He smiled shyly and looked at the papers on his desk. "I know that all sounds very cut and dried." He glanced at them, and his eyes twinkled. "Rather like a tidy algebraic formula—but that, quite simply, is how it works. The power of God Himself cuts the bond that binds one to Satan."

"Well?" Kathy said, looking at him frankly. "Do you think we need to be exorcised?"

George looked at her sharply. Was she buying all this? Did she actually think this nice old fellow could somehow help them? Certainly there was a—a feeling, some sort of charisma about the reverend, but still . . . exorcism?

The reverend looked at George as if he could see his doubts quite clearly. "What do you think?" he said, and his gaze seemed to take in both George and Kathy.

"I don't think it's necessary," George said bluntly. "But I suppose you do."

The Reverend Johnstone was unflappable. He smiled broadly and gave a small, almost delicate shrug. "I've been doing this quite a long time, Mr. Lutz. I think I can see—or perhaps feel—when someone needs my help." He leaned forward again and looked at George and Kathy intently. "Shall I be blunt?"

"Please do," Kathy said, and George glared at her.

"I see a dark presence—a sort of cloud—emanating from you two. I think you need my help, and I think you need it rather badly."

George was shaking his head. It was just too much. Too much. The next thing he knew, they'd be speaking in tongues and smearing themselves with ashes. "No," he said, angrily, "not exorcism."

Kathy reached over, took his hand, and said, "Babe . . ." very gently. He pulled his hand away while a small part of him wondered why he was getting so upset about it.

Because it was stupid. Stupid and pointless.

"Call it what you like, Mr. Lutz. I often call it

deliverance. That describes it very well, I think."

"It's the same thing. It's—" He wanted to say *bullshit*—it almost came out before he could stop it. At the last moment he settled for, "Nonsense. Just nonsense."

"Mr. Lutz, there is a strong aura of bad feeling—of negativeness, if you will—that hovers about you. Is it possible that you feel so adamant about this because of some influence from . . . outside?"

George exploded. "Oh, come on! Now I can't even disagree with you without being—what? Possessed?"

"George," Kathy said, "he's only trying to help."

"Of course he is! Everybody tries to help, Kathy! Haven't you noticed? And what good has it done us? Are we any better off now?"

She was doing her best to stay calm. "In some ways, yes. A lot better." She tried to take his hand again, but he resisted. "George, what's the matter?"

He didn't want to hear her; it was all too crazy, too ridiculous. "What makes you so special?" he demanded. "Why do you think you can help us, when others have tried and failed?"

The reverend looked puzzled. "Have you already been exorcised?"

George looked stubborn. "Well, no. Not in so many words, I guess. But what difference does that make? We've had the house blessed, and Mass said; we've even had psychic investigators—"

"Exorcism is a very different thing, Mr. Lutz. It's not anything I do myself. I am a channel, a conduit, and that is all. It is the spirit of God that helps you, not science or even the ritual of the Church, as important as they may be. It is *God* who cuts the connection between you and the power—in this case, the power that first touched you in the house in Amityville. And God has never failed you, has He?"

George felt something crumble inside, but he couldn't give up. The reverend was demanding an answer.

"Has He?"

George shrugged. "No, I guess not."

Reverend Johnstone was almost whispering now. "Call it what you like, George. Call it 'the laying on of hands.' The Bible says Jesus threw out devils by laying on his hands. It's the same thing."

George wanted to agree. He wanted, needed someone to help them. But something held him back—something kept him from accepting what the reverend had to say, no matter how right it felt.

Kathy tried to take his hand a third time, and this time he held it tightly. "George, I think he's right. He can help us. I'm sure of it."

The reverend stood and came around the desk. "At least come into the church with me. We will pray together; that's all."

George sat huddled in the chair as if an invisible hand held him there. He didn't know what to do, to say—he didn't know what to think anymore.

The minister was only inches away from him now, and the power that came from him was almost visible, almost tangible in the dim illumination of the study. "George, you want my help. I can see that. Forget your doubts. Come into the church and pray with me."

With an effort he thought was beyond him, with the help of some power he didn't know he had, George nodded his head and stood up. "All right," he said, his voice harsh and brutal in the silence.

Reverend Johnstone beamed. "I'm glad," he said. "Very glad. Shall we go, then?"

Diane Aldous told Kathy she would wait in the study, and the Lutzes followed the Reverend Johnstone out of the vicarage, into the garden, and through a thick oak door that led into the sanctuary itself.

A small series of rooms led into the church on the left side, near the altar. It was a huge stand covered in clean white linen, encrusted with gold and decorated with candlesticks cast in the same precious metal. Above it hung an image of Christ that glowed softly in the light that streamed through a stained-glass window above and behind it. Near the door itself, some twenty feet from the altar, a wooden railing ran the width of the church. Before it, on the floor, was a leather kneeling pad.

Reverend Johnstone asked them to kneel at the railing and wait for a moment. He entered a small room beside the altar and put a crimson mantle around his shoulders. When he returned to them, he had a small bowl of holy water in one hand.

George watched as the reverend stood in front of the altar and used a small brush to draw a cross of holy water on his forehead. He saw him stretch out his arms, spread-eagle, and invoke the power of the lord. His thin voice boomed with power as he asked God Himself to break the connection between George and Kathy Lutz and the dark force centered in their home.

George still didn't want to believe it. Something urged him to stand up, to leave the sanctuary. But a small, objective part of his mind held him there.

Something was happening. A force, a presence was in St. John's with them.

Timothy Johnstone turned and came toward them. In his hands was the bowl of holy water, and slowly, reverently, he wet his fingers and drew the sign of the cross on their foreheads.

At the touch of his hand, something rippled through George—a wave of power, a force that made his muscles twitch and dance. Something inside him—something awful—was flinching at the reverend's touch.

The Reverend Johnstone moved to Kathy first. He laid aside the wooden bowl and stood before her as if gathering strength. Then he crossed his palms one on top of the other and pressed them on the crown of Kathy's head with tremendous force.

The words came quickly, in a swift and continuous stream that made them hard for George to understand. But the words had barely begun when Kathy started to shake. Long, painful vibrations ran through her, as if rumbling up from the floor beneath, and gradually, inevitably, the shaking spread up the Reverend Johnstone's arms and captured him as well.

First his hands quivered. Then his shoulders twitched back and forth as if held in the grip of huge, violent fists.

Later, Kathy told George what she had felt

herself. The words, she said, were unimportant. It was the shaking that terrified her. It seemed to come from outside her and deep within her at the same time. She was a thin shell, a wall between two forces that were using her as a fragile battleground.

Moments after the trembling took her, a fierce, numbing cold began in her toes and slowly crept upward. She was shaking too violently to cry out, and for one horrible instant she thought that life itself was draining out of her, being sucked up through the palms of the reverend's hands. But as the coldness climbed past her knees, her thighs, her waist, as it twisted like a living thing in her solar plexus, she knew that something vital had been left behind—a life, a purity, an energy that was cleansed of the stench of Amityville.

It ended in a single instant, in a *snap* of electricity and violence. The cleansing cold rushed upward from stomach to skull in a fraction of a second and burst from the top of her head. Kathy felt weary and dizzy . . . so light that she thought she might float away.

George saw the moment it happened quite clearly. A tension that had lived in Kathy for years, a weight and darkness that had become part of her in the long hard months since Amityville, was suddenly, inexplicably gone. She straightened and smiled, almost glowing with sudden strength. Reverend Johnstone's words became less forced, slower, more distinct. He nearly sighed as he straightened and gave the final blessing, and when Kathy opened her eyes, there was a new life and hope flowing from her that George loved and envied and hated all at once.

Because the darkness was still in him. The thing from Amityville still had him tightly in its grip.

When the Reverend Johnstone turned from Kathy Lutz and looked at her husband, he found himself hesitating. The time he had spent with Kathy had been short—a few minutes at best—but it had drained him terribly. The spirit inside her was strong, incredibly strong, and at the moment of her liberation he had experienced a familiar, frightening impression—a thing almost seen, almost heard, that lifted out of her body and rushed from the sanctuary.

It often happened at the crucial moment of freedom. He heard the entities cry out as they fled, and oddly, for reasons he could only guess at, the cries he almost-heard were frequently words of thanks.

It had not been a thank-you this time. It had been a wordless, hostile howl of pain and defeat, and he knew it was far from over.

The demon inside George would be far worse. Everything pointed to it—his reluctance to enter the church, his violent outbursts, the intensity of the evil he had experienced at Amityville and in the months since their flight from that awful place. It might be too powerful, too much for him to exorcise when he was already drained and weary.

But there was no other alternative. He would face it. He would win.

He stood before George and took in a long, slow breath. Then he raised his hands slowly, carefully, put one over the other. For a moment he stared blindly at the knuckles, the fingers, the tendons and bones, as he gathered his strength.

In one violent motion he moved forward and clamped his hands on George's head.

"I *bind*, by the True God, the Living God, the Holy Ghost, in the Name of the Father and of the Son and of the Holy Spirit, any evil force that they may not intrude, interfere, disturb or distort your life!"

George exploded with a violent trembling. His hands gripped the rail until his knuckles were white. He felt the muscles bend and flutter inside him as if they were being pummeled from inside and out.

A deep and penetrating cold, more intense than ever before, engulfed his toes, his feet, his ankles, inching toward his knees. It stopped there, held back by some invisible barrier. Then it began to spread upward through his body.

The reverend twitched and jumped, and for an instant, the words of the ritual caught in his throat. His head was pounding. His hands were moving over George's skull as if the contact were too vibrant with power to hold steadily. He seized it with all his strength, held it tightly, and began again.

"I *cut*, with the sword of the Holy Spirit, all psychic links with the house in Amityville, that they may not intrude, interfere, disturb, or distort your life!"

The pressure that built inside the minister grew too strong. Blood poured from his nose and ran in a thick stream down his chin.

It had happened before. Often the pure power that coursed through him grew too strong to
control. I should have warned the Lutzes, he
thought distantly. I should have told them what
to expect. But he had never dreamed of anything this powerful.

He stopped a second time and cleared his
throat. His heart was thumping like a mad-
man's; he felt light-headed, giddy. His knees
were beginning to buckle.

When George looked up through the tremors
and the cold, he couldn't believe his eyes. Blood
had splashed over the minister's face and was
pouring down his neck and chest. His mouth
was wide open, and he was gasping for breath
with a sound like torn cloth. He was white as
bone—pale, pasty white. The only color in his
face was the blood itself.

He's going to die, George thought, panicking.
He tried to speak, to stand, to help.

*"No!"* the reverend cried. *"Stay where you
are!"* He steeled himself and forced his heart to
slow. The blood stopped flowing from his nose.

His hands came away from George's head,
but the tremors continued. Contact was no longer
necessary, he knew. A battle was being waged in
the young man's body, a battle he could scarcely
control.

He took a handkerchief from a pocket and
wiped his nose. Then he took George's hands in
his own and spread them wide, like the arms of
the cross itself.

His voice rang out in defiance. A light as
strong as the sun glowed in his eyes. "I *cut* with
the sword of the Holy Spirit, all psychic links
with the house in Amityville, that they may not

389

intrude, interfere, disturb, or distort your life!"

The shaking grew worse. It slapped them, jerked at them, threw them from side to side. Kathy screamed and tried to touch them, but the muscles flowed beneath her hands like water. They were trapped in some ritual dance, flying in all directions at once.

The cold inside George was more cutting and brutal than ever. It slashed at him, burned him. It turned him brittle and weak.

The reverend's nose burst with blood a second time. His face quivered, his eyes seemed to start from his head, but the words kept on, rattling one after the other, marching from his mouth as if falling from a broken automaton.

The cold resolved itself into a border at George's waist. Below was the brilliant, crystalline purity of peace; above the torrent of power boiled and burst within him.

The cold began to lift to his chest, his shoulders, his neck. It stopped, reversed, retreated to his stomach.

It fell. His thighs were recaptured. His groin was hot and turgid. Then it lifted again—upward, higher, the borderline trembling and flexing in his chest.

It was an insane tug-of-war, and George groaned at the power within him. It had to stop soon. It had to, or he would be torn to pieces.

The light fixtures that hung at the back of the church began to rattle, the vibrations thundering and receding in point and counterpoint. Their mad rhythm beat in time with the dance of the exorcist and his subject.

Kathy shouted and reached for them— Everything stopped.

The lights ceased their movement. George's trembling cut off. The reverend's body was still, and deep inside George Lutz's mind, buried under layers of panic, a tiny voice said:

*It's over. I'm finished with it. I'm—*

No! He could feel the evil still twisting inside him. It had only retreated for a moment. It wanted him to relax, to let down, to make it easier.

Timothy Johnstone felt it, too. His hands gripped George's more tightly than ever, and he said, "Oh, God, Son of God, unconquered Might..."

George felt as if he would lift off the floor. A force beyond comprehension seized him by the head and tried to pull him to the ceiling, but the priest pushed him down, forced him to stay on the floor, and continued.

"...unconquered Might who keepeth all those, even those who are against Thee, and by His death has destroyed Death and overcome the Prince of Death, BEAT DOWN Satan under our feet, and cause any evil forces to DEPART, and give praise to Christ, His power, and His peace!"

The light fixtures whipped about madly. Something rumbled at the far end of the church, as if the stained-glass window was flexing in its frame. The door to the church swung open wide.

The noise grew louder, as if on silent command, and the door slammed shut, and opened again, and slammed again. The minister had to shout to be heard above the chaos.

Waves of cold and heat snapped through George, tugging at him, tearing at him, making his head swim and his eyes blur with pain. For an instant, he was sure he was going to black out, and then the cold enclosed him, end to end, like the grip of a huge hand.

The reverend reared back as if he were being forced away from George, but he held tight to his hands. It happened again and again—a force shoved at the minister, pushed at him, tried to tear them apart, but they held fast to each other.

In one last, desperate move, Reverend Johnstone threw himself forward and thrust every ounce of strength up his arms. It grew from the pit of George's stomach and built in his chest. It rushed down his arms and through his hands, and in a single, massive, crushing wave, the cold leapt upward through George and exploded through the top of his head, flashing into the darkness above him.

He could feel the force hanging there, inches away. He could feel the icy, immovable grip of the minister holding it from him. "Under God's gracious mercy and protection we commit you," the minister breathed, still tense, still waiting. "The Lord bless you and keep you. The Lord make His face shine upon you in Grace, and may the Lord light the light of His Kindness and give you His protection and His peace. Now and forevermore. *Amen.*"

It happened in an instant: George felt a huge weight lift from him. Timothy Johnstone heard the torn and wretched moan of a thing in agony. The door to the church swung wide and waited, and the reverend saw something both insubstantial and deadly rise from George's shoulders and race the length of the sanctuary. It flew from the church, still screaming, and the door slammed shut with a crash.

The cathedral was cool and quiet. The fixtures that had danced in their fittings were silent. Light poured in through the stained-glass window above them, and the exorcist, standing over George like a statue, swayed and began to collapse.

He caught himself on the railing as he fell and refused to let his knees buckle. "I'm all right," he said. "Just give me a moment."

It had been hard for him—as hard as anything had ever been. Timothy Johnstone had been exorcising spirits for more than thirty years, and, God willing, he planned to do it thirty years more, and still, he had never felt anything remotely like it.

He prayed that it was over for them, that the evil had been driven from the Lutzes. Sometimes it wasn't so easy. Sometimes it took two, even three 'clearings' to put things right. Still, at the very least, the force plaguing them had been drastically weakened. And perhaps it was over entirely. God willing.

George held Kathy tightly in his arms. It was over now; he knew that. The evil was as far from him as it had been in months, in years. He held his wife and listened to her heart beat. He kissed her and said, "I love you, Kathy."

She hugged him fiercely and held back tears. "I love you, too, babe." The reverend came to them and put his arms around them both, and after a long moment they walked from the sanctuary of St. John's.

When they returned to the study, they found Diane Aldous pale and strangely upset. Kathy talked with her as the Reverend Johnstone wiped the drying blood from his face and wearily took his seat in the overstuffed leather chair behind his desk.

George collapsed into the other chair still available in the room. He was tired, drained, as weary as he had ever been. But Timothy Johnstone looked as if he had aged ten years.

"Reverend, are you *sure* you're all right?"

He nodded. "Just very tired, George, but that's normal." He smiled and straightened in his chair, and seemed to draw on some hidden source of strength. "Now tell me, George. You were reluctant to discuss the details with me before the clearing. Have you any questions now? Anything you'd like to know?"

At first George could think of nothing to say. The calm he felt, the certainty that something fundamental had changed for them, that some door had been unlocked, made the questions unimportant. But there was one thing that had always nagged at him.

"Reverend, maybe this will sound silly, but . . . *why us?* I mean, we're not especially pure, but we're not terribly bad. We're just normal. Why should we be singled out?"

Reverend Johnstone shook his head. "I wish I could answer that. I wish I had some simple explanation that could make your acceptance of it easier, but I don't. I can't." He sighed and passed a hand across his face. "It might be that some people are simply more psychically available—more open to such things, and therefore more apt to be influenced, tampered with. But frankly, George, I don't know."

"'Psychically tampered with?' Do you mean

that all the things we saw, all the things we felt were just *illusions?* That none of it was real?"

Timothy Johnstone smiled and spread his hands. "At the risk of sounding terribly trite, George, what is reality? Perhaps the dark forces at work in the world project their evil directly into the mind. Whether the things you saw—the things you experienced—fall into the tightly enclosed area we call 'reality,' or whether they were somehow, in some way, something else . . . who can tell?" He leaned forward and put his weight on his knees. His hands were folded before him, and George saw them tremble slightly with exhaustion. "Reality is only what you see and feel, George. What you perceive. The dreams you had, the things that appeared to you, the sicknesses and the fear and the impossible occurrences were as real to you as any reality we know in this world."

They left the warmth of the study and walked together into the cool, gray afternoon. Reverend Johnstone said his good-byes to Diane Aldous, and he asked the Lutzes to talk with him again before they left for America.

George and Kathy stood by Diane's car and exchanged final embraces with the exorcist. It was hard to let go, hard to leave him behind so quickly. But they knew they had to leave.

"Go with God," the reverend said. "If you're ever back this way again, please come and visit."

"Of course we will," George said. "And we'll let you know how things are getting along in America."

Timothy Johnstone smiled broadly. "I'd like that."

"Good-bye," Kathy said. "Thank you."

The car started and they moved slowly down the street until the minister was a dark smudge against the wide gray expanse of the church. Then they turned a corner and he was gone.

George put an arm around his wife, and Kathy nestled closer to him.

Tomorrow they would be on a plane to the United States. The day after that, only moments before sunrise, they would be home.

# 'SALEM'S LOT
# by Stephen King

Almost overnight, the population of 'Salem's Lot has gone from 1319 to nothing. *At least to nothing human!*

Thousands of miles from the small New England town of 'Salem's Lot, two terrified people still share the secrets of those clapboard houses and tree-lined streets.

One is an eleven-year-old boy who never speaks. Only his eyes betray the grotesque events he has witnessed.

The other is a man with recurring nightmares of a placid little township transformed into a tableau of unrelenting horror, a man who knows that soon he and the boy must return to 'Salem's Lot for a final confrontation with the unspeakable evil that lives on there . . .

NEW ENGLISH LIBRARY

# SMART AS THE DEVIL
## by Felice Picano

A twelve-year-old boy given to fits of devastating rage.

A case of dual personality? Or something even more evil? Without warning the child becomes a whirlwind of obscene ferocity, a nightmare fury fuelled by the very flames of hell . . .

'This psychological thriller wraps itself around your terror mechanisms and keeps squeezing till you find yourself limp with fear. You have my word for it; you've *never* been to the dark fearful places Felice Picano will take you with this stunning novel of extraordinary power.' — *Harlan Ellison*

**NEW ENGLISH LIBRARY**

# NEL BESTSELLERS

NEL P.O. BOX 11, FALMOUTH TR10 9EN, CORNWALL

Postage charge:

U.K. Customers. Please allow 40p for the first book, 18p for the second book, ▌for each additional book ordered, to a maximum charge of £1.49, in addition cover price.

B.F.P.O. & Eire. Please allow 40p for the first book, 18p for the second book, ▌per copy for the next 7 books, thereafter 7p per book, in addition to cover price

Overseas Customers. Please allow 60p for the first book plus 18p per copy for ea additional book, in addition to cover price.

Please send cheque or postal order (no currency).

Name ........................................................................................................

Address ....................................................................................................

..................................................................................................................

Title ........................................................................................................